Instant
ActiveX Web Database
Programming

Alex Homer

Wrox Press Ltd.®

Instant ActiveX Web Database Programming

© 1996 Wrox Press

Published by Wrox Press Ltd. 30 Lincoln Road, Olton, Birmingham, B27 6PA.
Printed in USA

ISBN 1-861000-46-4

Trademark Acknowledgements

Wrox has endeavored to provide trademark information about all the companies and products mentioned in this book by the appropriate use of capitals. However, Wrox cannot guarantee the accuracy of this information.

Credits

Author
Alex Homer

Contributing Authors
Darren Gill
Steve Jakab

Editor
Gina Mance

Development Editors
Graham McLaughlin
David Maclean

Technical Reviewers
Andrew Enfield
Robert Barker
Mark Harrison
Jon Bonnell
Ron Picard
Bruce Hartwell
Christian Gross

Design/Layout
Andrew Guillaume

**Proof Reading
and Index**
Simon Gilks
Dominic Shakeshaft

Cover Design
Third Wave

For more information on Third Wave, contact Ross Alderson on 44-121 236 6616
Cover image by David Maclean

Web Database Programming

Summary of Contents

Web Database Programming

Table of Contents

Introduction

What This Book Is About

The Internet has grown in ways that the original founders could never have imagined. Its roots were in a network designed simply as a way for the US government to communicate securely with its defense suppliers, and the underlying concept was a pure information-exchange and electronic messaging system. Even the gradual take-up in the early years by government-sponsored organizations, colleges, and other educational institutions, did little to change this.

In recent years, however, the explosion in its popularity has been no less than amazing. The World Wide Web, which allows simple access to colorful and interactive pages, has been the main factor fueling this incredible growth. Now, the viewer has an almost seamless and unending panorama of sites to visit, situated all over the world.

But what are these sites actually there for? Why do companies, organizations, and individuals go to all the trouble and expense of maintaining a presence on the Web? While we aren't going to devote this book to a sociological investigation into Web publishing, we will be considering the tasks that a web site is supposed to achieve. And more importantly, of course, how you achieve these tasks as easily, cheaply, and efficiently as possible.

In the great majority of cases, information you want to publish on the Web is stored in some kind of database. This could be anything from a mainframe that fills an office block, to a PC database application which runs on your office server. There is a raft of emerging technologies which form the link between this data and your Web pages, and that's the core of what this book is about.

The other side of the coin is to consider *where* you publish the information. Do you want to talk to the whole world out there, or is there a more specific need—to make it more available inside your own organization? Can your company become more efficient, and more customer-oriented, by having the right information available? More to the point, can that information be delivered at the right time, to the right place, and always be up to date?

Internal or external information publishing, we'll look at the background to the technology, show you what kinds of things are possible, and of course—in the best Wrox tradition—we'll take you through the whole process in detail. By the time you've read this book, you'll be in a position to take decisions on how, and why, you should be setting up your own corporate information system now.

Who This Book Is For

This book is about publishing information from a database on the Internet or your company intranet, using the latest technologies from Microsoft. It's aimed at everyone who needs to understand more about the background to the technology, the hardware and software required, and how to set it up and use it to achieve optimum results. If you are responsible for setting up and/ or maintaining a World Wide Web site, or a corporate intranet, you will find this book invaluable.

We'll be looking at the more recent main-line technologies, including:

- Internet Database Connector
- Internet Server API and OLEISAPI
- Microsoft dbWeb data retrieval tool
- Microsoft Index Server search engine

and we'll also give you a first glimpse of one of the newest server-side technologies: Active Server Pages.

What You'll Need To Use This Book

Web Publishing is one of the fastest growing areas of Internet development, with new technologies appearing all the time. We've chosen to concentrate on the major players, and so the hardware and software we'll be using will reflect this.

The Hardware and Software You'll Need

To build your own applications, like the ones you'll see in this book, you will require:

- A server computer running Microsoft NT Server. We are using version 4.0, though you can use earlier ones. This will mean that some components of the software will not be included in the package by default.
- A database management system such as SQL Server, Access or any other database for which there is an ODBC driver available.
- Microsoft Internet Information Server, version 2.0 or higher. Again, you'll find that earlier versions do not accommodate all the functionality you'll be seeing in this book.
- Internet Explorer Version 3.0, or a compatible browser which supports VBScript and ActiveX technology.
- Microsoft Index Server.
- Microsoft dbWeb.
- Microsoft Active Server Pages.
- A connection to the Internet, or an internal intranet, using TCP/IP protocol.

Note that some of these elements are included as part of later versions of IIS.

You can download many of the software components and upgrades from the Internet directly, and this is especially useful to ensure that you have the latest versions. Check out Microsoft's site at `http://www.microsoft.com/` for more details.

If you don't have access to all of our list of requirements, you can still see the results—as long as you have an Internet connection of some type and a browser. All the examples are available on our Web site at `http://www.wrox.com/books/0464/samples/webdb.htm`, and you can load them and see how they work. We've also included the **Wrox Information Manager** there, complete with some fictitious data for you to try out.

The Previous Experience We'll Assume

As for previous experience, we'll be assuming you already have a reasonable grasp of the basics of web pages. We won't be teaching you how to set up the hardware, or the web server software, either. Our aim is to look at the ways you actually *use* the technologies to their best advantage.

So we'll be assuming you are reasonably familiar with:

- The terminology of server hardware and software, and some appreciation of the way networks operate.
- Microsoft Visual Basic (VB), Visual Basic for Applications (VBA), or a similar language.
- VBScript and ActiveX controls, and the way the browser can be programmed using it, or similar methods.
- Structured Query Language (SQL) in at least its simplest form.
- HyperText Markup Language (HTML).

If you want to catch up on any of these subjects, look out for other books from Wrox Press, such as *The Beginner's Guide to Visual Basic, Beginning Access 95 VBA Programming, Instant VBScript, Instant SQL* and *Instant HTML*.

How This Book Is Organized

Because there are so many new technologies appearing, and the whole Internet scene is changing so quickly, it's easy to get lost in a sea of jargon and abbreviations. Before we even begin to look in depth at the technologies themselves, we'll spend some time helping you get to grips with the background to it all.

The first chapter talks about why you need to understand web database publishing, then goes on to broadly introduce the technologies, and how they all fit together. We then move on to cover the three main technologies, giving each a chapter of its own.

In the second half of the book, we look at some of the other mainline technologies, and see how they can be combined to produce high performance, attractive, and interactive web applications.

At the same time, and throughout the book, you'll see a real business application in use. We'll also show you some of the ways these techniques are used to construct this application. By the time you've worked through this book, you'll be in a position to build applications like this for your own company intranet or web site.

Tell Us What You Think

We've worked hard on this book to make it useful. We've tried to understand what you're willing to exchange your hard earned money for, and we've tried to make the book live up to your expectations.

Please let us know what you think about this book. Tell us what we did wrong, and what we did right. This isn't just marketing flannel: we really do huddle around the e-mail to find out what you think. If you don't believe it, then send us a note. We'll answer, and we'll take whatever you say on board for future editions. The easiest way is to use e-mail:

feedback@wrox.com

You can also find more details about Wrox Press on our web site. There, you'll find the code from our latest books, sneak previews of forthcoming titles, and information about the authors and editors. You can order Wrox titles directly from the site, or find out where your nearest local bookstore with Wrox titles is located. The address of our site is:

http://www.wrox.com

Customer Support

If you find a mistake, please have a look at the errata page for this book on our web site first. The full URL for the errata page is:

http://www.wrox.com/Scripts/Errata.idc?Code=0464

If you can't find an answer there, tell us about the problem and we'll do everything we can to answer promptly!

Just send us an email to **support@wrox.com**.

or fill in the form on our web site: **http://www.wrox.com/Contact.htm**

The Background To Web Databases

It's relatively easy to create a few Web pages. There are plenty of tools around that will build simple pages automatically, and allow you to add extras like graphics or sounds. There are also tools emerging which help you structure a whole site, and assist you in defining the relationships and links between the individual pages.

It's when you go beyond these basics that life gets a little more complicated; for instance, trying to keep the published information up-to-date soon becomes a major headache—you'll need to find ways to make the task as 'automatic' as possible. The answer lies, as you'll see in this chapter, in the use of the information-retrieval properties of a database, together with the easy publishing techniques of HTML, and the technologies of the Internet.

As we go through this book, we'll be developing some applications which use a web browser as the 'front end', but draw the information for the page's content from a database management system. You may well be surprised at the different ways this can be done, and you'll see each method used to advantage—in a different way.

Before we really roll up our sleeves, though, we'll use this first chapter to develop an outline view of all the technologies we'll be covering, and see how they fit together. Without this, it's easy to get lost in the flood of new technologies that's inundating the market place. Even the ever-increasing use of abbreviations can make your head spin. Just what are OLEISAPI, IIS and IDC anyway?

So in this chapter, we'll be looking at:

- Why creating and maintaining a web site can be 'hard work'.
- What **information** is, and where it comes from.
- Ways of getting information into your web pages.
- Some of the new technologies that are becoming available.
- Some of the possibilities they offer for publishing information.

First, then, we'll investigate some of the problems of publishing information on the Web....

Why the Web is 'Hard Work'

Maintaining a presence on the Web is hard work. It doesn't matter whether you use it to publish corporate information, sell your company's products, disseminate your own kind of propaganda, or just display pictures of your dog—creating and maintaining a web site involves a lot of time and energy, and generally a lot of money.

A recent survey of major web sites in the US revealed that, on average, each one requires fifteen people just to maintain it (remember that these sites may hold 25,000 pages or more; StarWave's ESPNet site, for example, has 75,000+ pages). And that doesn't include the original design and construction! So it can be a frighteningly expensive process, and unless it produces some long-term benefits, it's very difficult to justify the cost and effort that it requires.

Finding the Benefits

The Web, and its associated technologies such as an intranet, *can* bring enormous benefits to corporations. They can also be highly cost-effective. For example, distributing promotional material by post is costly, and traditionally has a very low 'hit-rate'. If the letter goes straight from the letter-box to the trash can like most junk mail does, without being read, you've wasted your money on that particular mailing. However, if someone passes through your web site without buying, you aren't going to have to pay directly for their visit (as long as you get enough benefit from the rest to cover the overheads, of course!).

If your site is non-profit making then, in theory, life is easier. You don't have to justify the cost by making sales. However, there must still be a reason for being there, and anything you can do to reduce the cost, while increasing its effect, has got to be worth looking into. For example, if you are promoting a cause, such as saving whales, you can benefit from reducing the effort required to create each page. You can use the recouped resources to create more pages, or rescue some other endangered species as well.

But it's the fast-growing world of the corporate intranet where web publishing costs are often under the most intense scrutiny. While you can write off a few million dollars for a web site as 'advertising' or 'marketing', you won't get away with this when you are using the technology as an internal resource-provider. Every company is looking for ways to save money, and the Information Technology (IT) department is fast becoming the place to start. You need to be sure that you are using the most efficient methods of creating and disseminating information within your organization.

If you *are* just publishing pictures of your dog, though, we probably can't offer you much help in this book. However, if your site turns into the home of the National Alsation Appreciation Society, for instance, then you will certainly need to know a lot more about web database publishing. So you'd better read on now, and be ready....

Where Information Comes From

Year after year, the world gets more complex as we find more and more 'really important' things that we need to know. In a company environment, it's no longer enough to know that you sell 150,000 sprocket nuts a month. You have to know who you sold them to, where they live, what their income is, which social category they fall into, and what they eat for breakfast. The simple accounting systems of years back have been supplemented and superseded by Executive

Information Systems, Management Information Systems, Data Warehouses, and Online Transaction Monitoring. Accurate data about your market is often the key to survival in today's competitive world.

In fact, the whole world is hell-bent on collecting information. Each time you reply to a magazine advertisement, you can bet your bottom dollar that your name and address is added to many other lists. Each list helps advertisers and marketing people to better target you with just the right promotional literature—or junk mail. All this information is stored in huge database systems, across the world.

So, It's Databases Then?

Although it's the databases that hold all the facts and figures, they don't actually store *information* as such. If they did, they would be called 'informationbases'. What they do store is data—or, to be more precise, just numbers. It's only when these numbers are translated into characters, words, and pictures, that they really mean anything. By combining, extracting and interpreting data in different ways, it becomes information.

The value of any information depends on the needs of the recipient, and in many situations a good database system can make the difference between success and failure—be it a corporate marketing campaign, a government department, a political pressure group, or just your own address book. For example, if you want to know someone's phone number, and it only tells you their birthday, it's not exactly useful. To be of benefit, you must be able to get information that is precisely targeted to meet your need.

Different Kinds of Databases

Database systems vary from the desktop PC applications, like Microsoft Access or IBM/Lotus Approach, to the enterprise-oriented systems like Microsoft SQL Server, Sybase, Informix and Oracle. Each one is specifically designed to meet particular needs, such as the number of users, the amount of data to be handled, and the speed of response. For simpler, individual needs, you may use another type of application, such as a spreadsheet, an electronic diary, or a financial software package.

Most of these are well supplied with their own methods of extracting useful information from the data they contain. For example, in Microsoft Access, you can use the built-in query generator to summarize data in an almost endless number of permutations. Larger corporate database systems will generally contain pre-written modules which provide specially designed reports, together with tools to create user-defined ones. And the more specialist data storing applications will provide at least some different views of their data. An electronic diary, for example, could offer views of your commitments by day, week, month, or year; plus a list of all the people's birthdays you need to be sure not to miss again this year.

Providing Access to Information

Here's the crunch. If you only want to publish the information within your own company, you can distribute it over the network by letting each user fire up a copy of the database software and run the report. Alternatively, you can print it out and give them a copy for their information folder. Why do you need to put it in a web page, anyway? Here's a few things to think about:

If the data is viewed in the application that created it:

- You pay for extra user licenses, so that some people can just view it.

- You have to be sure only the authorized users modify it.

- The server and network must cope with multiple copies of large files.

- Several copies of each file will be open, so updating can be difficult.

- Casual users may have to learn the application, just to view the data.

If the data is on paper:

- Someone has to actually look after copying and distributing it.

- You can never be sure that everyone is using the latest version.

- If staff need to use the information in a document, they have to copy it.

- It's easy to lose it under all the other papers on your desk.

- It's hard to maintain security, for example preventing photocopying.

Using a browser and related technologies can produce added advantages. While a separate application presents information in terms of its intended purpose, and paper reports are expensive, slow, and often limited as to what can be displayed, browsers can present graphics, sound, video, and text in a common format, across multiple platforms, and at a relativity low cost. All in all, there are a lot of benefits in using this method of disseminating information throughout your company. The continuing growth of the corporate intranet bears witness to this.

What Can You Do With Information?

The way you actually provide access to information is basically the same whether you are pumping it around your own company's intranet, or making it available to the whole world over the Internet. But, of course, the nature of the content could well be different.

Publishing Information on the Web

For example, we provide a huge amount of general and specific information about our range of books on our web server at `http://www.wrox.com`.

It's mainly there for visitors from outside the company, though there are also many occasions when our sales staff use it to look up details on a particular book. The data is retrieved from a single database that stores all the information about the books and authors.

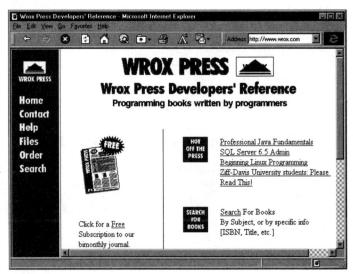

Using Information on an Intranet

In our production facility, however, we have very different needs. Maintaining control over the whole book publishing operation, getting projects completed on time, and ensuring that our high standards of quality and accuracy are met—all this needs an internal communications system which can handle all kinds of information. We are going to be working with this application throughout the book.

You can try all the pages for this book, or download them to run on your own server from our Web Site at:

http://www.wrox.com/books/0464/samples/webdb.htm

// www.wrox.com /store / Download.asp ? Code = 0464

For example, we can monitor the amount of resources expended on each project on a daily basis using a web page which collects details from each of the staff. Our accounts department can use this information to tightly control project costs.

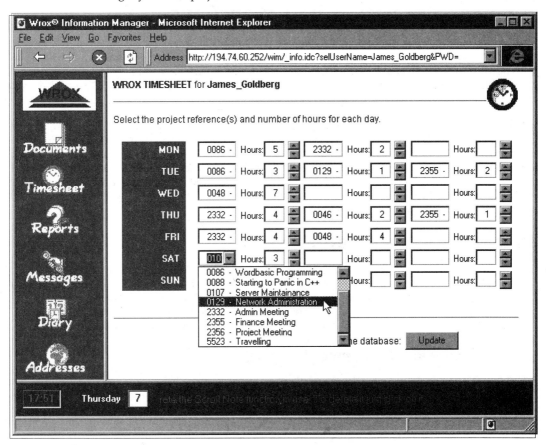

The Timesheet page that you can see in this screen shot is one frame of the browser window, and the other frames provide more information. For example, the bottom frame allows each person to send short notes to others in the form of a scrolling message which appears automatically. It also displays the 'system' time—taken from the server's clock rather than the client machine that is running the browser. This means that everyone is working to the same time. The application can also display other pages within the main frame, as you'll be seeing throughout this book. Of course, these pages aren't normally available outside our own local area network. They contain information which is not for general use.

The point is, that there are many different kinds of information that you may want to display, and even allow the user to manipulate, which can all be combined into web pages. Distributing this information using web technologies, and viewing it in a normal browser, provides a consistent interface and seamless links between the different types of information. Users can jump to a page that contains data from a different server on our local area network, then across to our external web site, and from there go out on to the Net in search of the information they need. The concept of universal access to all these disparate types of information has been around for a while. Now, however, it's a practical reality.

Getting Information into Web Pages

The beautifully formatted product sales report that you can display on screen in Access, or print out as hard copy, isn't a lot of good when it comes to getting the information into a web page. Yes, you can copy it into a new HTML page using one of the many editing tools that are available, or output it to a disk file, using a converter or filter to turn it into HTML; but how do you keep it up to date?

If the information changes every day, as sales figures do, you're faced with the decision of how often you want to update the page. Doing it weekly would probably satisfy the marketing department, but you can be pretty sure that the accounts department would prefer it done daily. And what if the information is used directly by customers placing orders for sprocket nuts, or by passengers booking seats on a plane? In these cases, you need to update it each time you make a sale or booking. It's no good updating the page once a week. You'll soon have shortages in your deliveries, or chaos at the check-in desk.

Creating Dynamic Web Pages

What we need is a way to connect the database itself to the Web, so that each page is created *dynamically*, using the values stored in the database at that actual moment. This is the core subject that we're devoting this book to. There are several technologies which offer this kind of integration, some old and some new. We're going to be looking in depth at some of the more recent products, and showing you how they can be used in a variety of situations.

What's Required for Dynamic Web Pages

The theory is simple enough. You just link your Internet server to your database system, so that it sends out the contents of the database on demand. Then, each time a user opens a page, they see the latest values from the records in the database. For example, if they place an order, the quantity will be subtracted from existing stocks. Then they, and all the other viewers, will only see the amount of stock that's still available.

*This is a little over-simplified, of course. Pages which are **already** open aren't usually updated automatically. It's only when the viewer refreshes the page, or comes back to it again, that they'll see the latest figures. This is only likely to be a problem if you have several viewers placing orders at the same time, and you can protect against this by validating the order against remaining stocks when they actually submit it.*

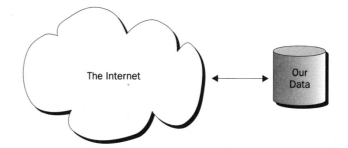

So here's what we're looking for:

Making the Connection

The problems come thick and fast now. Creating a direct physical connection for data to travel between the Internet and your database is not only difficult, but also leaves you open to security risks. Unless there's a proper translation layer, with appropriate controls applied, it's like placing a terminal on a street corner, and connecting it directly to your corporate network. Obviously, we need some combination of hardware and software which will sit between our database and the outside world.

So, how can we form this physical connection? To start with, our database server machine has to run some type of software interface to the Internet, which can handle user requests and supply pages. This might be Microsoft Internet Information Server (IIS), Website, NCSA httpd, CERN httpd, or similar, and it could be running on Windows NT, OS/2, Mac OS, Linux or any of the other UNIX-based operating systems.

Then, what about the Database Management System software (DBMS)? For a relatively small site, this could be Access, running on Windows 95 or Window NT, or perhaps File Maker or Clarion on an Apple Mac. In larger organizations, it's likely to be something more enterprise-oriented, such as SQL Server, Sybase, DB2 or Oracle—again running on an appropriate operating system of its own.

So we provide a bridge which can link the DBMS to the Internet, using some kind of Internet server application:

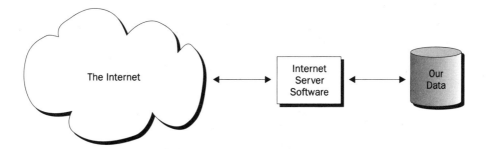

Of course, the database and the Internet Server software can be running on different machines, linked together by your network.

The actual combination you use depends on several factors. If you already have the hardware and the DBMS, then you need to find suitable bridging software. If you are starting from scratch, though, you can specify all the equipment so as to exactly match your projected needs. Choosing the hardware and a database on which to run your company is outside the scope of this book. Instead, we're going to look at what is likely to be the most flexible solution at present.

We are using **Microsoft Internet Information Server (IIS)** because many of the new technologies are actually core parts of the latest version. And we're basing this on the only operating system which is specifically designed for it: **Microsoft Windows NT Server.** As for the database, we're using **Microsoft Access** and we'll be accessing it only through the **Open Database Connectivity** driver **(ODBC).** This provides an abstraction layer between the database and the Internet software. As long as there is an ODBC driver available for your DBMS, you can access it with IIS. (We told you there would be a lot of abbreviations flying about!)

So the kind of configuration we're starting with looks something like this:

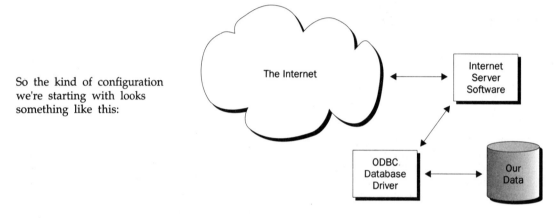

Looking at the Possibilities

It's pretty clear from what we've seen so far that the main problem we face is finding the 'something' that fits between the Internet and our data sources. It has to take instructions from the browser, which will generally occur when a `<FORM>` section of a page is submitted, and retrieve the information from the database. It then needs to format this information in HTML and return it to the browser on the client machine.

You won't be surprised to know that there are several ways we can do this, all based around a feature of Internet Information Server called ISAPI, or Internet Server Application Programming Interface. This interface is standard across many web servers, and allows other software to query it for the details of the browser's instructions, and persuade it to return a particular HTML page in response. This software becomes the 'something' in the middle.

An Overview of the Technologies

There are several new web products and development tools all competing for the role of the 'something' that sits between a web server and a database, and in this chapter we'll be looking broadly at all of them. Then, in the rest of the book, we'll be examining the front-runners in detail. To understand more about how the different technologies fit together, take a look at the next diagram. It's not intended to show the physical connections between the technologies, or to be an exact 'real life' view of the structure. It just shows how the different products are related in basic design.

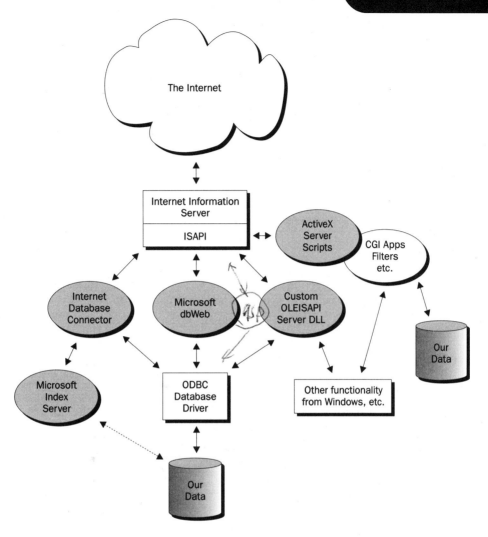

So there are several different products that sit between Internet Information Server and the Open Database Connectivity (ODBC) driver—and we haven't included all of them by any means. We've indicated the ones that we'll be looking at in this book by shading them. One of them, Active Server Pages, is difficult to position in the diagram. At the time of writing, it is in early Beta. However, we'll be spending some time in Chapter 6 looking at it, and you'll see why we've had trouble describing it accurately in the terms of the other technologies.

There's a couple of things we should consider from the diagram above. The Common Gateway Interface is more connected with older methods of creating interactive web pages, and there are also new methods which allow you to use similar techniques. As well as just retrieving data, the CGI and OLEISAPI methods are, in effect, separate executable programs. This lets you take advantage of all the other functionality available from your operating system, and even other applications on your system. For example, you can use mathematical and string handling functions, or retrieve the system date and time, from within your CGI or OLEISAPI applications.

Secondly, there is one technology which doesn't actually *extract* data from a database. Microsoft Index Server provides an indexing facility for almost any type of document on your system, not just HTML pages. As your web site grows in size and complexity, a search feature helps visitors to quickly find the location of the particular information they want. On a corporate intranet, the ability to index all kinds of documents makes it easier for staff to find the resource they need quickly and efficiently.

The other 'something' in the diagram, Microsoft dbWeb, is a specialist product which makes building a data query facility into a web page a simple task. We'll be looking at dbWeb in Chapter 4. We'll start, however, with the Internet Database Connector.

You can check out the new Microsoft technologies we've talked about here at their web site **http://microsoft.com**. *The ISAPI interface is also supported by other web servers. You can get more information from* **http://rampages.onramp.net/~steveg/isapiven.htm**

Internet Database Connector (IDC)

The Internet Database Connector (IDC) is a mechanism introduced with Microsoft Internet Information Server. It acts as a bridge between any ODBC data source and IIS, and hence the client browser. IDC is relatively straightforward, quick to set up and use, and can easily transform static web pages into dynamically generated HTML documents.

An Overview of IDC

IDC uses a script which is stored on the server in an **.idc** file, and which defines the parameters required to extract and format the information. These parameters can include the name of the data source, a user name and password to access it with, an SQL query to execute against the data, and the name of a template which contains the formatting information.

Along with the script, we create an Extended HTML Template (HTX) file. This is similar to standard HTML, but also contains 'placeholders' for the returned data. IDC uses the SQL query in the script file to extract the data from the database into a recordset. It then replaces the placeholders in the HTX template with the values from the matching records, and returns it to the user as an HTML file.

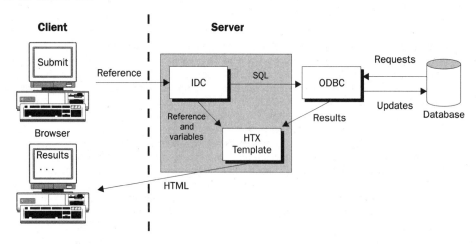

The fact that the HTX template is really just a normal HTML page, but with placeholders instead of actual values, means that converting an existing site to use this technology is relatively straightforward. You can just modify the existing **.htm** pages, and save them with an **.htx** extension, as you'll be seeing in later chapters.

Initiating an IDC Process

To initiate the process of retrieving information with IDC, you just have to reference the IDC script file on the server. This can be done from a normal **<A>** tag, or in the opening **<FORM>** tag of a form section on the page. The resulting HTML page is then returned to the browser.

Of course, it's most likely that you'll want to supply parameters to the query using information from the page currently being viewed. For example, you may have a text box where the user enters a part number. Your IDC script can retrieve the details of that part from your inventory database, format it using the HTX template, and provide a web page for the user with information about just that part.

Here's a query page in Internet Explorer, followed by the code that produces it:

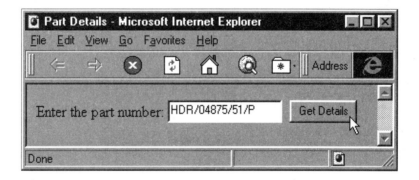

```
<HTML>
  <HEAD><TITLE>Part Details</TITLE></HEAD>
  <BODY>
    <FORM ACTION="http://myserver.com/inventory/part.idc" METHOD="POST">
      Enter the part number:
      <INPUT TYPE="TEXT" NAME="PART_NO">
      <INPUT TYPE="SUBMIT" VALUE="Get Details">
    </FORM>
  </BODY>
</HTML>
```

Clicking **Get Details** sends the contents of the controls in the form to the server and starts the script named **part.idc**. This extracts the details from the database, formats them using an HTX template, and returns the result to the browser:

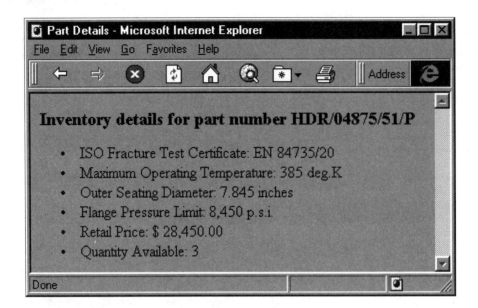

Using IDC in an <A> Tag

It's also possible to start an IDC process by referencing the script in an **<A>** tag, rather than as the **ACTION** in a **<FORM>** tag. However, this is only useful if you know the required parameters beforehand, or if you don't actually need any parameters at all. With a link created by an **<A>** tag, there are no controls whose content you can submit to the IDC; instead the browser just references the URL in the **HREF** attribute of the tag:

```
<A HREF="http://myserver/inventory/partlist.idc"> . . . </A>
```

This will execute the IDC script **partlist.idc**, without specifying any parameters, so the result will be broadly the same each time it is clicked. However, the page *will* automatically reflect any changes made to the records in our inventory database since the last time the user opened it. If we supplied the returned page as an ordinary static HTML file instead, i.e. as **partlist.htm**, it would need to be updated manually each time the data changed.

We can add parameters to the end of the **HREF** attribute, which are then passed to the IDC. For example, the following link will execute the **partlist.idc** script, but send it the parameter **widget07** as well:

```
<A HREF="http://myserver/inventory/partlist.idc?partno=widget07"> . . . </A>
```

In this case, IDC can use the parameter and make sure that the returned page just contains the information about the size seven widgets.

Using IDC in Applications

We use IDC in several different ways for the pages in our sample Wrox Information Manager application. One of these pages provides a user-definable set of links to other resources which can be on the user's own hard drive, stored on one of our network servers, or out on the Net itself. And these resources can be any type of file—such as a web page, spreadsheet, text document, zip file, or graphic.

The links themselves are descriptions that the user supplies for the resources, and they can add or remove links as required. The actual addresses of the resources are held in a database table in Access, so we can use a simple IDC script to retrieve them each time, and create the page.

Clicking a link opens that file or resource in a new browser window, or downloads it and opens it directly in the relevant application. Because some browsers can use in-place activation to host a copy of mainline applications such as Word and Excel, the file may even be displayed in this way:

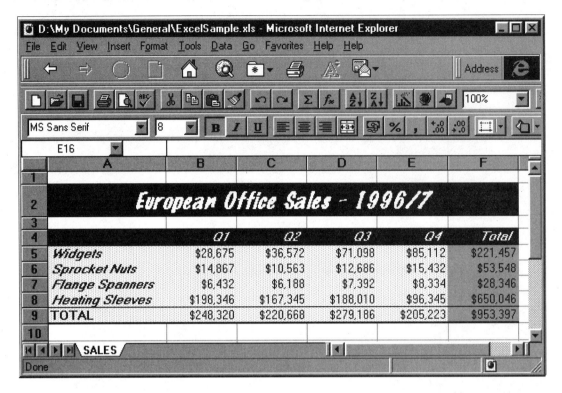

The links on the page can also be to a folder, rather than to a specific file or resource. In this case, the new window works just like the normal Windows Explorer, displaying a list of contents and allowing the user to double-click one to start the application, or navigate to other folders.

So IDC is quite simple to use from the browser's point of view, yet it can provide quite sophisticated functionality. In the next chapter, you'll see how easy it is to set up and use when it comes to looking after the server end of the process, and we'll show you how we created this application for Wrox Information Manager as well. Basically, once you've created the `.idc` script file and the matching `.htx` template, you're flying. IDC looks after the complexities itself, and you can just get on with developing even better client-side applications

An Introduction to dbWeb

To make data retrieval even easier, and allow users to query a database in different ways direct from their browser, Microsoft have released a utility called dbWeb. This connects to Internet Information Server and uses ODBC to retrieve the data it needs from any suitably enabled database system. Its major strength is the ease with which you can create your own personalized query system.

An Overview of dbWeb

To use dbWeb, you create one or more schemas which hold the details of the query that's required. When the user references a schema, via the dbWeb control DLL **dbwebc.dll**, the data is retrieved from the database, formatted with HTML tags, and returned to the client browser.

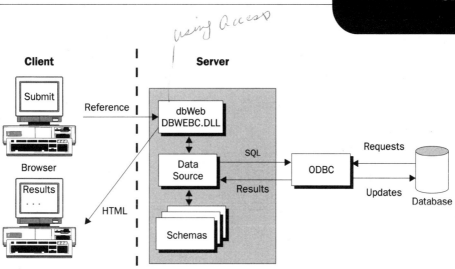

The key to each dbWeb query process is the schema. It holds details of the tables, fields, and joins required to extract the information from the database. It also contains a set of properties for each field, and the layout details which define how the finished page will appear. All in all, it's a bit like using Microsoft Access to display data from a table. So it's no surprise to find that dbWeb is, in fact, based on Access technology. The schema and data source details are stored in an Access-format database file.

Schema Wizard in dbWeb

One of the things that makes dbWeb so easy to use is the Schema Wizard. This allows you to step through the process of creating a schema, defining all the parameters required for the query system. The wizard is surprisingly powerful in that you can include drill-down fields in the returned pages. This means that the list of results in the page are actually hot-links instead of normal text. Clicking on one displays the data in the 'next level down'. You can set up query systems which allow the user to explore the database contents using several pre-defined queries, rather than just a single one.

You can also create schemas by hand, rather than with the wizard, and create your own return page formats. Of course, you can design this type of multilevel query process using, for example, IDC—but dbWeb makes setting it up a lot easier.

Initiating a dbWeb Process

To initiate a dbWeb query you would normally use an **<A>** tag to create a link in the page. The **HREF** attribute of this tag is the path and name of the dbWeb DLL, plus the name of the schema and the method you want it to use. For example, to reference a schema called **part_details**, and display the 'query by example' grid, we could use:

```
<A HREF="http://myserver/dbweb/dbwebc.dll/part_details?getqbe"> . . . </A>
```

In this case, the parameter is **getqbe**, which is the name of the built-in dbWeb method that creates the query-by-example page. To display the results, once the user has entered the criteria for the query and clicked the start button, dbWeb automatically calls the built-in **getresults** method. From there, each link in the page uses parameters to display the next level of detail, and by linking schemas together we can provide a whole range of levels.

Using dbWeb in Applications

We use dbWeb in one of the pages of our Wrox Information Manager application. Our staff provide details of the time they spend on each project using the Timesheet page you saw at the beginning of this chapter. When it comes to examining the results, so that we can cost each project, we use the Reports page in our application.

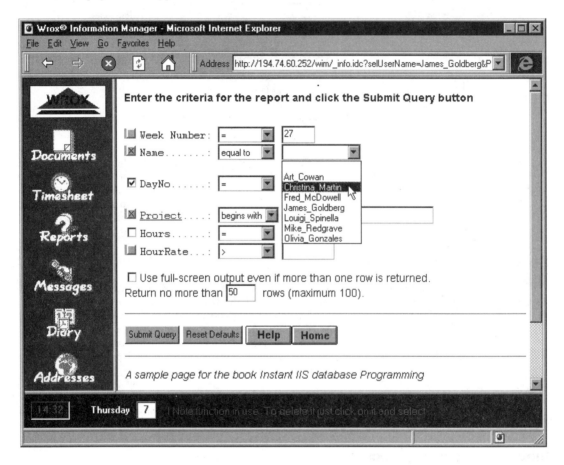

The initial Reports page uses the **getqbe** method to display a list of the available fields in the schema. By entering criteria in the text boxes, we can select the records we want to see. For example, here, we're interested in projects worked on by Christina Martin.

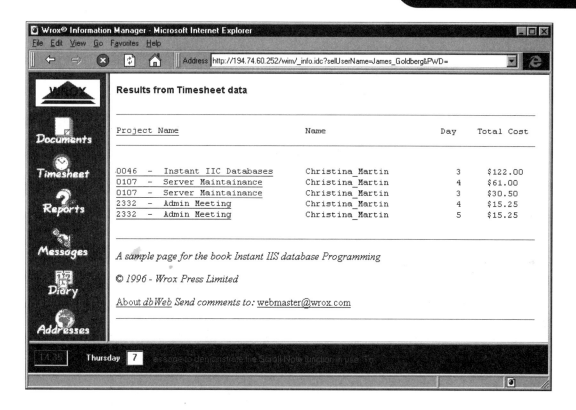

The query returns a list of all the projects, and the total cost for each one. Notice that the project names are actually hyperlinks. By clicking on one, we can get to see a different view of the data. In this case, we would see a listing of all the people who worked on that project.

You can see what we mean when we say that dbWeb is like using a normal database application directly. You'll see more on how this page is created, and some other ways of using dbWeb, in Chapter 4.

Accessing your Web Server Directly

The two methods we've seen so far provide an easy way to communicate with Internet Information Server and your ODBC database driver, without having to know much about what's going on behind the scenes. However, to get the most control over the data-retrieval process, you have to go a little more deeply into the workings of the process.

There are also limitations on what you can achieve with both IDC and dbWeb. To get real power, you have to deal direct with your web server software, either by using its Application Programming Interface, or by using the Common Gateway Interface (CGI). There are different ways you can approach the task, depending on the web server and operating system you are using.

Microsoft Internet Information Server (IIS), running on Windows NT Server, provides both a standard CGI interface and the ISAPI. We can attack either of these directly, using a programming language like C/C++, Pascal, Visual Basic, Perl, or Fortran. Alternatively, we can access the ISAPI using OLE/ActiveX methods. In this section, we'll look at the various possibilities.

23

OLE has now officially been re-titled ActiveX. However, this all-encompassing word is now applied to almost everything that is connected to the Internet. In this book, you'll see OLE used where we feel it helps to better pinpoint the actual technology we're discussing at the time.

The Common Gateway Interface

It's long been possible to create web pages dynamically using some kind of database or application which is running on the server. Traditionally, these use the Common Gateway Interface (CGI), which is a mechanism that allows web clients to execute programs on a web server, and the server to communicate the results back to the client. Through the use of CGI programs, the server can process input from an HTML form and dynamically produce HTML documents.

The CGI is, in fact, a cross-platform and cross-application standard. All web servers should implement CGI in the same way, so that the same CGI application can be run on any system. In reality this isn't quite true—they are source-compatible, but a UNIX server won't be able to execute a program which has been compiled for an Intel processor, for example. However, in general, CGI applications are portable between different web servers at software level. This is one of their main attractions, and source code for most of the common requirements is freely available.

How a CGI Application Works

Notice, first, that the CGI uses an *application*, i.e. an executable file. This can be a normal **.exe** program, or the equivalent in another language such as a Perl script (**.pl**). Instead of reading from the keyboard and outputting to the screen, however, it uses the standard C language input and output streams, **stdin** and **stdout**.

The web server sends it the information from the client browser as a string, and the CGI application returns a coded string containing the HTML for the page that is to be returned to the viewer. The application can take advantage of any of the features of the language used to write it, except outputting information to the server's screen.

Initiating a CGI Application

To start the application running, the browser just references it, like we saw with an IDC script. The name of the CGI application is placed in an **<A>** tag, the **ACTION** argument of a **<FORM>** tag, or anywhere else that a normal URL would be referenced (such as an **HTTP-EQUIV** statement which refreshes a page automatically). For example, to execute the application **mycgiapp.exe** we could use:

```
<A HREF="http://myserver/cgi-bin/mycgiapp.exe"> . . . </A>
```

We can also send parameters to the application if required. This example sends the parameter **showcolor** to the **mycgiapp.exe** application:

```
<A HREF="http://myserver/cgi-bin/mycgiapp.exe?myparam=showcolor"> . . . </A>
```

And, of course, if we reference it in a **<FORM>** tag, the values of the controls in that form are sent as arguments as well. Here, we're sending the values of the controls in our form to the **mycgiapp.exe** application:

```
<FORM ACTION="http://myserver/cgi-bin/mycgiapp.exe" METHOD="POST">
```

It's also possible to map, or redirect, a normal web page on the server to the application. For example, you could map the page **siteview.htm** to the CGI application **siteview.exe**. When the browser references this page, the application runs instead, and creates the return page dynamically:

```
<A HREF="http://myserver/cgi-bin/siteview.htm"> . . . </A>
```

Hitting the Internet Server API Directly

Whereas the CGI is a universal interface, common across different platforms, ISAPI is often less universally compatible. In Microsoft Internet Information Server, however, ISAPI provides a set of functions which can be called from most programming languages, and which are used to communicate with IIS directly. They can retrieve the information coming from the client browser, and transmit dynamically generated pages back to it.

This is probably the most efficient way to work with IIS, and for C++ gurus with major server-side programming tasks to accomplish, it's the only answer. However, unless you are used to programming Windows at a low level, ISAPI presents a quite formidable task which deserves a book all to itself.

How an ISAPI Application Works

The first important point to note is that to work with ISAPI directly, you have to create a Dynamic Link Library (DLL) and *not* an executable application. This immediately presents a problem for Visual Basic users as, at the time of writing, you can't create standard Windows DLLs using VB. (You can create OLE Automation Server DLLs, however, as you'll see later.)

Inside the DLL, you use a range of functions which can interrogate IIS to obtain all kinds of information about the client and the data it supplied. For example, the ISAPI functions **GetServerVariable** and **ReadClient** return information which is supplied when the DLL is referenced by a browser, and **WriteClient** sends a data string back to it to provide the returned page.

Initiating an ISAPI Application

Although the internal workings of ISAPI are very different to CGI applications, the way they are referenced in an HTML page are similar. To reference a DLL called **myisapi.dll**, we could use:

```
<A HREF="http://myserver/isapi/myisapi.dll"> . . . </A>
```

To send parameters to it, we just add them after a question mark separator:

```
<A HREF="http://myserver/isapi/myisapi.dll?myparam=doitnow"> . . . </A>
```

And to reference it in a **<FORM>** tag, we could use:

```
<FORM ACTION="http://myserver/isapi/myisapi.dll" METHOD="POST">
```

Using OLE/ActiveX Methods - OLEISAPI

To get around the problem of creating a standard Windows DLL to work with ISAPI, we can instead create an In-process OLE/ActiveX Automation Server as a DLL. This is a similar technique to creating OLE servers which operate as part of another application's functionality. For example,

25

the Equation Editor supplied with Microsoft Word is an OLE Automation Server, and so Word can act as the client and take advantage of the functionality it provides. Most Windows programming languages, including Visual Basic 4, let you create OLE Automation Server DLLs.

How an OLEISAPI Application Works

The background to OLEISAPI is very similar to that of dbWeb, which we looked at earlier. Communication with Internet Information Server is simplified by a system DLL which sits between IIS and our custom application. In the case of dbWeb this was **dbwebc.dll**, and in this case it's called (not surprisingly) **oleisapi.dll**.

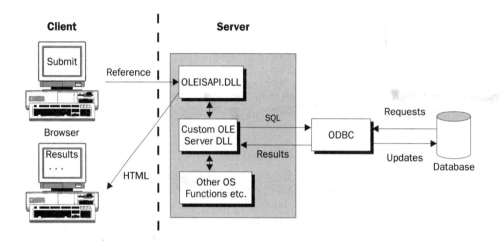

The OLEISAPI DLL interrogates IIS to get the data coming from the client, and sends it to our custom DLL. This manipulates the data, queries the database as required, performs any other processing necessary, and then returns a new HTML page to the OLEISAPI DLL. This page is passed back to IIS, which returns it to the client's browser.

Again, this method allows us to create custom solutions based on all the functionality available in that language (apart from routines which write to the server's screen). All we need is a class definition containing at least one method, which must accept two string-type parameters. The first one is the data coming from the browser, and the second one is set within the DLL to a string containing the HTML of the page we want to return. This example shows how we could implement it in Visual Basic:

```
Sub DoItNow(strDataIn, strPageOut)
  'code to decipher the data in strDataIn
  . . .
  'code to manipulate the database and get the results
  . . .
  'code to create the page in strPageOut
  . . .
End Sub
```

Initiating an OLEISAPI Application

To initiate our custom OLE server, we place a call to it in an **<A>** tag on the page or in the **ACTION** attribute of the **<FORM>** tag, so that it executes when the form is submitted. We have to specify the name of the class and the method in that class that we want to execute:

```
<A HREF="http://myserver/oleisapi.dll/myole.dll.myclass.doitnow"> .. </A>
```

To reference it in the **ACTION** attribute of a **<FORM>** tag, we could use:

```
ACTION="http://myserver/oleisapi.dll/myole.dll.myclass.doitnow"
```

Using OLEISAPI in Applications

We'll show you just how useful OLEISAPI is in Chapter 3. Many of the pages in our Wrox Information Manager application use OLEISAPI behind the scenes, so you'll learn a lot more about how the DLLs are built and how they can be used. As an example, the Timesheet application you saw, near the start of this chapter, uses OLEISAPI extensively to process the multitude of data returned each time a user updates their timesheet.

Before we leave the web server API, we should briefly consider two more aspects. One is how the various methods affect performance of the server, and the other is how one of the most recent technologies can make working with the API easier.

CGI versus ISAPI

Although both CGI and ISAPI (which includes OLEISAPI) are used to manipulate the web server software directly, they operate in very different ways. CGI applications are executable programs which can be written in a variety of languages. They tend to be standardized across platforms, so pre-written and tested ones are easily available for everyday tasks.

ISAPI and OLEISAPI methods use DLLs, rather than executable applications. At present there are fewer of these available, although the list is growing. As you've seen, dbWeb is a specialist ISAPI-based system underneath, as is (in the broadest sense) IDC itself.

It's the way that the two methods are implemented that gives rise to major performance differences. A CGI application is loaded each time it is referenced by a client, and so a separate copy is running for each one. An ISAPI DLL, however, can be dynamically loaded and unloaded by the operating system, as memory and resources require. And because DLLs can be multithreaded, one can handle several simultaneous browser requests.

So the server must have memory space to load and execute several copies of a CGI application on a busy site, and complex ones which take a while to run can cause problems. They are also slower to load and execute than a DLL, which is likely to already be in memory. It's also a lot quicker to send the parameters to a DLL, which executes in the same address space as the web server software.

However, this sharing of address space can be the downfall of ISAPI DLLs. If a CGI application fails, it only breaks itself. Because it is in a separate address space, it can't cause failure of the web server software. An errant ISAPI DLL can, however, so you need to be very sure that it is properly tested and verified before use.

Active Server Pages

Before we move away from the server API, we must mention one of the newest web server technologies. Creating ISAPI DLLs and CGI applications generally requires a programming language which can produce executable files or DLLs. However, there are some script-based languages, such as Perl and Awk, which use an interpreter to 'execute' the code in a script when it is referenced. For small and simple tasks, this is an easy way to create server-side applications.

With the arrival of VBScript in the browser, it's not surprising to find that Microsoft has produced a server-side implementation. It offers a lot more features than pure VBScript, because it has to be able to manipulate databases, files, and other system objects. It can also host other scripting languages, and run other applications directly. However, it works in essentially the same way as client-side VBScript and, of course, its predecessors Perl and Awk.

Server-side scripting is a big enough subject to warrant a book of its own (look out for *Instant Active Server Pages Programming* from Wrox); here, we'll just be giving you an overview and introduction to it. At the time of writing, Active Server Pages is still in development, and you'll find it changing quite considerably as time goes on. However, what you'll see in our brief introduction will help you to decide if it's suitable for your needs. It's quite an impressive new technology, and offers to make server-side scripting a lot less of a 'black art' than it has appeared to be in the past.

Index Server Search Engine

Lastly, in this chapter, we'll take a brief look at another of the new technologies which are available to make life much easier for both you and your users—Index Server. We are not going to cover this in detail in this book, but will provide an introduction to it in Appendix C.

Finding information within a large web site, or corporate intranet, can be a real headache. While users can (hopefully!) remember which drive, and with luck which folder, they left a file in on their own machine, it's not as easy when someone else is administering the entire system. Web sites and intranets are reorganized, and things get moved around regularly. So, when the poor user comes to download the latest fix to their favorite software, or check out some information in the corporate color scheme documentation, they can be left browsing around for ages.

The answer, of course, is good site design; but a search engine can make life even easier. It can index not only the titles and filenames of documents, but also the contents of all kinds of files as well. These could be word processor documents, text files, spreadsheets, etc. By supplying a set of search criteria, the user gets a list of all the matching documents, and they can open the one they want with a single mouse-click.

Index Server is Microsoft's search engine, and is an add-on to IIS and Windows NT server. In total, it's a highly versatile system which covers almost all searching requirements, allows you to set up customized forms for the original query, and supports several foreign languages. It also has automatic indexing facilities and a range of administrative tools.

How Index Server Works

In an earlier section, we looked at Internet Database Connector, and saw how it used a script and an Extended HTML Template to create a results page. Index Server is a similar type of technology, and is used in a very similar way—offering the same mix of flexibility and simplicity. This, alone, accounts for the huge potential it offers for creating personalized search applications within your own web site or company intranet.

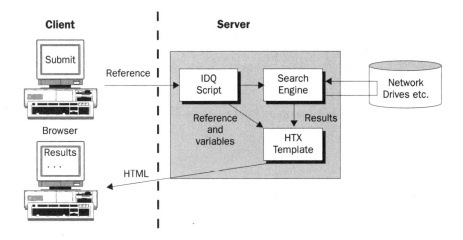

Looking at the diagram, you can see that the only real difference in the way it's used, when compared to IDC, is that the **.idc** script is replaced by an **.idq** file. The parameters and syntax used in these files are different because the nature of the information being sought is very different, but the working structure of the components is similar. And there are only minor differences between the two HTX templates types.

Using Index Server

We've included a simple example of Index Server in our **Wrox Information Manager** application. It allows users to search our multiserver site to find specific documents by supplying the name or part of the document's content. Here, we've specified all documents which contain the words **Widgets** or **Sprocket Nuts**.

After a few moments, a new browser page reveals that four documents match the criteria. Each one is displayed as a hyperlink, and clicking on one opens that document directly.

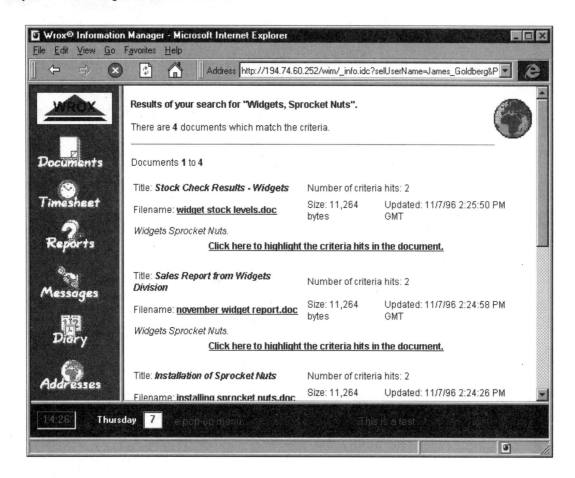

Summary

In this chapter, we've taken a broad overall look at the technologies which provide methods of publishing data dynamically on a web page, while reducing the time and effort it involves. We looked at the reasons why you need the technology, some of the more recent additions to the range of products available, and how they can be used.

This book will concentrate on three of these technologies: Internet Database Connector (IDC); OLEISAPI; and Active Server Pages (as it stands at the time of writing). We'll also spend some more time on dbWeb. These are the most efficient ways for the newcomer to web publishing to start, while still encompassing the power needed for all but the most intensive server-side processing tasks.

We've also shown you some of the pages from our sample application, **Wrox Information Manager**. This provides an excellent illustration of how the various technologies can work together to provide web applications of quite surprising power and effectiveness.

In the next chapter, we'll go back to IDC, and show you—from the ground up—how quick and easy it is to get started with interactive web database publishing.

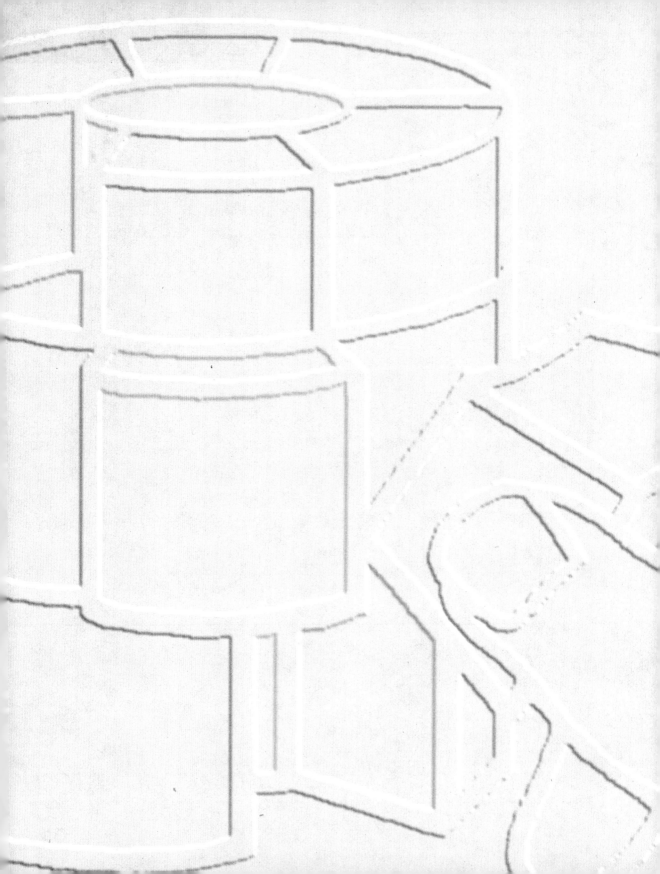

Internet Database Connector

In the last chapter, we introduced you to several techniques that we can use to extract information from a database and create dynamic web pages. In this chapter, we will be concentrating on the **Internet Database Connector** (IDC) technology, which is an integral part of Microsoft **Internet Information Server** (IIS).

IDC is one of the easiest ways to start building your own dynamic pages using database information. The inherent flexibility of IDC means that you have plenty of opportunities to fine tune your pages to meet your precise needs. It therefore compares favorably with application-based systems such as dbWeb (which you'll be seeing more of in Chapter 4).

In this chapter, we'll show you how we use IDC as the basis for our Wrox Information Manager application—to retrieve, insert, and update records in our database. We'll also show you how you can take advantage of other functions that are part of IDC, to allow all kinds of data management tasks to be accomplished.

> *We are using version 2.0 of IIS, and if you have an earlier version, you will find that some of the techniques we describe will not work. In particular, Version 1 only allows one SQL statement per IDC script.*

So in this chapter, we'll be looking at:

- The basic principles behind Internet Database Connector
- How we use it to retrieve, insert, and update records in a database
- Some of the issues of security and controlling user actions
- A brief look at some of the other possibilities of IDC technology

We'll start with the basic principles of IDC, and show you how a simple dynamic page can be created.

What is IDC?

IDC is just one of the technologies which allow you to execute an SQL statement against a database and turn the results into useful information in a web page. If a request that the Internet Information Server receives from the client's browser is a reference to an IDC script, it passes it on to the Internet Database Connector.

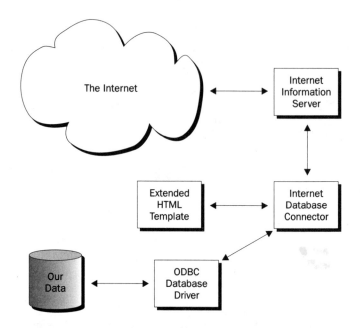

Here, the database is queried to retrieve or update the information as required; at the same time, an Extended HTML template (HTX) is referenced. This template contains the outline of the page that is to be returned. IDC combines the two, and sends it back to the client.

From the point of view of the client, the browser just requests a web resource which happens to be an IDC script—a text file with the extension **.idc**. The server processes the request, and the client gets the results back as HTML formatted information—just like any other web page.

There are two main parts to the process—a script file, and the Extended HTML template (**.htx**) file. The next figure shows the process in a little more detail; it's worth keeping this model in mind, because you'll be meeting other technology implementations, later in the book, which are (broadly) very similar.

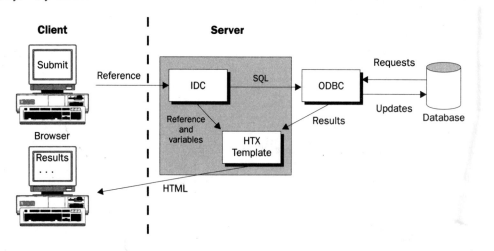

Taking the Server-Side View

So, from the client's point of view, things are simple. Just referencing a URL that includes a reference to an IDC script will download the formatted HTML page. From the point of view of the server, of course, things are a little more complex, because it's here that all the work is done. We'll start with the basics that you need to consider when you create your first scripts.

Executable Directories

An IDC script is just a text file. So, as with any other file resource, pointing a browser at a reference to it in an HTML page should simply download it to the client machine. This isn't terribly useful, however, because we want the server to *execute* it. To do this, we have to make the server directory in which the script is stored an 'executable' directory, so that scripts of all types (not just **.idc** ones) will be passed to the correct script interpreter—in the case of IDC, this is **httpodbc.dll**. By default, IIS will have created a **/Scripts** directory when it was installed, and will automatically have made this executable. If we place our IDC scripts (or any other scripts) in another directory, then we have to make sure it's executable as well.

To create an executable directory, or to make an existing directory executable, we have to first set up a virtual path, or **alias**, to that directory. In Internet Service Manager, open the Properties dialog for the WWW Service, and select the Directories page. Here, you can see the **/Scripts** directory, plus any others you have created. To add another one, just use the Add button, and select the directory and the Alias you want to use for it.

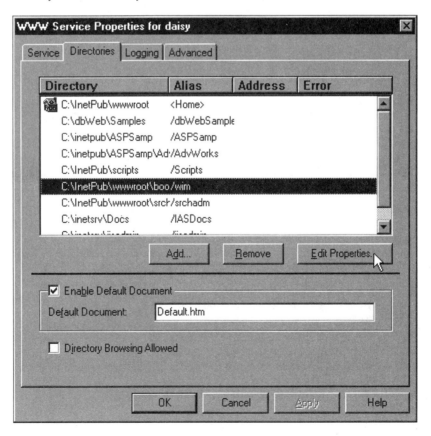

35

To make the selected directory executable, all we need to do is click the Edit Properties... button and check the Execute option at the bottom of the dialog. In the screenshot below, we've left the Read option checked as well, because we want to be able to store the HTX templates and HTML documents there as well. IIS will automatically execute scripts, but let the browser download other files. If the Read option is not set, IDC will not work correctly.

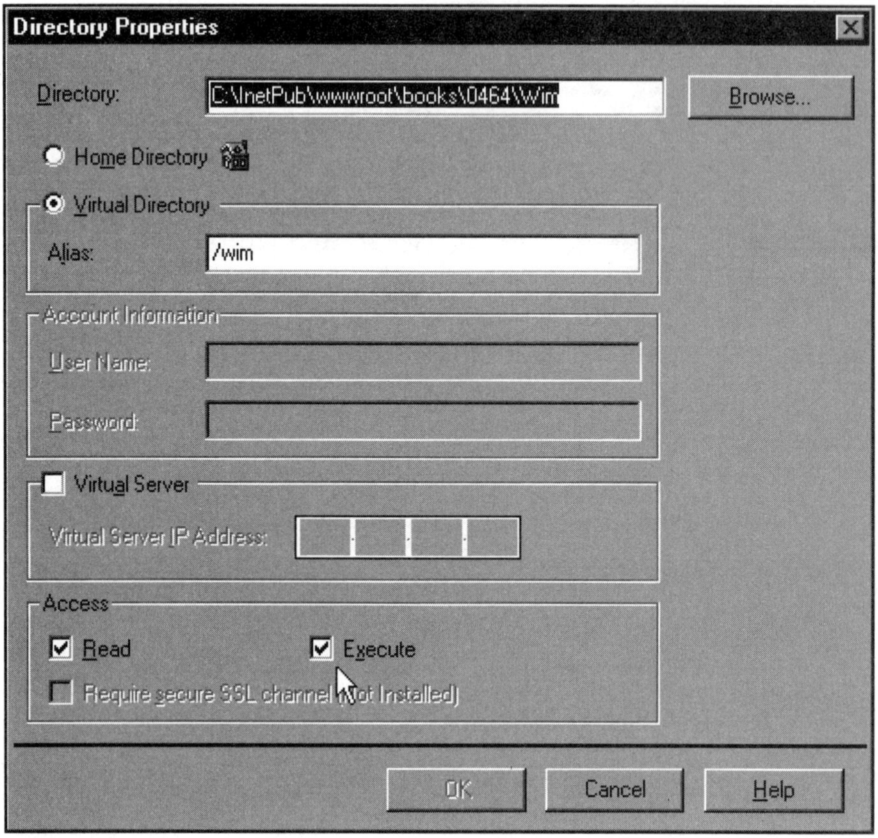

The IDC Script File

To create an IDC script, we just need a text editor—Notepad will do fine. In it we have to specify all the information that IDC needs to locate the data source and matching template, and extract the right information. The format of a simple IDC file is:

```
Datasource: <An ODBC Data Source Name>
User: <Name of the User Account to Access Database>
Password: <User Account Password>
Template: <URL of an HTML Template file>
SQLStatement:
+ <Lines of SQL Statements>
+ <Lines of SQL Statements>
```

The **Datasource** specifies the database from which to retrieve data. Since the connection is made using Open Database Connectivity (ODBC) methods, this can be just about *any* database system for which there are ODBC drivers. When configuring your server to access the database through ODBC, you need to have previously defined a **System Data Source Name** that relates to the data source, so that any script you create will run correctly.

> *Because this has to be done for almost all the IIS database technologies, we've supplied full instructions separately, in Appendix A of this book.*

The **User** and **Password** lines of the script contain the security information that is passed to the database through the ODBC connection layer. In our initial examples, we are being very lax, and just using the database administrator account **sa**. Be warned: doing this may allow a visitor to view your script, and hence see the passwords and other details. We'll be looking at security issues in Chapter 5.

Next come the **Template** and **SQLStatement** entries. These are the bits that do all the work.

Defining the SQL Statement

The **SQL Statement** line holds any SQL statement, in a dialect that is appropriate for the ODBC driver and database combination in use. In fact, you can do almost anything in this statement—if your knowledge of SQL is up to it! Any data that is returned by the query can then be used in the **Template**.

> *This book isn't an SQL primer, and we'll assume you have at least some grasp of its syntax. We'll be using relatively simple SQL statements, and concentrating on the server technologies instead. If you want to learn more about SQL, look out for Joe Celko's book, Instant SQL Programming.*

To connect the values returned from the SQL query (if there are any) to the template, we use the field names of the returned records. For example, the following script lines execute a query against our data source, which returns a list of all the values in the **UserName** field of the **Person** table in our database:

```
SQLStatement:
+ SELECT UserName FROM Person
```

This returns a set of records containing just the names of the users. To refer to them in the template, we would use the name **UserName**. Of course, we can re-name the result fields in SQL, like this:

```
SQLStatement:
+ SELECT UserName AS Employee FROM Person
```

This returns the same values, but now we refer to them with the name **Employee**. This gives us extra flexibility if we have to match the SQL statement to an existing HTX template, and saves having to edit all the placeholders in the template.

Defining the Template

The HTX template is simply a text file which is used to produce the page that is seen by the client browser. It looks just like a normal HTML page, except that we add tags which act as placeholders for the data returned from our SQL query, plus a few other pieces of information that the server gives us access to.

37

To refer to the values returned by the IDC script, we use the names we created in the SQL statement as placeholders. The syntax is **<%variable_name%>**. When the template is interpreted by IDC, before being sent back to the client, these placeholders are replaced by the actual values.

*You might as well get used to the **<% ... %>** syntax, because you'll be seeing it in a lot of other places in this book, besides IDC.*

We can also access the values that are sent to the IDC script directly, as well as those retrieved from the database through the SQL statement. Adding **idc.** to the beginning of a variable name tells IDC to use the value sent to it from the browser. For example, while **<%UserName%>** could be the value of the user name retrieved from the database, **<%idc.UserName%>** could be the value of the control named **UserName**, on the form in the browser which initiated the request.

Of course, we often expect our SQL query to return more than one value from the database tables. In the example SQL statement we used above, we'll get a list of all the users defined in the **Person** table. To place the list of users in the page that's returned to the client, we use a loop which is defined in the template with **<%BeginDetail%>** and **<%EndDetail%>** tags. This effectively tells IDC to repeat all the stuff between the tags, once for each record, putting in the respective values from each of these records in turn.

So, to build a list of employee's names, where we've extracted them from the database with the SQL statement **SELECT UserName FROM Person**, we could use:

```
<PRE>
  <%BeginDetail%>
    Employee name is: <%UserName%>
  <%EndDetail%>
</PRE>
```

The result is a nicely formatted list:

```
Employee name is: Christina_Martin
Employee name is: Fred_McDowell
Employee name is: Joe_Spinolla
. . .
```

Notice that we've included the **<PRE>** and **</PRE>** tags, which indicate to the browser that the text is pre-formatted. It should use a fixed pitch font, and respect the carriage returns, to ensure that we get a properly formatted list. If we don't take steps like this, the names will all be on the same line, because in HTML the browser doesn't recognize carriage returns. Of course, as an alternative, we can use:

```
<%BeginDetail%>
  Employee name is: <%UserName%><BR>
<%EndDetail%>
```

If we are creating lists in columns, we'll need to either use **<PRE>** tags and the correct number of spaces, or insert the results into a table. For example, if **PartNum** and **PartDesc** have been extracted from a database table using a query, such as:

```
SELECT PartNum, PartDesc FROM PartList WHERE PartNum > 4167
```

we can use an HTML `<TABLE>` like this:

```
<TABLE>
  <TR>
    <TH> Part Number </TH>
    <TH> Description </TH>
  </TR>
  <%BeginDetail%>
    <TR>
      <TD> <%PartNum%> </TD>
      <TD> <%PartDesc%> </TD>
    </TR>
  <%EndDetail%>
</TABLE>
```

IDC Examples from Wrox Information Manager

Like all things in life, the best way to learn is by doing. In our Wrox Information Manager application, we have a page which displays a list of documents and resources which are defined by, and for, each user. They can maintain this list to suit their regular working pattern, and it makes it easier for them to find regularly used files.

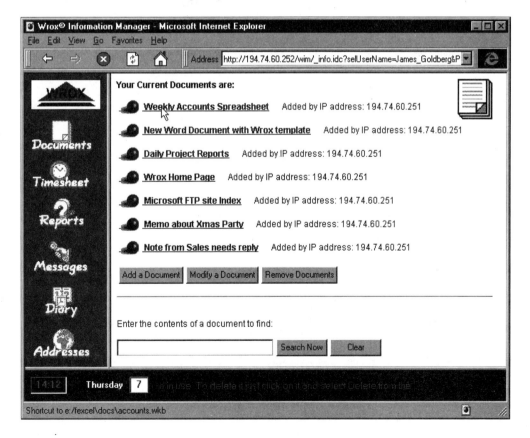

You can load this page from the samples index page on our web site at `http://www.wrox.com/` `books/0464/samples/webdb.htm`

The samples index page allows you to go directly to any of the samples supplied for this book. You can also download the files and run them on your own system. There's a file called `Setting Up.txt` *which gives instructions of how you should set the application up if you want to run it on your own web server.*

Creating the Current Documents List

Each entry in the list of documents contains a graphic and a hypertext link to the document, so the user can open it with a single click. (For the time being, take no notice of the other parts of the page—we'll come to them later.) The links are stored in a table **CurrentDocument** in our database, so each time we want to create this page we just have to extract them.

Displaying the Hyperlinks

The fields in the **CurrentDocument** table hold the **UserName** of the link's owner, a **Description** of the document to use as the text of the link, the **Location** (URL) of the document to allow the browser to fetch it, and an **IP** address string which shows where the document link was added from. We'll look at how documents are added to the table in a moment. In the meantime, though, here's the SQL statement that extracts the values for our page:

```
SQLStatement:
+SELECT ALL Location, Description, IP FROM CurrentDocument WHERE
+ UserName='%UserName%' ORDER BY Description
```

The purpose of **UserName** is to make sure we only extract values for the correct user, and here we're using the value of the **UserName** parameter directly in the SQL query as part of the **WHERE** clause. **%UserName%** (without the **<** and **>** characters) returns the value of the parameter, or the control on a form, with that name. Because it's a text value, we have to enclose it in single quotes in the SQL query.

In our case, the value itself comes directly from the **HREF** attribute of the **<A>** tag that loads this page. We'll come back to this in a while, but for now just accept that the SQL query gives us a recordset which contains just the records for our current user.

For each record returned from this query we need to write a new line in the HTML page that the template generates, like this:

```
<%BeginDetail%>
  <A HREF="<%Location%>" TARGET="Workspace">
    <IMG SRC="ball_red.gif" ALT="<%Location%>" ALIGN=MIDDLE BORDER=0>
    <STRONG><%Description%></STRONG>
  </A>
       Added by IP address: <%IP%><P>
<%EndDetail%>
```

The **Location** field in each record is used for the **HREF** attribute of the hyperlink. Notice that we are targeting documents to a new window which will be named **Workspace**, rather than just loading them into the main application frame. The **Description** in each record is used for the text of the link, and the **IP** address shows that we can retrieve other interesting information for use in our scripts. Again, we'll look at some of these server variables later in the chapter.

*To place extra spaces in our page, we've used the code ** **. This is one of the standard codes (like **©** for the copyright symbol) that you can use for characters which are not supported directly in HTML. Normally, browsers ignore multiple repeated spaces in the HTML code. ** ** inserts a non-breaking space in the text, and you can use several to give more room between words without resorting to the **<PRE>** or **<TT>** formats.*

Conditional Directives in a Template

Of course, there will be times when no data is returned from our query. For example, if we ask for the links for a user who has doesn't have any defined, we won't get any records returned. In this case, it would be good to be able to tell the user that there are no records.

IDC allows us to create template files where some conditional tests are done, and the HTML code which is generated can be varied depending on the results of these tests. What we do is use a conditional **<%If .. %> <%EndIf%>** statement in the HTX template:

```
<%If CurrentRecord EQ 0%> <!-- No Documents defined -->
   There are no documents currently defined for <%idc.UserName%><P>
<%EndIf%>
```

CurrentRecord is a reserved variable provided by IDC. It indicates the relative position of the record currently being accessed in a **<%BeginDetail%> <%EndDetail%>** section, within the returned recordset. For example, it will have the value 3 when the third record in the recordset created by the SQL query is being combined into the template. If there are no records returned by the SQL query, it will still be zero *after* the **<%BeginDetail%> <%EndDetail%>** section of the template has been evaluated.

> *Note that **CurrentRecord** has an undefined value until after the **<%BeginDetail%> <%EndDetail%>** section of the HTX template has been interpreted.*

In our example, we've tested for equality with **EQ**. IDC defines four comparison operators for use in conditional tests:

Operator	Comparison
EQ	Equality
LT	Less than
GT	Greater than
CONTAINS	True if the right hand side expression is a substring of the left hand side

As you might expect, we can also use the **<%If .. %> <%Else%> <%EndIf%>** construct for conditional tests:

```
<!-- place this AFTER the BeginDetail/EndDetail section -->
<%If CurrentRecord EQ 0%>     <!-- No Documents defined -->
   There are no documents currently defined for <%idc.UserName%><P>
<%Else%>
   <%idc.UserName%> has <%CurrentRecord%> documents defined.
<%EndIf%>
```

While it's possible to use nested `<%If .. %> <%Else%> <%EndIf%>` statements in IDC under IIS version 2 or later, you'll get an error message if you try it under earlier versions.

Conditionally Creating Control Buttons

The Current Documents page also has three buttons which Add, Modify and Remove documents. These allow the user to customize their list of working documents. However, it only makes sense to include Modify and Remove when there are some existing documents. In cases where there are no current documents, we've used an `<%If .. %> <%EndIf%>` construct so that only the Add button is defined. The HTX for this part of the template is:

```
<!-- Now the buttons to Modify, Add and Remove documents -->
<TABLE>
  <TR>
    <TD>
      <FORM ACTION="AddDocs.idc" METHOD="POST">
        <INPUT TYPE="HIDDEN" NAME="UserName" VALUE="<%idc.UserName%>">
        <INPUT TYPE="SUBMIT" VALUE="Add a Document">
      </FORM>
    </TD>
<%If CurrentRecord GT 0%>
    <TD>
      <FORM ACTION="ChangeDocs.idc" METHOD="POST">
        <INPUT TYPE="HIDDEN" NAME="UserName" VALUE="<%idc.UserName%>">
        <INPUT TYPE="SUBMIT" VALUE="Modify a Document">
      </FORM>
    </TD>
    <TD>
      <FORM ACTION="DeleteDocs.idc" METHOD="POST">
        <INPUT TYPE="HIDDEN" NAME="UserName" VALUE="<%idc.UserName%>">
        <INPUT TYPE="SUBMIT" VALUE="Remove Documents">
      </FORM>
    </TD>
<%EndIf%>
  </TR>
</TABLE>
```

You can see that each cell of the table will contain a **`<FORM>`**, which has a hidden control and a button. The **`VALUE`** attribute, and hence the content, of the hidden control is set to **`<%idc.UserName%>`**. When the page is created by IDC, therefore, this will be the user's name, as defined in the **`Person`** table. For example, the HTML generated could be:

```
<INPUT TYPE="HIDDEN" NAME="UserName" VALUE="Olivia_Gonzales">
```

Each **`<FORM>`** section also has a different **`ACTION`** attribute. This defines the particular IDC script that will be used when that button is clicked. We'll look at these scripts in a while, but first we'll just take a quick look at one other way of using the **`<%BeginDetail%> <%EndDetail%>`** section of the HTX template.

Filling List Controls from a Database

Our Wrox Information Manager application starts with a Logon screen, where the user selects their name from a drop-down list, and enters their password. (In the sample we're using in this book, we haven't actually implemented the password, so anyone can use it.) To create this page, we have to find a way of transferring the values from the **`Person`** table in the database into the drop-down list.

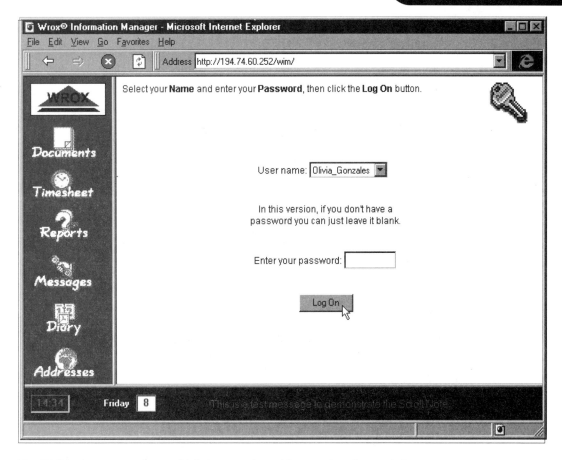

The IDC script **logon.idc**, which is run when this page is referenced, is:

```
Datasource:WroxInfoManager
Username: sa
Password:
Template: logon.htx
SQLStatement:
+ SELECT DISTINCTROW UserName FROM Person
```

As you can see, the SQL we use is very simple, just returning a recordset which contains a single field. There is a record for all the user names in our database, and these are passed into the template file. The drop-down list in the template is defined as a **<SELECT>** tag, and so to add all the users to it, we just need to place their names in **<OPTION>** tags within the **<SELECT>** tag:

```
...
<SELECT NAME=selUserName>
   <%BeginDetail%>
     <OPTION VALUE="<%UserName%>"><%UserName%>
   <%EndDetail%>
</SELECT>
...
```

This is similar to the way we created the list of links in the Current Documents page. The difference, here, is that the **<%BeginDetail%>** and **<%EndDetail%>** tags are inside the **<SELECT>** and **</SELECT>** tags which create the list box, and the value of the **UserName** field is within an **<OPTION>** tag for that list box. When the page is sent to the client, it looks like this:

```
...
<SELECT NAME=selUserName>
   <OPTION VALUE="James Goldberg">James Goldberg
   <OPTION VALUE="Fred McDowell">Fred McDowell
   <OPTION VALUE="Olivia Gonzales">Olivia Gonzales
   <OPTION VALUE="Mike Redgrave">Mike Redgrave
   <OPTION VALUE="Christina Martin">Christina Martin
   <OPTION VALUE="Louigi Spinella">Louigi Spinella
   <OPTION VALUE="Art Cowan">Art Cowan
</SELECT>
...
```

The HTML between the two detail tags has been repeated for each row of data, or record, returned by the SQL query. In each of these rows, IDC has substituted the current data from that record for the placeholder. You can see that we've used the **UserName** twice—once for the **VALUE** attribute of the **<OPTION>** tag (so that we can retrieve it later as the selected option), and then again for the text that's actually shown in the list.

> *Remember that you can view the results of an IDC script/HTX template in your browser by selecting the* View Source *option. In Internet Explorer, just right-click on any blank area of the page and select* View Source *from the short-cut menu. This is a handy way to see what's going on, and will help you to debug troublesome HTX templates.*

Understanding Variables and Parameters

We've used variables and parameters in several places in our scripts and templates so far, and talked about the forms which call our scripts. In this section, we'll look at how we use the different types of variables that are available, and then walk through the different ways that we can initiate a script so that a results page is created.

Query Result Variables

As we've seen in previous examples, we can refer to any of the values that are returned from the SQL query in the IDC script, by using the field name. So the query

```
SELECT PartNum, PartDesc FROM PartList WHERE PartNum > 4167
```

provides us with the two variables, **PartNum** and **PartDesc**, which we can use in our template:

```
<%BeginDetail%>
   Part Number <%PartNum%> is described as <%PartDesc%>
<%EndDetail%>
```

However, take a look at our SQL statement. We've hard-coded the part number **4167** into it. If we wanted to find information about a particular part, or a different range of part numbers, we would have to edit the script each time.

To produce a properly interactive Web page, we need to allow the user to specify information that affects the outcome of the query, such as (in this case) supplying the part number themselves. The obvious way to do this is to use a text box or other control on a **<FORM>** in the browser.

Forms and Parameter Variables

When a **<FORM>** section on a page is submitted to the server, the values of all the controls are sent as parameters to the script or application referenced in the **ACTION** attribute of the form. Here's a simple **<FORM>** section:

```
<FORM ACTION="ChangeDocs.idc" METHOD="POST">
   <INPUT TYPE="TEXT" NAME="DocName">
   <INPUT TYPE="TEXT" NAME="Desc">
   <INPUT TYPE="SUBMIT">
</FORM>
```

Clicking the Submit button references the script **ChangeDocs.idc**, and sends it the values of the two text boxes. This is done by assembling the contents of all the controls in the format:

name1=Value1&name2=Value2 .. etc

These are normally referred to as **name/value pairs**. In our case, if the user has entered **MyLetter.doc** and **Letter to my bank**, we would get:

```
DocName=MyLetter.doc&Desc=Letter to my bank
```

This string is then appended to the URL of the script, separated by a question mark. So *in theory*, the browser sends the whole lot off to the server as a request like this:

```
http://www.wrox.com/doit.idc?DocName=MyLetter.doc&Desc=Letter to my bank
```

URL Encoding

However, things aren't quite that simple. Sending information appended to the URL address like this requires that the information is **URL encoded**. First of all, any spaces in the string are replaced with plus (**+**) characters. Of course, if the spaces become pluses, then the actual pluses must become something else. Special characters like this need to be replaced with a token holding their ASCII code—in the format **%hh**, where **hh** represents the hexadecimal code value. A listing of the characters that need to be replaced like this is included in Appendix B, at the end of this book.

There are also two different methods that can be used to submit the values from a form. The **METHOD** attribute in the **<FORM>** tag can be either **GET** or **POST**.

The GET Method

GET is the default method by which a form sends its data to the URL specified in its **ACTION** attribute. When the Submit button is clicked, the data in all the various form controls is URL encoded, and appended to the **ACTION** URL. You can see this when you click the Log On button in our application. If you select the user name **Fred_McDowell**, then the address that your browser navigates to is:

```
/wim/info.idc?selUserName=Fred_McDowell&PWD=
```

Notice that the last piece of data is missing. Even if you don't enter a password, you still get the **PWD=** part of the name/value pair.

Data in the name/value pairs appears here in clear text for all to see, and travels across the Net in the same way. If we had entered a password, it would be there for the whole world to see. This is why your browser will generally warn you when submitting forms over the Internet. It is relatively easy for programs to watch for password data like this, and it makes for easy hacking into your site or files.

There is another serious limitation with using the **GET** method. The maximum length of the query string sent by this method is typically limited to 256 characters. For anything other than a simple user name and password combination, you could quite easily lose information when the string becomes truncated in transport. Worse still, you may not even be aware that a string of data has been truncated.

The POST Method

Fortunately, there is another method available for sending data from a form. When you specify **POST** for the **METHOD** attribute, the data is sent to the server in a separate block, within the HTTP packets. As well as the data itself, the server will receive information specifying the format of the data (URL encoded just as with **GET**), the total length of the data included, and finally the data itself.

If you need secure communications, such as for credit card information, you should implement this separately. IIS and NT4 can provide a secure transport layer for browsers that are suitably equipped.

Using Parameters in Scripts and Templates

Once the request arrives at the server, it is automatically decoded, and we can access it in our scripts and HTX templates.

For example, our initial logon page contains a list box named **selUserName** which holds all the user names and a password box. When the Submit button is pressed, we need to know which user name has been selected. If we were implementing the password function in this example, we would also want to collect the password that has been entered. The **ACTION** attribute of the page references the following script, **Info.idc**:

```
Datasource:WroxInfoManager
Username: sa
Password:
Template: Info.htx
SQLStatement:
+ SELECT ALL UserName FROM Person WHERE UserName='%selUserName%'
```

Here, the SQL statement must return just one record—for the user whose **UserName** is selected in the list. The list box on the page is named **selUserName**, and we retrieve its value using the syntax **%selUserName%**. As it's a text value, we need to enclose it in single quotation marks so that it matches the correct SQL syntax.

Each control value is returned in a variable like this, so we could create a page where the whole of the SQL statement was built up from values input by the user. Mind you, this might not be very helpful for database security, or ease of use!

As we mentioned earlier, we can use the values from the controls directly in our HTX template, as well as in the IDC script. In this case, we add the prefix **idc.** to the name of the control e.g. **<%idc.selUserName%>**.

Protecting Scripts from Misuse

When you are gathering numeric user input, rather than text, you can leave yourself open to attack. As an example, imagine you have an IDC script which displays the salary of an employee when they enter a secret code number—so that you are using an SQL statement like this:

```
SELECT Salary FROM Staff WHERE EmpCode = %txtEmpNumber%
```

Since a user can type anything into the text box on your form, they could enter an SQL expression when you expect a simple value. For example, if they entered:

```
0 OR UserName = 'Olivia_Gonzales'
```

they could retrieve the salary of someone else.

One way of preventing this from happening is to evaluate the entry with the **Val()** function, before applying it to the database tables:

```
SELECT Salary FROM Staff WHERE EmpCode = Val('%txtEmpNumber%')
```

OK, so it's a simple example, and you would normally use some client side scripting language like JavaScript or VBScript to help deter such an easy abuse of your web page by a casual hacker. Although it couldn't be classed as a secure method, it's a technique that's worth bearing in mind when you are prompting for numeric values.

Built-in IDC Variables

There is another kind of variable we can use in our templates. This is one that contains values from the environment of the Internet Information Server. For example, we can retrieve the IP address of the client making the request by using the built-in variable **<%REMOTE_ADDR%>**. There are a great many of these built-in variables that we have access to, and the following table lists the popular ones:

Variable	Description
CONTENT_TYPE	The type of information supplied by a **POST** request.
HTTP_ACCEPT	Special case HTTP header. Values of the **Accept:** fields are concatenated, separated by "**,**". For example, if these lines are part of the HTTP header: **accept: */*;q=0.1** **accept: text/html** **accept: image/jpeg** the **HTTP_ACCEPT** variable will have a value of: ***/*; q=0.1, text/html, image/jpeg**
PATH_INFO	Additional path information as given by the client. This is the trailing part of the URL after the script name but before the query string (if any).

Table continued on following page

47

Variable	Description
`QUERY_STRING`	The information following the ? in the URL that referenced this script.
`REMOTE_ADDR`	The IP address of the client.
`REMOTE_HOST`	The host name of the client.
`REMOTE_USER`	The user name supplied by the client and authenticated by the server.
`REQUEST_METHOD`	The HTTP request method.
`SERVER_NAME`	The server's host name (or IP address) as it should appear in self-referencing URLs.

Referencing Scripts with Parameters

One way of starting an IDC process, as we saw earlier in the chapter, is to reference the script in the **HREF** attribute of an **<A>** tag. However, by doing this, we can't send the values of controls at the same time, as we can with a form. Instead, we add them to the **HREF** string ourselves when we create the page with IDC, like this:

```
<A HREF="MyScript.idc?UserName=<%idc.selUserName%>"> Run the script <A>
```

IDC will substitute the value of the variable when it creates the HTML, resulting in something like:

```
<A HREF="MyScript.idc?UserName=Olivia_Gonzales"> Run the script <A>
```

We can also use this method to target a script to a frame inside a **<FRAMESET>** tag:

```
<FRAME SRC="Menu.idc?UserName=<%idc.selUserName%>" NAME="Menu" NORESIZE>
```

Again, IDC will plug in the value, so the browser sees something like this:

```
<FRAME SRC="Menu.idc?UserName=Olivia_Gonzales" NAME="Menu" NORESIZE>
```

And, of course, we can add more parameters to the end of the **HREF** or **SRC** attributes, up to the maximum length of a URL string.

Adding, Deleting & Updating with IDC

So far, we've only used IDC to retrieve values from our data source, using **SELECT** queries. However, you can also quite easily add new records, or modify existing ones. In fact, you can even use it to execute SQL statements which modify the structure of your database—if the ODBC driver and SQL dialect you are using support this. We'll show you some examples by examining how our Wrox Information Manager allows you to add new document links to the Current Documents page, and modify ones you've previously added.

Selecting a Script to Execute

As we saw earlier, we can choose to add, delete or modify a link by clicking the relevant button. The code that generates the three buttons looks like this:

```
<!-- Now the buttons to Modify, Add and Remove documents -->
<TABLE>
  <TR>
    <TD>
      <FORM ACTION="AddDocs.idc" METHOD="POST">
        <INPUT TYPE="HIDDEN" NAME="UserName" VALUE="<%idc.UserName%>">
        <INPUT TYPE="SUBMIT" VALUE="Add a Document">
      </FORM>
    </TD>
<%If CurrentRecord GT 0%>
    <TD>
      <FORM ACTION="ChangeDocs.idc" METHOD="POST">
        <INPUT TYPE="HIDDEN" NAME="UserName" VALUE="<%idc.UserName%>">
        <INPUT TYPE="SUBMIT" VALUE="Modify a Document">
      </FORM>
    </TD>
    <TD>
      <FORM ACTION="DeleteDocs.idc" METHOD="POST">
        <INPUT TYPE="HIDDEN" NAME="UserName" VALUE="<%idc.UserName%>">
        <INPUT TYPE="SUBMIT" VALUE="Remove Documents">
      </FORM>
    </TD>
<%EndIf%>
  </TR>
</TABLE>
```

Adding New Document Links

Clicking the Add a Document button runs the **AddDocs.idc** script, and passes to it the value of the hidden control named **UserName**. The script looks like this:

```
Datasource:WroxInfoManager
Username: sa
Password:
Template: AddDocs.htx
SQLStatement:
+ SELECT ALL Count(DocumentID) as NumRec FROM CurrentDocument WHERE
+ UserName='%UserName%'
```

The SQL we have here just gives us a value in a variable, **NumRec**, which is a count of the number of records owned by the current user. Their name will already have been substituted for the **<%idc.UserName%>** placeholder in the **<INPUT>** tag by the IDC script that created the original Current Documents page, and we use it in the **WHERE** part of the SQL statement.

The template we use is **AddDocs.htx**, which creates a page containing two text boxes and two buttons, plus some general text. We've used **<%idc.UserName%>** again to get the user's name, and the built-in variables **<%REMOTE_HOST%>** and **<%REMOTE_USER%>** to get the address of the host machine and the user name, if available. This is here purely to show that we can get this sort of information from the client.

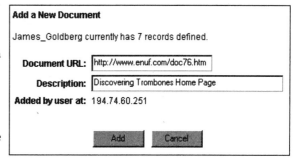

49

Here are the parts of the HTX template that really interest us. You can see how we've used the value of **NumRec** to decide whether to add an 's' to the end of 'document', in the first line. OK, so you could just use 'document(s)', but sometimes that little extra effort in making the page aesthetically pleasing is worth the effort:

```
<%idc.UserName%> currently has <%NumRec%> record
<%If NumRec EQ 1%><%Else%>s<%Endif%> defined.
  <FORM ACTION="AddAction.idc" METHOD="POST">
    <TABLE>
      <TR>
        <TH ALIGN=RIGHT> Document URL: </TH>
        <TD> <INPUT TYPE="TEXT" Name="txtLocation" SIZE=30> </TD>
      </TR>
      <TR>
        <TH ALIGN=RIGHT> Description: </TH>
        <TD> <INPUT TYPE="TEXT" NAME="txtDescription" SIZE=50> </TD>
      </TR>
      <TR>
        <TH ALIGN=RIGHT> Added by user at: </TH>
        <TD> <%REMOTE_HOST%> <%REMOTE_USER%> </TD>
      <TR>
        <TD COLSPAN=2 ALIGN=CENTER>
          <INPUT TYPE="HIDDEN" NAME="UserName" VALUE="<%idc.UserName%>">
          <INPUT TYPE="SUBMIT" VALUE="Add">  
          <INPUT TYPE="Button" VALUE="Cancel" onClick="history.back();">
        </TD>
      </TR>
    </TABLE>
  </FORM>
```

You can see that virtually the whole thing is a **<FORM>**, and it has an **ACTION** which is yet another IDC script, **AddAction.idc**. Again, there is a hidden control containing the user name, and a button to Submit the form. We've also implemented a Cancel button, using a simple JavaScript statement which is equivalent to clicking the Back button on the browser.

Inserting the New Link Record

When the Add button is clicked, the **AddAction** IDC script is run. This script is a bit different to the ones we've seen so far, in that it has two tasks to achieve. The first is to actually add a new record to the database, and the second is to return the user to the original Current Documents page, but with the new document displayed as well as the existing ones.

We already have a script and template to produce the Current Documents page, so it makes sense to reuse what we can. To this end, the **AddAction** IDC script uses the same template file as the **CurrentDocs.idc** script used earlier:

```
Datasource:WroxInfoManager
Username: sa
Password:
Template: CurrentDocs.htx
SQLStatement:
+ INSERT INTO CurrentDocument (Location, Description, IP, UserName)
+ VALUES ('%txtLocation%','%txtDescription%','%REMOTE_ADDR%','%UserName%')
SQLStatement:
```

```
+ SELECT ALL CurrentDocument.* FROM CurrentDocument
+ WHERE UserName ='%UserName%'
```

What is really interesting, here, is that there are two SQL statements. The first one is an **INSERT** statement. Three of the values to be entered in the new record are taken from the HTML controls of the page, and the third—the IP address—is taken directly from one of the built in variables we've used before.

The second query just fetches all the records for that user again, including the new one we've just added. And because the template is the same **CurrentDocs.htx** that we used originally, we get the original page back again—but now with the new value added to it. It is the values returned by the second SQL query that are used in the **<%BeginDetail%>** **<%EndDetail%>** section of this template.

The IDC engine is intelligent enough to realize that the first query didn't return a recordset, and so it will not attempt to use it in the template file. Each query that returns records is matched to the next **<%BeginDetail%>** **<%EndDetail%>** section of the template. For example, if you have three queries, and only the first and third ones return any records, the third query will use the second **<%BeginDetail%>** **<%EndDetail%>** section.

> *Note that this is NOT the case if you are running IIS 1.1 on NT 3.51. On this release, you were limited to just one SQL statement in any IDC script.*

Because we have used the same template file as the initial documents page, you have a very nice cyclic application where the Add a Document page is just like a dialog. Whichever button the user presses to dismiss the page, they end up back at the original Current Documents page.

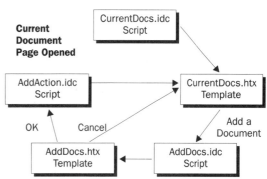

Removing Document Links

In the previous section, you saw how we can use two SQL statements in a single IDC script. The first one didn't return any values, and so the results of the second one were used in the template. It's also possible, however, to use multiple result sets in our templates. We've done this with the script that runs when the Remove a Document button in the Current Documents page is clicked.

We've chosen to allow the user to select the documents they want to remove from a multiple select list box. One of the attributes that can be set for such a list box is the **SIZE**, which represents the number of lines that are visible. We use an IDC script that first calculates the number of documents currently stored for that user, like this:

```
Datasource:WroxInfoManager
Username: sa
Password:
Template: DeleteDocs.htx
SQLStatement:
```

```
+ SELECT ALL Count(DocumentID) as NumRec FROM CurrentDocument
+ WHERE UserName ='%UserName%'
SQLStatement:
+ SELECT ALL Description, DocumentID FROM CurrentDocument
+ WHERE UserName='%UserName%' ORDER BY DocumentID
```

The first query returns just one record, which is a count of the number of document links owned by that user. The second query retrieves the details of these documents, which we use to fill the list box. Here's what the Remove Documents page, that this script uses, looks like:

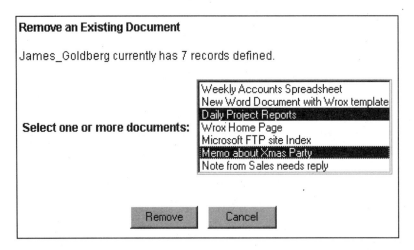

These are the relevant parts of the template, **DeleteDocs.htx**, which produces the page:

```
<%idc.UserName%> currently has <%numRec%> record
<%If NumRec EQ 1%><%Else%>s<%Endif%> defined.
  <FORM ACTION="DeleteAction.idc" METHOD="POST">
    <TABLE>
      <TR>
        <TH ALIGN=RIGHT> Select one or more documents: </TH>
        <TD>
          <SELECT MULTIPLE NAME="selDocs"
            SIZE=<%BeginDetail%><%NumRec%><%EndDetail%>>
            <%BeginDetail%>
              <OPTION VALUE="<%DocumentID%>" ><%Description%>
            <%EndDetail%>
          </SELECT>
          <INPUT TYPE="HIDDEN" VALUE="<%idc.UserName%>" NAME="UserName">
        </TD>
      </TR>
      <TR>
        <TD ALIGN=CENTER COLSPAN=2>
          <INPUT TYPE="SUBMIT" VALUE="Remove"> 
          <INPUT TYPE="Button" VALUE="Cancel" onClick="history.back();">
        </TD>
      </TR>
    </TABLE>
  </FORM>
<%If CurrentRecord EQ 0%> <!-- No Documents defined -->
  <H3>Some Error has occurred for <%idc.UserName%></H3>
```

```
      You should not be able to get here if there
      are no records for the user!
<%EndIf%>
```

This template has two **<%BeginDetail%>** **<%EndDetail%>** sections. These correspond to the two queries executed by the IDC script, which both return values. The first one returns the number of links defined, and we use it to set the size of the list to match the number of items available.

The second detail section fills out the entries for the list, just as we did with the original logon screen. Notice that the **DocumentID** is being stored in the **VALUE** attribute of each entry. This will be used to actually delete chosen links from the table. Again, we are storing the user name in a hidden input control, and we have a Cancel button with a little JavaScript.

We've also included a test at the bottom of the code, which will display an error message if something goes wrong. While it should never appear, it's easy enough to implement, and may assist us in debugging stubborn pages.

Deleting the Record from the Table

The Remove button on this form executes the **DeleteAction.idc** script. This is similar to the **AddAction.idc** script we used earlier, and also makes use of the original **CurrentDocs.htx** template to make the process operate like a dialog. The interesting feature of this particular query is that the list box allows multiple selections to be made. This means we need to handle multiple deletes from the table in one action. Fortunately, the method by which the selection is passed to the IDC script makes life easy.

The data passed to a script from a list box is the **Value** attribute of the selected entry. In our case, this is the **DocumentID** field value that we originally extracted from our database table. When more than one item is selected, the values are sent as a comma separated list. Traditionally, Web programming languages, such as Perl, are particularly good at handling list data, and SQL also makes light work of it. The query we use simply deletes all the records which are in the list **selDocs**, by parsing the comma-separated values and matching these to the **DocumentIDs** in the table. The **IN** predicate of the **DELETE** query takes the list of comma separated values, and does all the work of matching them to the table contents and deleting the records:

```
Datasource:WroxInfoManager
Username: sa
Password:
Template: CurrentDocs.htx
SQLStatement:
+ DELETE * FROM CurrentDocument WHERE DocumentID IN (%selDocs%)
SQLStatement:
+ SELECT ALL CurrentDocument.* FROM CurrentDocument
+ WHERE username ='%UserName%'
```

Once the records have been removed, the second query retrieves the updated list of links and feeds them into the original **CurrentDocuments.htx** template. This leaves the user back in Current Documents page again.

If you need to send a list of string data to a template, you must remember to insert quotes around the list variable in the HTX template, like this:

<OPTION VALUE = "'<%YourData%>'">

This prevents any misinterpretation of the data.

Modifying the Document Links

The other button that we have to consider is the Modify a Document button. What we do here is a combination of the techniques we used for the Add and Delete buttons. This is what the Modify a Document page looks like:

```
Modify an Existing Document

User is James_Goldberg.

Select document:  |Weekly Accounts Spreadsheet   e:\excel\docs\accounts.wl ▼|

      New URL:    |e:\excel\sheets\accounts.xlw|

New Description:  |Weekly Accounts Spreadsheet, Updated November|

    Modified by:  194.74.60.251


              [  Update  ]   [  Cancel  ]
```

You can see that we have a list box, as in the Remove Documents page, and text controls for the **URL** and **Description** like in the Add a Document page. Even the IDC script that runs when the Update button is clicked is quite similar to the others we've looked at. In fact, the only difference is that we've added some security checking in the **UPDATE** query:

```
Datasource:WroxInfoManager
Username: sa
Password:
Template: CurrentDocs.htx
SQLStatement:
+ UPDATE CurrentDocument
+ SET Location = '%txtLocation%', Description = '%txtDescription%',
+ IP = '%REMOTE_ADDR%'
+ WHERE (DocumentID = %selDoc% AND UserName = '%UserName%')
SQLStatement:
+ SELECT ALL CurrentDocument.* FROM CurrentDocument WHERE UserName ='%UserName%'
```

This checks that the **UserName** previously associated with the selected **DocumentID** and stored in the table is, in fact, the same as the one from the current user. If not, there will be zero rows returned from the **WHERE** clause, and so no update will take place. This may seem a little pointless, since the **DocumentID** is selected with the **UserName**, but you should remember that anyone can create an HTML form that references your IDC script. By ensuring that the **UserName** matches, you help to prevent casual security breaches.

Of course, in a 'real' system, this would be checked against a password or similar, rather than just a name. This is also the reason that the IP address field is placed into the table. By recording the address of the person who made the change, you always have somewhere to start looking when things go belly-up.

Finally, after we've updated the record, we just reload the **CurrentDocuments.htx** template, and the user gets to work with the new version of the records.

Joining the Scripts and Pages Together

In the previous section, you saw how our Current Documents pages use scripts and templates to achieve a dialog-like effect. You start off clicking buttons to achieve some task, and end up back where you started.

Our Wrox Information Manager application uses similar techniques with all the pages, so that the user starts off with a logon screen, and ends up being able to select and cycle through a whole range of other task-oriented pages. (In our sample application only four of the tasks are fully implemented—the Current Documents, Timesheet, Messages, and Reports pages.)

Starting the Application

So how do we actually start the application? We've created a page that contains the **<FRAMESET>** for the introductory screen, called **Default.htm**. IIS recognizes this name and will load it if the browser doesn't specify an actual document from that directory. We can load it by just specifying the address of the server, and the alias, or virtual path, of the directory where the starting page is stored. Because this is on a different server to our normal Wrox site, however, you will have to use the samples index page to run it. This is located at:

http://www.wrox.com/books/0464/samples/webdb.htm

> *Some web servers use* **Index.htm** *(or* **Index.html**) *for the default document. In IIS, you can specify the default document name for any directory using the same WWW Service Properties dialog, as you do when specifying virtual directory mappings.*

All **Default.htm** does is load the following: a static HTML page into the left-hand Menu frame; a dummy Messages Bar into the lower frame; and the file **logload.htm** into the Main frame. This last file is a normal HTML document, but it contains a single inline JavaScript statement which starts the logon process by referencing the IDC script **logon.idc**. (We could equally well use VBScript, but JavaScript is natively supported in a wider range of products.)

```
<SCRIPT LANGUAGE="JavaScript">
<!--
location.href="logon.idc";
-->
</SCRIPT>
```

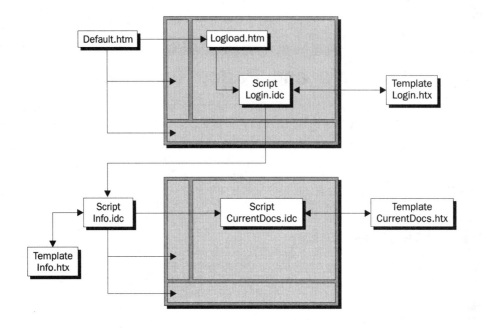

The **logon.idc** script is one that we saw earlier. It loads the logon page using a list of the users from the **Person** table and the template file **logon.htx**. At this point, the dummy page that is loaded into the menu bar contains all the images of the application pages, but these are not actually hyperlinks. So the user can do nothing, except click the Log On button.

Loading the Main Application Page

The Log On button is actually a **SUBMIT** button on the form which contains the user name and password controls. This form references the script **info.idc**, using the code:

```
<FORM ACTION="info.idc" Target="_top">
```

So, it sends the values of the user name and password to the script as name/value pairs. Notice that the return page is loaded in place of the original **<FRAMESET>**, replacing the complete browser window contents, because we've included a **TARGET** attribute which is set to **"_top"**.

56

The **info.idc** script queries the database to extract the user name again, as a single record. (In the secured version of the application, it validates the password against the table as well.) Then it loads the **info.htx** template:

```
Datasource:WroxInfoManager
Username: sa
Password:
Template: info.htx
SQLStatement:
+ SELECT ALL UserName FROM Person WHERE UserName='%selUserName%'
+ ORDER BY UserName
```

This template is just a copy of **Default.htm**, that created our original **<FRAMESET>**. However, now the menu bar is the 'real thing', with images which are hyperlinks. It also loads a working copy of our Messages Bar into the bottom frame, and the Current Documents page into the main frame. Each of these is itself a script, rather than a normal HTML document, and each receives the value of the user name which is substituted into the page before it is sent to the browser. (You'll see what **Mesg.asp** is in Chapter 6.)

Here's the **info.htx** template in full:

```
<HTML>
<HEAD>
<TITLE>Wrox&#169; Information Manager</TITLE>
</HEAD>
<FRAMESET ROWS="*,45">
  <FRAMESET COLS="120,*">
    <FRAME SRC="Menu.idc?UserName=<%idc.selUserName%>" NAME="Menu"
        SCROLLING=NO NORESIZE>
    <FRAME SRC="Documents/CurrentDocs.idc?UserName=<%idc.selUserName%>"
        NAME="Main">
  </FRAMESET>
  <FRAME SRC="message/Mesg.asp?UserName=<%idc.selUserName%>"
        NAME="Mesg" SCROLLING=NO NORESIZE>
</FRAMESET>
</HTML>
```

When it reaches the browser, of course, the **<FRAMESET>** will contain the actual user name, like this:

```
<FRAMESET ROWS="*,45">
  <FRAMESET COLS="120,*">
    <FRAME SRC="Menu.idc?UserName=Olivia_Gonzales" NAME="Menu"
        SCROLLING=NO NORESIZE>
    <FRAME SRC="Documents/CurrentDocs.idc?UserName=Olivia_Gonzales"
        NAME="Main">
  </FRAMESET>
  <FRAME SRC="message/Mesg.asp?UserName=Olivia_Gonzales"
        NAME="Mesg" SCROLLING=NO NORESIZE>
</FRAMESET>
```

Loading Application Pages from the Menu

Each script that creates one of the pages for the **<FRAMESET>** receives the current user name as a parameter. So, to change to a different page, all we need to do is ensure that we keep passing on this parameter. In the cases we've seen so far, the IDC scripts have been referenced by either submitting a **<FORM>**, or as the **SRC** of a **<FRAME>**.

In the main application menu, we use images which are hyperlinks to select the new application page. In the **HREF** attribute of the **<A>** tag, we include the script name that creates that application page, and we append the user name again. It's just like using it in the **SRC** attribute of our frames. Here's part of the **menu.htx** template:

```
<BODY LEFTMARGIN=8 TOPMARGIN=8 BGCOLOR=#FF0000>
  <IMG SRC="Images/Wrox.gif" WIDTH=100 HEIGHT=42 ><P>
  <CENTER><B>
  <A Target="Main"
    HREF="Documents/CurrentDocs.idc?UserName=<%idc.UserName%>" >
    <IMG SRC="Images/mnu_doc.gif" BORDER=0 ALT="Documents">
  </A><P>
  <A Target="Main"
    HREF="Timesheet/Tsheet.idc?UserName=<%idc.UserName%>">
    <IMG SRC="Images/mnu_ts.gif" BORDER=0 ALT="Timesheet">
  </A><P>
  <A Target="Main"
    HREF="/scripts/dbweb/dbwebc.dll/TS_Query?getqbe">
    <IMG SRC="Images/mnu_rpt.gif" BORDER=0 ALT="Reports">
  </A><P>
  . . .
```

You can see that the last option is nothing like an IDC script. The **HREF** points to a dbWeb schema, that allows our staff to query the Timesheet information; this is the one case where we don't need to actually pass on the user name. You'll see more about the Timesheet page in the next chapter, and we'll be looking at dbWeb in Chapter 4.

Controlling User Access

As a little food for thought, here's one way that we could change the behavior of our menu, depending on who the current user is. Each IDC script passes on the user name to the next one, and we've seen how it's available in the menu page.

If we need to limit access to some parts of the application, for particular users, we can check the value of **UserName** in the template, using an **<%If..%> <%Else%> <%EndIf%>** construct. Remember that it's only the code in the relevant section that is actually returned to the browser, not the whole template. The contents of the **<%If..%>** tag are never included in the returned HTML code, and so users who don't pass the **<%If..%>** test will only ever get to see the code that's included when the condition test is **False**.

```
  . . .
  <%If UserName EQ 'Admin'%>
    <A Target="Main"
      HREF="/scripts/dbweb/dbwebc.dll/TS_Query?getqbe">
      <IMG SRC="Images/mnu_rpt.gif" BORDER=0 ALT="Reports">
    </A>
  <%Else%>
    <IMG SRC="Images/mnu_rpt.gif" BORDER=0 ALT="Reports">
  <%EndIf%>
  . . .
```

So, if they are user **Admin**, they get a hyperlink to the dbWeb Report page. If not, they just get a pretty graphic which isn't 'hot', and they can't navigate to the page unless they know the address and the correct syntax for it.

Of course, you should implement a more secure system than this in 'real life'. Store your pages in different folders, depending on who should access them, and set the Read permissions in NT's User Groups dialog for those directories as required.

Advanced IDC Script Techniques

There is more to IDC than we have so far experimented with. Up to now, we've kept mainly to the simple tasks of selecting, updating and deleting records in our data source tables. As well as this, we can use far more complex SQL statements to get at the data in our tables, and add extra parameters to the IDC script. We can even use variables in places other than the SQL statement.

Logging ODBC Calls

We can find records based on fairly general criteria, using the SQL **LIKE** predicate in our query statement. Consider the situation where the user is asked to supply a search criteria for text that is *within* the document's location in our **CurrentDocs** table. A simple text control is used to enter the text, and we implement a query like this in our IDC script:

```
SELECT Description FROM CurrentDocs WHERE Location LIKE '%%txtInput%%'
```

Because we know the syntax for our data source uses a percent sign as the 'any characters' wildcard, we expect to get a match to any record where the text in **txtInput** matches anywhere within a record's **Location** field. What we actually get is nothing. The query has been swallowed up!

The strange combination of percent symbols we've used is required with many database systems, when accessed with ODBC. They use the percent symbol as a wildcard meaning 'any number of characters'. This may not be the case with your data source, however. Remember that your SQL statement must be written using a syntax that matches the particular ODBC driver/database language combination that you are using.

To investigate the monster that's eaten this very simple query, it would help if we could look under the hood and see what happens within the IDC script's SQL query. To do this, we need to trace the ODBC calls, and there are various options that can be set in the IDC script to achieve this. Adding the line:

```
ODBCOptions: SQL_OPT_TRACE = 1, SQL_OPT_TRACEFILE=\sqlTrace.log
```

to the top of the IDC script causes the system to log all the function calls made to our ODBC driver through the dynamic link library **httpodbc.dll**, which is responsible for translating IDC requests to ODBC. Executing the script now, with a suitable value in the text box, writes a whole bunch of reporting details to the log file. This simple query causes fourteen lines to be written to it, but luckily, the answer to our problem lies in the first two:

```
SQLAllocStmt(hdbc001D0058, phstmt001E8500);
SQLExecDirect(hstmt001E8500, "SELECT Description FROM CurrentDocs WHERE Location
LIKE '%txtInput%'", 116)
```

59

The second line reports the executed query. Look at the actual value passed to the **LIKE** clause. It's certainly not the text value we entered in the text box on the form. The problem is in the way that the percent symbol is used both as the substitution variable, and also as the ODBC pattern match for any number of characters.

When our SQL statement is interpreted by **httpodbc.dll**, and passed to the ODBC driver, a double percent symbol is interpreted to be a single percent, and used as the wildcard operator. A single percent symbol, however, is just passed on as a literal character. Although we started off with double percent symbols, the 'inner' ones are used as part of the substitution variable **%txtInput%**. This just leaves us with single percent symbols. What we actually need is this:

```
SELECT Description FROM CurrentDocs WHERE Location LIKE '%%%txtInput%%%'
```

Needless to say, it follows that if you want to find records that have the value entered by the user at the start of their Location field, you could use:

```
SELECT Description FROM CurrentDocs WHERE Location LIKE '%txtInput%%%'
```

Other IDC Script Options

The ODBC options are not the only thing that we can tweak in our scripts. There are other parameters that can be added to control how information is used within the SQL statement or the HTX template. We'll look at the two popular ones here.

The RequiredParameters Option

One particular IDC option that is very useful if we want to control how our scripts are used is **RequiredParameters**. As the name suggests, this allows us to specify the names of variables that are essential to the success of the query. For example, if we have a control on the form named **txtImportant**, we can use an IDC script like this:

```
Template: MustBeThere.htx
RequiredParameters: txtImportant
SQLStatement:
+ SELECT Description FROM CurrentDocs
+ WHERE Location LIKE '%%%txtImportant%%%'
```

If the user fails to enter any data in the **txtImportant** control, IDC automatically creates a warning message and cancels the query. They just see a message like this:

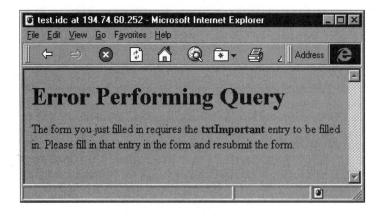

The DefaultParameters Option

We can also use the **DefaultParameters** option in our IDC scripts. This is similar in nature to the **RequiredParameters** option—but rather than having an error returned to the casual browser, we can ensure that something useful is always returned. If the parameter is to be used as part of a search criteria, then we might assume a default of **%** to give a match against all the records. The IDC script:

```
Template: MightBeThere.htx
DefaultParameters: txtImportantValue=%
SQLStatement:
+ SELECT Description FROM CurrentDocs
+ WHERE Location LIKE '%%%txtImportantValue%%%'
```

will ensure that, where no search criteria are entered, all the records are returned. Of course, we can be a lot more ingenious than this. If we want to return a default set of documents from a specific source, we can use:

```
Template: MightBeThere.htx
DefaultParameters: txtImportantValue=http://MyCompany.com/Documents%
SQLStatement:
+ SELECT Description FROM CurrentDocs
+ WHERE Location LIKE '%%%ImportantValue%%%'
```

This will select only those document files whose **Location** is the specified server and directory.

Conditional IDC Scripting Techniques

As well as using values from form controls in the SQL statement lines, it's possible to use them for the other entries within an IDC script. For example, we could place four text boxes on the form named **txtUser**, **txtPassword**, **txtTemplate**, and **txtSQL**. In the IDC script, we use the values from the browser directly:

```
Datasource: WroxInfoManager
Username: %txtUser%
Password: %txtPassword%
Template: %txtTemplate%
SQLStatement:
+ %txtSQL%
```

From the browser, the user can provide the user name, password, template, and SQL statement they want to use in the IDC script. Of course, the values they specify will be sent over your network, or the Internet, as plain text for all to see: so you might like to restrict your use of this technique for passwords!

It also leaves your system wide open to misuse in other ways. Earlier, we saw the dangers of allowing users to enter their own SQL statement. On top of this, they may specify, as the template, a file which normally has restricted access. IIS will quite happily retrieve it using its own permissions, and return it to the browser.

Even worse, if they specify a script or executable application of some type, it will be run, rather than downloaded, if the directory is marked as executable. So you have no idea what they are actually doing behind the scenes.

Allowing Users to Select a Template

Allowing the user to select a particular template is a very useful technique, however. One way of controlling which ones they can select is to add the **.htx** file extension to whatever they enter in the **txtTemplate** box:

```
Datasource: WroxInfoManager
Username: sa
Template: %txtTemplate%.htx
SQLStatement:
...
```

We can be even more restrictive. If all our HTX templates for a particular IDC script have the same partial name, we can make sure only the correct ones are used. For example, if the available templates are **SalesDept_ByMonth.htx**, **SalesDept_ByName.htx**, and **SalesDept_Outstanding.htx**, our IDC script could be:

```
Datasource: WroxInfoManager
Username: sa
Template: SalesDept_%txtTemplate%.htx
SQLStatement:
...
```

On the form, the user has a drop-down list, or a set of option buttons, where they select which template to use. Although the templates will use the same values from the records, because they all use the same SQL statement, they can format it and report it in different ways. If we allow users to select carefully controlled parts of the SQL statement as well, they can easily obtain even more accurately tailored reports.

Here's an example where they can select the template, the sorting order, and the criteria for inclusion in the results:

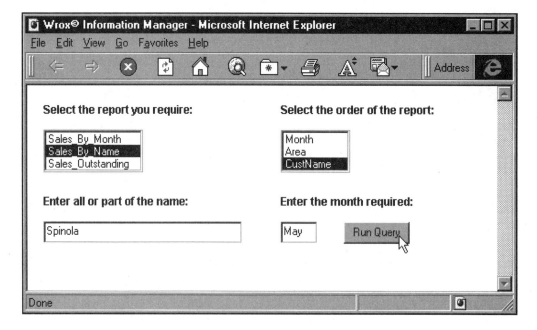

In the IDC script, we just substitute the values from the controls on the form into the various parts of the script:

```
Datasource: WroxInfoManager
Username: sa
Template: SalesDept_%lstTemplate%.htx
SQLStatement:
+ SELECT Sales.* FROM Sales
+ WHERE Sales.Month='%txtMonth%'
+ AND Sales.CustName LIKE '%txtName%%'
+ ORDER BY Sales.%lstSort%
```

Finally, the HTX templates can make use of any of the values in the **Sales** table records that are returned by the SQL query, because we've included the asterisk, which indicates that we want all the fields.

Summary

In this chapter, we've looked at the **Internet Database Connector** (IDC) technology which is an integral part of Microsoft **Internet Information Server** (IIS). We've also shown how IDC was used as the basis for our Wrox Information Manager application.

We've looked at the different parts that make up an IDC script, and seen how **.idc** files can be used to retrieve records from a database. We also talked about the different variables that are available for use in your scripts and looked at how you can add, update and delete records using IDC. In the last section of the chapter, we looked at some more advanced IDC script techniques, such as logging ODBC calls and using options such as **RequiredParameters** and **DefaultParameters**.

In the next chapter, we'll move on to an entirely different technology. OLEISAPI is a method of linking custom applications to your Internet Server, so that they can create dynamic Web pages. And it's very different from the way we've been using IDC in this chapter.

Internet Server API

Microsoft Internet Information Server (IIS) provides an Application Programming Interface (API) which allows programs written in other languages to communicate with it directly. This enables software suppliers to create tools and add-ins to extend the functionality of IIS. In this chapter, we'll be seeing how we can use the API to create our own interface between Internet Information Server and an ODBC data source.

This frees us from the limitations of using the Internet Database Connector (IDC) methods which you saw in the last chapter. We can, instead, introduce more complex ways of manipulating the information, and at the same time exert more control over the HTML pages that are returned to the browser following a database query operation.

It's possible to interface directly with the Internet Information Server API by creating a standard Windows Dynamic-link Library (DLL). In our case, however, we'll be using ActiveX (OLE) technology. This is referred to as OLEISAPI (OLE Internet Server API), and requires the creation of an OLE Automation server. This is essentially a collection of objects that you can program to perform certain tasks. You can use Visual Basic 4 onwards (Professional and Enterprise editions) to create OLE Server DLLs.

As well as the extra control OLEISAPI offers us, over and above that of most Internet database technologies, it has another advantage. Once we are using a 'real' programming language (rather than a scripting language like IDC), we have the rest of that language's functionality available as well. For example, if we are using IDC there is no easy way to include the current time and date in the page we return to the client browser. However, we can quite easily find this information in Visual Basic with the built-in **Date()** and **Time()** functions. So if our interface between the client and the data is an OLE Automation server, using OLEISAPI, we can include a call to these functions and place the result in the HTML page we return.

So in this chapter we'll be looking at:

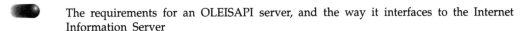

- The requirements for an OLEISAPI server, and the way it interfaces to the Internet Information Server

- How we can translate and manipulate the information received from an HTML form in the browser

- How we create the returned HTML page within the server

- An overview of the methods of creating classes and objects in Visual Basic

How we cope with errors, and debug the OLE server

 How we use it within the Timesheet section of our application

Before we actually dive in to see how OLEISAPI works, we'll take a look at the task we have to perform.

An Overview of OLEISAPI

Using OLEISAPI to provide interactive web pages is a distinctly more complex technique than IDC. With IDC, we could just write a text script and HTML-type page, and leave all the interface problems to IIS. With OLEISAPI, we have to carry out, and therefore understand, a lot more of the background tasks.

OLEISAPI uses a dynamic-link library (**OLEISAPI.DLL**) which is specifically designed to let you make interface calls from HTML to OLE servers. The point of ISAPI is to enable the development of extensions to IIS. OLEISAPI facilitates this, further, by allowing the extensions to be OLE Automation servers that can be created in Visual Basic, C/C++, etc.

In the course of this chapter, we'll take you through the process of using OLEISAPI to deal with the computation and database functionality for our sample Timesheet application. But first, we should take in some of the background.

Why we use OLEISAPI in our Application

Our sample Wrox Information Manager application includes a timesheet page which collects information about who has worked on each project over the week, allowing us to keep track of costs. However, our staff may work on more than one project in a day, and we also want to collect information about what other tasks they have to get involved in—such as attending meetings or fixing one of the network servers.

The page you see when you first open the Timesheet contains three sets of drop-down list boxes, text controls, and spin buttons for each day. All the users have to do is select a project in the list, and enter the number of hours worked on it. They can enter information on up to three different projects for each day.

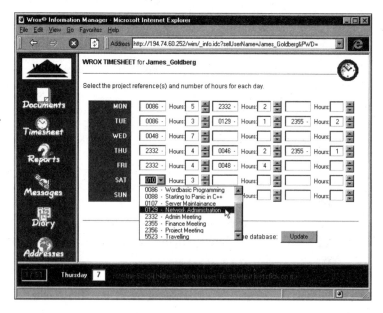

This page is actually created dynamically using a mixture of IDC, VBScript, and ActiveX controls. You'll see more of this in Chapter 5. In this chapter, however, we're interested in how we handle the information it returns, and how we go about updating the database.

Consider the problem here. We have up to 21 different items of information to store in the database table each time the user enters information. However, we don't know exactly how many items there will be. They might enter information for just one project for one day, or three different projects for one day, or (as in the screen shot) a different number for several days.

We also have to determine which week they are updating. Our application works on the principle that they will enter information for the current week, but how does our code know what the current week number is? There are obviously requirements here that can't be met using just IDC, which is really limited to collecting and retrieving data.

Understanding OLEISAPI

To understand what OLEISAPI has to do, we need to understand how information is passed from a client browser to the web server, and back again. We saw this outlined in the previous chapter—if a web page contains this simple form:

```
<FORM ACTION="ChangeDocs.idc" METHOD="POST">
    <INPUT TYPE="TEXT" NAME="DocName">
    <INPUT TYPE="TEXT" NAME="Desc">
    <INPUT TYPE="SUBMIT">
</FORM>
```

submitting it when the user has entered **MyLetter.doc** and **Letter to my bank**, will send this instruction to the server:

```
http://.../ChangeDocs.idc?DocName=MyLetter.doc&Desc=Letter to my bank
```

On top of this, the string is URL-encoded for transmission via HTTP. Spaces in the string are replaced with plus (+) characters, and special characters are replaced with a token holding their ASCII code—in the format **%hh**, where **hh** represents the hexadecimal code value.

In IDC, we let the web server, Internet Information Server, do all the work of translating the string back into normal text, and we could retrieve the values of the form controls simply by using the syntax:

```
<%idc.control_name%>
```

The bad news is that none of this is going to work when we use OLEISAPI! Instead, we have to manipulate the information directly in our own code. We'll be doing this in the course of the chapter.

Interfacing with the Internet Server API

When we write programs in other languages, such as Perl, through the Common Gateway Interface (CGI), we have to retrieve the information coming from the browser and send back our 'response' page. Languages such as Perl use a script which is passed to a separate interpreter application, and this interfaces directly with the CGI. An executable program, in such a case, can be a batch file or any registered executable.

As we saw back in Chapter 1, using such executable programs has one particular advantage—it allows our custom program, be it a script interpreter or a free-standing application, to execute in its own protected address space on the server, separate from the web server software. If it fails for any reason it will not affect the operation of the server software as a whole. Only that particular submit action will fail.

Using OLE methods to interact with the server doesn't offer this kind of protection, because the code execution operates in the same address space as the server software. If our OLE server fails, it could overwrite shared memory and cause the server software to crash. However, while this is an important concern, there are several advantages to using OLE methods:

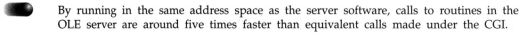

- By running in the same address space as the server software, calls to routines in the OLE server are around five times faster than equivalent calls made under the CGI.

- IIS caches DLLs and other server extensions by default, thus allowing them to be kept in memory for instant access.

- It's easy to build a small set of really useful generic routines that can be reused on future OLEISAPI servers, because of the simple interface.

- By using the same memory space as the IIS, the OLE server methods can have access to all resources, and they have much less overhead because they don't require the creation of new processes.

Internet Information Server and the ISAPI framework form the software backbone of Microsoft's Internet strategy, and new services are being produced all the time which will run under it. Accessing it using ActiveX technology, by using OLEISAPI, fits nicely into this communication framework.

OLE Servers in Outline

First, what's the difference between a normal DLL and an OLE server DLL? As a simple example, consider the way that Windows itself uses DLLs. The Windows operating system contains DLLs such as **MFC40.dll** and **MAPI32.dll**, which provide functionality in the form of callable routines which are directly available to the system. Each one contains a series of code routines which carry out specific tasks. To use one of these routines, we call it directly and supply the relevant arguments required. It acts like it is just part of our application's code:

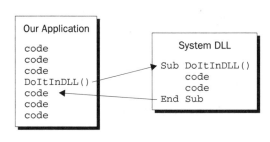

An OLE server is different. It's almost a complete object in its own right. It can store its own data, and contains the methods and properties necessary to communicate this information to the outside world. With most major Windows applications, you can use an OLE server which then effectively becomes part of that application. For example, the Equation Editor that comes with Microsoft Office is an OLE Server, and you can use it to insert an equation into your document.

Inside an OLE Server

To be able to communicate with other applications, OLE servers implement **properties** and **methods**. They are object-oriented in nature, and generally contain one or more **classes** which define different objects.

A **class** is a blueprint for an object. An object is an instantiated class. That is, an object is a copy of a class that's been executed and is running in memory. There can be more than one class in an OLE server. As an example, a class could be used to define a student object complete with properties and methods.

Properties are attributes of objects, and are usually represented as data that is maintained within the object. For example, our student object could have a **CourseTitle** property. Some properties can be changed from outside the class, while others might be read-only.

Methods are just routines within an object which carry out a particular task. For example, the student class could have an **IncrementYear** method that you could execute to increment the current course year. There can be more than one method in a class and they can accept parameters.

So an OLE server can be thought of as a collection of objects, rather than a series of code routines. We can execute parts of the OLE server by creating instances of the classes. The resulting objects can then be used as required.

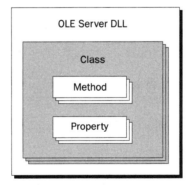

How IIS uses an OLE Server

All this explanation of OLE servers is OK, but how does it fit in with Internet Information Server? The answer is that there is an interface component called **OLEISAPI.DLL**, which itself is interfaced with the ISAPI. OLEISAPI acts as the translation layer between IIS and your own custom OLE Server DLL. It passes to it the incoming HTTP string, and transmits the response back to the client.

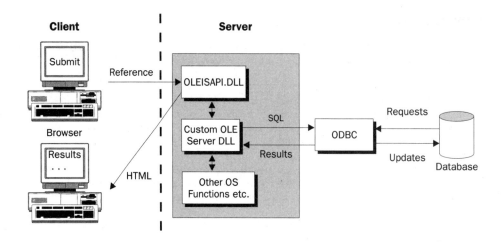

An OLE server used through ISAPI doesn't have to access a database, but for easily maintainable dynamic HTML generation, some form of database access is usually present.

An OLE server DLL which is used with Internet Information Server implements at least one **class** and, within this class, one **method** which acts as this join:

```
Sub CustomMethod(strFieldValuesIn As String, strHTMLResponse As String)
    'Processing of strFieldValueIn to get the individual field values
    'Processing of these values as required by the application
    'Mandatory formation of the return string in strHTMLResponse
End Sub
```

It's this method that is called by **OLEISAPI.DLL** to carry out the whole client-server interaction.

*The **OLEISAPI.DLL** is not included with NT Server or IIS. If it isn't already on your machine, you can download a copy from*

http://www.apexsc.com/vb/ftp1s.html

If you are running NT 3.51, and IIS in a version prior to 2.0, you'll also require the NT Service Pack 4.

Referencing an OLE Server in the Browser

To use an OLE server DLL in our page, we can reference it in the **ACTION** attribute of the **<FORM>** tag. We have to supply the path to **OLEISAPI.DLL** on the server, and the name of our own custom OLE server DLL. Also, we must send the name of the class and method that we want **OLEISAPI.DLL** to use:

```
ACTION="http://.../path to oleisapi.dll/our.dll/class.method"
```

Alternatively, as you've seen with IDC, we can reference a resource on the server from an **<A>** tag, or by using it as the **SRC** of a frame. With our OLE server, though, we need to add the values we want to work with to the end of the URL, like this:

```
<A HREF="http://.../path to oleisapi.dll/our.dll/class.method?field1=
                                    value1&field2=value2"> . . . </A>
```

or, for a frame:

```
<FRAME SRC="http://.../path to oleisapi.dll/our.dll/class.method?field1=
                                    value1&field2=value2">
```

The name of our custom OLE server must be registered within Windows before it can be used, and this is done using the Windows Registry. The Windows Registry has to provide a mapping of an object's name and type before it can be accessed by other applications, and our OLE server is no exception. We'll look at how this is done next.

Setting up an OLE Server in Windows

Once we've created an OLE server DLL, there are several steps involved in getting it up and running. The first consideration must be setting up all the files we need on the server system, and then registering them so that Windows knows how to use them. Lastly, we have to set up the access and launch permissions so that IIS can actually use them.

Creating the Setup Files

Unless the DLL is a stand-alone file, we need to install support files for it to work properly. For example, if it's written using Visual Basic we also need to install all the necessary VB support files (such as **VB40032.DLL**, **MFC40.DLL**, etc.). We'll also need some other files, such as **REGSVR32.EXE**, which are required to register the server.

The easiest way to make sure we have all the necessary ones, and get them on to the target system, is to use the Application Setup Wizard that comes with VB. This ensures that the appropriate components are correctly installed, in the right directories, and properly registered.

Registering an OLE Server DLL

Registration of an OLE server is just a way of letting the web server or other application know where the OLE server resides. Providing we have installed all the required files, it's simply a matter of running **REGSVR32.EXE** from a DOS command prompt. Before doing this, we must stop the WWW service in IIS running, using Internet Service Manager.

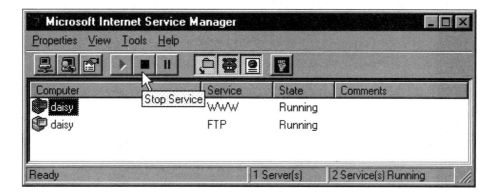

Then we can open a command window, and enter **regsvr32 *DLL_Path\Name*** at the DOS prompt. A 'success' message confirms that our OLE server has been loaded, and we can then restart the WWW service.

Updating an OLE Server DLL

If we need to update an OLE server DLL, we will normally have to de-register it first. This is because the new value of its **CLSID** (Class ID) will be different unless we've compiled the DLL in OLE Server Compatibility Mode, and we'll end up creating entries in the registry which are not current.

> *A Class ID is a unique value that's used by the Windows registry to keep track of system components.*

To de-register our OLE server, we just stop the WWW service, open a DOS command prompt, and enter **regsvr32 /u *DLL_Path\Name***. Then we replace our server DLL with the new one, and register it again by entering **regsvr32 *DLL_Path\Name***.

Controlling Server Caching

If we need to update the OLE server component on a regular basis, especially during development, it's a good idea to disable IIS caching. By default, IIS performs caching to ensure that our OLE server DLL is kept in memory after it's been loaded the first time. To disable caching, we set the value of the key:

HKEY_LOCAL_MACHINE\SYSTEM\CurrentControlSet\Services\W3SVC\Parameters\CacheExtensions

to 0 (Extension Caching disabled) with **regedit.exe**. This means that it will be unloaded after each use, and prevents Access Denied messages when attempting to overwrite the OLE server. Of course, once we've finished updating the component, we need to re-enable caching to get maximum performance, by setting the value of the key back to 1 again.

> *If you aren't comfortable with using **regedit**, you can reboot NT each time you want to try out a new version of your OLE server to clear out any cached extensions you may have.*

Setting Access and Launch Permissions

Once the OLE server DLL is installed and registered, we must make sure that NT will allow it to be accessed and launched when required. We use the Distributed COM Configuration Manager, **dcomcnfg.exe**, (in the **WINNT\System32** folder) to alter the permissions.

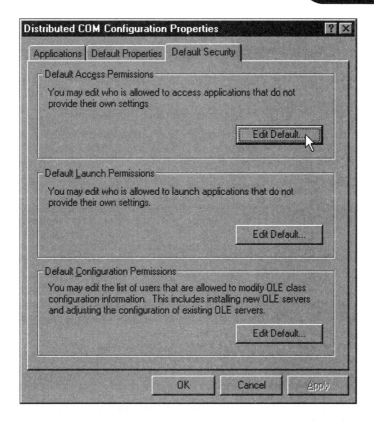

In the Default Security tab, we need to set the Default Access Permissions and Default Launch Permissions. We use each of these sections of the dialog to add Registry values that will allow us to run our OLE server uninhibited. First, in the Default Access Permissions section, click the Edit Default... button. The Registry Value Permissions window opens.

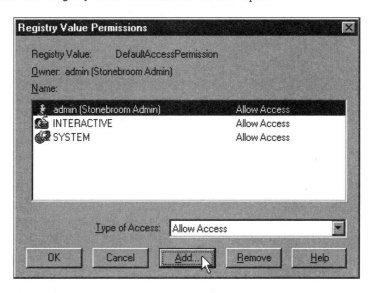

This shows the groups and users that have default access to applications that don't provide their own settings, such as our OLE server DLL. We want to allow the system to launch our OLE Automation server, so we need to add a permission for the Internet Information Server 'anonymous' user (the default name of this user is IUSER_*machine_name* or IUSER_*domain_name*).

In the Registry Value Permissions window, select the Add button; the Add Users and Groups dialog then provides a list of groups. Select Show Users and, in the list, select the entry for your Internet Information Server user. Make sure the Type of Access list is set to Allow Access and click Add. This will allow IIS, and hence our Internet visitors, access to the OLE server.

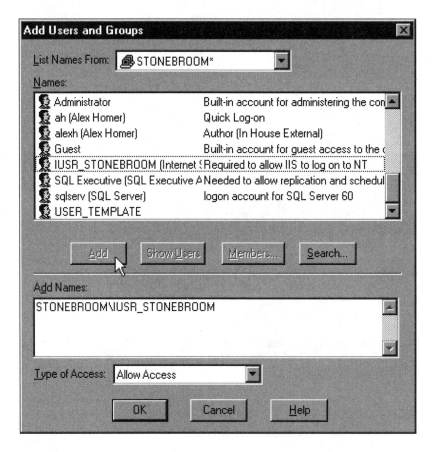

In a similar manner, back in the main Distributed COM Configuration Manager window, change the Default Launch Permissions so that IIS and our visitors can invoke and execute the methods in our OLE server.

Building ActiveX/OLE Server DLLs

Now that we've covered some background to OLE servers, let's see what a simple one looks like. Recall how we suggested that they could easily achieve tasks that were not possible using IDC or other methods. We'll look at a couple of simple examples first.

A Minimal OLE Server

In its minimal form, we can easily create an OLE server using almost any programming language. Here we're using Visual Basic 4. All we need to do is start with a blank project, then add a standard **code module** (with an empty **Sub Main()** routine), and a **class module**. Inside the class module, we write the code for a **method** which can be called from the **ACTION** attribute of a **<FORM>** tag.

The general structure of the method, as we saw earlier, takes two string parameters. Inside the method subroutine, we carry out the processing required to set the value of the second string. This will be an HTML page, which is returned to the browser:

```
Public Sub CustomMethod(strFieldValuesIn As String, strHTMLResponse As String)
    'Processing of strFieldValueIn to get the individual field values
    'Processing of these values as required by the application
    'Mandatory formation of the return string in strHTMLResponse
End Sub
```

So, if we just wanted to return 'Hello World!', then all that we need to do is set the value of **strHTMLResponse**. This becomes a *virtual* document in the browser, since it is being created by a process, rather than residing as a file on the hard disk. As far as the browser is concerned, though, it's just getting back HTML.

As the document has no filename (and hence no filename extension), we have to inform the browser that the type of the document we are returning is indeed an HTML document, and not plain text. We do this by including the content-type of the document. This isn't actually displayed in the page:

```
strHTMLResponse = "Content-Type: text/html"
```

So all that this does is give us an empty HTML document—clearly not very useful! We can send back 'Hello World!' by using:

```
strHTMLResponse = "Content-Type: text/html" & vbCrLf & "Hello world!"
```

Of course, an HTML document should have the appropriate **<HTML>**, **<HEAD>** and **<BODY>** tags in it to conform to the HTML specification, but straight text like we've used will work OK.

And, of course, we haven't got any values coming from the browser to take account of in these simple examples, so all we need in our method is:

```
Sub ReturnHello(strValuePairsIn As String, strHTMLResponse As String)
    strHTMLResponse = "Content-Type: text/html" & vbCrLf & "Hello world!"
End Sub
```

The only other thing we must provide is a **Sub Main()** routine. This is called automatically when the server DLL is first loaded, and can be coded to initialize variables or routines in the DLL ready for use. In our case, we have no initializing to do, so it's just an empty subroutine:

```
Sub Main()
End Sub
```

Finding the Server Time

We often need to find the current time and date within an application, and our Wrox Information Manager is no exception. We need the current week number to be able to update our Timesheet records, and the date and time for the Messages Bar in the lower frame of the main window. Here's how we can build an OLE server DLL which returns the current time and date from the server's internal clock.

```
Sub ReturnTimeDate(strValuePairsIn As String, strHTMLResponse As String)
   strHTMLResponse = "Content-Type: text/html" & vbCrLf_
                   & "The time and date are: " & CStr(Now()) & "."
End Sub
```

That's all there is to writing a basic OLE server. However, we can't actually compile our projects into OLE server DLLs yet, as there's still some groundwork to do. We need to define which methods from our classes are meant to be used by outside applications, and which ones aren't, as well as which classes we intend to expose for use by a client.

Setting the Class Properties

Visual Basic classes have three properties: **Name**, **Public** and **Instancing**. Together, these provide information as to how the class is to be created.

The Name Property

When we want to use a method of a class, we must refer to it explicitly as **classname.methodname**. So, it's a good idea to name the class to be representative of the functions that it will provide through its methods. The name we use is important as it determines **classname** when invoking the method.

The Public Property

We want **OLEISAPI.DLL** to be able to use one or more methods that are defined in our classes. We make a class's methods available by setting its **Public** property to **True**. In fact, we need to have at least one class within our project which is **Public**, otherwise our OLE server would be useless because applications couldn't use any part of it through the objects created! Of course, it's possible to create classes that will just be used internally in our OLE server, and which we don't want the outside world to see or use. In this case, we set their **Public** property to **False**.

So this is how we select which *classes* are to be visible from a client program that uses our OLE server (**OLEISAPI.DLL** is one such client). But how can we make sure that only the methods in a **Public** class which we want to expose are available for use, and not all of them? We can do this in two ways:

Make use of **Public** and **Private** keywords when defining methods in our classes. **Private** methods are available only to the class in which they reside, while **Public** methods can be accessed by any client that is using that class.

 Include a Visual Basic module which houses all the global subroutines that will be available to our classes, but not to the outside world.

Quite often, combining both of these mechanisms provides the best results. For example, we can introduce as many **Private access routines** (intermediate subroutines and functions introduced to break down programming tasks into manageable steps) as necessary in the appropriate class, and make sure that they are used only internally by that class. An example may be a routine to get the next word from a text file. We wouldn't want other applications to use this directly, so we define the routine as **Private** like this:

```
Private Function GetNextWord() As String
```

However, the method that will make use of this routine can be declared as **Public**, so that *it* will be accessible by other applications. Omitting the **Public** and **Private** keywords makes it **Public** by default:

```
Sub ReturnNextWord(strValuePairsIn As String, strHTMLResponse As String)
    strHTMLResponse = "Content-Type: text/html" & vbCrLf & GetNextWord()
End Sub
```

Internal routines that are specific to a particular class should be written within that class. Routines that are generic, however, and that can be used across the whole OLE server, should be declared as **Public** and put into a separate code module. This will allow these routines to be available from anywhere inside the project. But remember, it's only **Public** methods that are written inside *class* modules, that are exported and available for use outside the OLE server.

The Instancing Property

Finally, we need to set the **Instancing** property so that our classes can be turned into objects when necessary. For classes that are going to be used via OLEISAPI, we need to set the property value to be **2 - Creatable MultiUse**. This means that **OLEISAPI.DLL** creates the OLE server in memory before the method is invoked, and leaves it available for future use. We only have one copy of it in memory. All client application requests will be serialized so that the server only services one request at a time

Wrox Information Manager OLE Server

The core functionality of the Timesheet page of our application is implemented in the **Timesheet** class of our OLE Server **WroxInfoManager.dll**. This functionality is, in fact, just a part of the whole OLE server that we've created. Other classes and methods are added to provide flexibility and support for the sample application, where other technologies such as IDC are inadequate. As such, we can use each technology to the best effect, rather than trying to 'patch' them to achieve functionality they were never designed to achieve.

For the remainder of this chapter, we'll show how the **Timesheet** class works, and introduce you to some interesting concepts in using OLE servers. For example, we've implemented some nice generic routines and some interesting debugging techniques.

Creating the Timesheet Class

The Timesheet page of our application provides a set of values for a user's daily and weekly project work. Our **Timesheet** class has to accept these values and use them to add or update records in the **Timesheet** table. The method that does this is **Update**, and to call it from the application we just need to reference it in the page's **<FORM>** tag:

```
<FORM NAME="frmTimeSheet" ACTION="/OLEISAPI.DLL/WIM.DLL/Timesheet.Update"
METHOD="POST">
```

When the form is submitted, an object of type **Timesheet** is instantiated, the **Update** method is called, and it receives a string containing the name/value pairs from the controls on the form. When it has finished updating the database, the **Timesheet** object is destroyed, though the DLL code remains in memory. Here's a schematic view of the tasks we need to perform, showing the main steps we need to carry out. You can see how we are using **Class_Initialize()** and **Class_Terminate()** to open and close the database each time our **Update** method is invoked. **Sub Main()** is the entry point of the DLL and is executed only when the DLL is first loaded into memory.

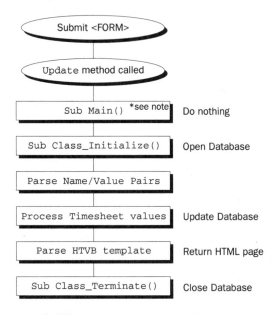

*Sub Main() is only used as an entry point to the OLE Server DLL

So, in our **Timesheet** class, we can simply set up the references to the database using:

```
Private Sub Class_Initialize()
  OpenWroxDB
End Sub

Public Sub OpenWroxDB()
  Set WS = Workspaces(0)
  Set DB = WS.OpenDatabase(App.Path & "\..\Database\WroxInfoManager.mdb",
                                                        False, False)
End Sub
```

And close them with a routine which clears all our references to the database when the class terminates:

```
Private Sub Class_Terminate()
  CloseWroxDB
End Sub
```

```
    Public Sub CloseWroxDB()
      Set DB = Nothing
      Set WS = Nothing
    End Sub
```

*We're using a Microsoft Access database here, so we can't use ODBC methods to manipulate it directly. If
you are implementing the database on SQL Server, or another system, you will instead use the particular
functions of your specific ODBC driver/database combination.*

Overview of the Update Method

The main work of our OLE server is done in the **Update** method, which is structured around the
following outline:

```
    Public Sub Update(strValuePairsIn As String, strResponseOut As String)
      'parse the name/value pairs coming from the Timesheet page
      'process the values and update the database table
      'parse the HTV template, and build the return page in strResponseOut
    End Sub
```

We are going to provide an implementation for all three parts, making use of three access routines.
One will be responsible for each part of the total task:

```
    Public Sub Update(strValuePairsIn As String, strResponseOut As String)
      ParseNameValuePairs strValuePairsIn, objNameValuePairs
      ProcessUpdate
      strResponseOut = ParseTemplate(App.Path & "\Template\TimeSheet.htvb",
                                             objNameValuePairs)

    End Sub
```

In our **Timesheet** class, we want to convert the name/value pairs that are automatically passed
in by **OLEISAPI.DLL**, in the string **strValuePairsIn**, and so we need a way of both decoding
them from the input string, and storing them for use when we come to update the database. To do
this, we've implemented a special class just to hold the name/value pairs. After this, we
dynamically produce the HTML document to return, which can use any values we've computed in
the DLL, intermingled with standard HTML code.

Making Life Easier with the HTVB Template

We've actually specified a **template file** as a parameter to the **ParseTemplate** subroutine. This
template file has the extension **.htvb** as it represents an HTML VB template. Before you get too
excited, this is not a standard use of OLEISAPI. While IDC (and other technologies) use a template
to format the output HTML code, OLEISAPI forces you to create the whole return page as a string,
stored in the output parameter of your method.

However, we've added this functionality to our OLE server ourselves, in Visual Basic code. Why?
Well, you'll have seen how much work is involved in de-registering and re-registering a
component each time you want to change it. And, of course, you also have to recompile the source
files each time. So regular minor changes are, to say the least, a headache.

However, most of these minor changes are likely to come from changes in the HTML code
requirements, rather than the functionality of the application. It could be something as simple as

wanting a different background color to match your corporate color scheme. By using a template like IDC, with placeholders for the calculated values, we allow changes to the HTML code to be made without the need to recompile our OLE server DLL. You can even use your favorite HTML authoring utilities!

Getting Data into the OLE Server

The names and values of the controls within the `<FORM>` tag on our page are passed to the **Update** method of our DLL by **OLEISAPI.DLL** when it invokes the method. These will arrive as name/value pairs, which are still URL-encoded. So our first task is to decode them, and split them up into individual values, ready to use when we come to update the database. The string we get looks like this:

PersonName=Valerie_Gonzales&1P1D=0048&1P1H=2&1P2D=0088&1P2H=2... etc

The first name/value pair is the actual name of the person who is submitting the information to the database. After that, each time period of each day that they've supplied values for consists of two name/value pairs. The first one defines the project, and the second one the number of hours. In the Timesheet page, each day allows up to 3 entries, and each entry is composed of a project code and the number of hours spent on that project. Monday is represented as day 1, and Sunday is represented as day 7.

Within the incoming name/value pairs, the first one denotes the project number, as *DayNo**P**Period**D**=ProjectNo*. So **1P1D=0048** means that the first entry for Monday is for project number **0048**. The next name/value pair contains the number of hours, as *DayNo**P**Period**H**=NumHours*. So **1P1H=2** means that for this project, the number of hours is **2**.

Storing the Name/Value Pairs

In order to store all the name/value pairs that come from the browser, we've defined a special object which we've called **FieldValues**. This object is created using the **New** keyword, as a global object within the class. So it's always available within our OLE server code once the **Timesheet** object has been referenced:

```
Private objNameValuePairs As New FieldValues
```

We can then pass the string of name/values pairs directly to it from our top-level **Update** method:

```
ParseNameValuePairs strValuePairsIn, objNameValuePairs
```

Since **ParseNameValuePairs** can be used for (potentially) all application class modules as they are added, it can be declared in the main module as a global subroutine. The object, **objNameValuePairs**, is passed by reference, so any changes made in the subroutine are to the actual data, not a copy passed by value.

> By default, Visual Basic passes all parameters by reference, but this can be explicitly ensured by including the*ByRef* keyword before the parameter name.

The **ParseNameValuePairs** routine takes the name/value pairs in string form. Its task is to place these into the **objNameValuePairs** object which will store them, and enable us to retrieve particular values easily later on. We won't be going into how this particular object is implemented in the book, though you may load the code from our web site into Visual Basic and examine it there. For the time being, you only need to know that it has an **Add** method, which we can call to add a name/value pair to it.

Here's the code of **ParseNameValuePairs**. To split the string into name/value pairs, we only have to look for the '**&**' ampersand character. If the **Position** is zero (an invalid position, as the first character is at position one) then we know that '**&**' is not present in the string, and so we have at most one name/value pair. In such a case, we skip the **While...Wend** loop:

```
Public Sub ParseNameValuePairs(strNameValuePairs As String,
                                   objNameValuePairs As FieldValues)
  Dim strToParse As String
  Dim strFieldName As String
  DIm strFieldValue As String
  Dim intMed As Integer, intEnd As Integer, intCount As Integer

  strToParse = strNameValuePairs
  intEnd = Position(strToParse, "&", 1)
  While intEnd > 0
    intMed = Position(strToParse, "=", 1)
    strFieldName = Left$(DecodeStrToHTML(strToParse), intMed - 1)
    strFieldValue = Mid$(DecodeStrToHTML(strToParse), intMed + 1,
                                            intEnd - intMed - 1)
    objNameValuePairs.Add strFieldName, strFieldValue
    strToParse = Mid$(strToParse, intEnd + 1)
    intEnd = Position(strToParse, "&", 1)
  Wend
```

While there are more name/value pair separators, '**&**', we continue to split up the field name from the field value by looking for the equals sign. As we do so, we **Add** each name/value pair to the object **objNameValuePairs**.

Once we've run out of '**&**' separators, or if we didn't find any in the first place, we may still have one name/value pair left over that we need to take care of:

```
    intMed = Position(strToParse, "=", intCount)
    If intMed > 0 Then      'get last name/value pair
      strFieldName = Left$(DecodeStrToHTML(strToParse), intMed - 1)
      strFieldValue = Mid$(DecodeStrToHTML(strToParse), intMed + 1)
      objNameValuePairs.Add strFieldName, strFieldValue
    End If
End Sub
```

We've used our own custom string handling routine, called **Position**, to find the '**&**' characters. It simply gives us the position in the string of the nth occurrence of the substring we specify. This is a very useful, generic routine, so it's best to define it in the main module. That way we can call it from any other routine. Again, you'll find it in the source code for this book.

Decoding URL-encoded HTML

We've now got the name/value pairs stored in the class wide object variable **objNameValuePairs**, but we have glossed over one small detail on the way—the fact that any name/value pairs are URL encoded as they are passed to our **Timesheet** method. This is done so that special non-alphabetic characters can be sent—such as **&** within a field name or value. If such encoding was not done, then separating out name/value pairs based on searching for '**&**' would have disastrous effects.

Our decode routine assumes that all we want back from it is a decoded version of the string we've sent in, and so this routine can be called on fragments of code such as a field name or value, as required. We've written it as a function called **DecodeStrToHTML**, and again, you can find this on our web site, in the code for this book.

Now that we've covered the preliminaries of getting the data from the Timesheet page, into a form that we can use, we can look at how we update the database and create the HTML output page that's returned to the browser.

Writing the Timesheet's Functional Parts

Now that we've gathered our input data, it's time for us to look at the next stage of the **Update** method. It calls a routine named **ProcessUpdate**, which has the task of updating the database, and calculating the total number of hours worked. There, we've also included code to calculate the total pay and overtime rates.

We've already got all our name/value pairs stored away in our custom **objNameValuePairs** object, so we can examine these in turn and add them to the database. The **FieldValue** class, which is the basis of the **objNameValuePairs** object, implements an **Add** method, which we've used previously, plus the **Item** and **Remove** methods. To examine a value, we call the **Item** method, providing it with the **Name** part of the name/value pair that we want. Passing the same parameter to the **Remove** item deletes that name/value pair.

So we can loop through all possible values of the name part for this week, and see if we have a name/value pair. If so, we retrieve the number of hours, and send it—together with the values of the user name, day number, and project code—to another routine which actually updates the database. This is named **ProcessUpdate()**.

Once we've completed updating the database, we execute another routine which gets the total number of hours worked for that person, and adds it as a new name/value pair in the **objNameValuePairs** object. This is a handy way of storing values we'll need later, when we come to build the return page. Lastly, we can calculate whether any overtime rate is due, and work out the total pay for that person, ready for use in the return page.

Updating the Database

Our **ProcessUpdate** routine uses three other subroutines and functions. The main one of these is the **UpdateDatabase** subroutine, which takes a user name, day number, project number, and number of hours, and updates the database table. Because the user could be updating an existing entry, we perform a **DELETE** query on it first, then an **INSERT** query to add the new record:

```
Private Sub UpdateDatabase(strName As String, intDayNumber As Integer, _
    strProjCode As String, strNumHours As String)
```

```
    Dim intWeekNumber As Integer
    Dim SQLQuery As String
    intWeekNumber = GetWeekNumber(Now)
    SQLQuery = "DELETE DISTINCTROW Timesheet.PName, Timesheet.WeekNo," _
            & "Timesheet.DayNo, Timesheet.Project From TimeSheet " _
            & "WHERE (((Timesheet.PName)='" & strName & "') AND " _
            & "((Timesheet.WeekNo)=" & intWeekNumber & ") AND " _
            & "((Timesheet.DayNo)=" & intDayNumber & ") AND " _
            & "((Timesheet.Project)='" & strProjCode & "'));"
    DB.Execute SQLQuery
    SQLQuery = "INSERT INTO Timesheet(PName,WeekNo,DayNo,Project,Hours)" _
            & "VALUES ('" & strName & "', " & intWeekNumber & ", " _
            & intDayNumber & ", '" & strProjCode & "', " _
            & strNumHours & ");"
    DB.Execute SQLQuery
End Sub
```

The other two routines are ancillary functions. The first one returns the hourly pay rate for that person, by extracting it from the **Person** table stored in our database. The other one just returns the current week number.

> *Again, remember that we're using a Microsoft Access database here, and so our SQL statements reflect the syntax expected by Access. If you are implementing the database on SQL Server or another system, you'll need to use the particular syntax of your specific ODBC driver/database combination.*

Now that the data submitted by the browser has been added to the database, and we've obtained some statistical figures on the total number of hours worked, etc., we need to create a return document which we'll send back to the user's browser. This HTML document will provide confirmation that the details have been successfully stored, and provide feedback on the number of hours worked to date this week.

Generating the Returned HTML Document

As you've seen earlier, we are not going to be building up a return document using lots of Visual Basic code to string parts together. What we'll do instead is use a template file that acts as a blueprint for the returned HTML—in a similar manner to the way IDC uses HTX templates to generate actual HTML. We'll look at how we *use* the template first, then see how it actually works.

Using our HTVB Template

The principle behind our template system is similar to that employed in IDC, however, we haven't implemented quite as much in the way of functionality. For example, we won't be handling the HTTP variables, such as **REMOTE_USER**, or using **<%If..%> <%Else%> <%EndIf%>** constructs (perhaps in a later version!).

What we need is for our template parser to pick out the value placeholders and substitute the appropriate value in their place. The placeholders are the names of the fields whose values are required, using the same syntax as IDC:

```
<HTML>
<HEAD>
<TITLE>New Page</TITLE>
</HEAD>
```

```
<BODY>
User name is <%UserName%>.<P>
Total Hours = <%TotalHours%><P>
Rate per Hour = $<%HourRate%><P>
Thanks
</BODY>
</HTML>
```

Given the template file above, we want to generate an HTML page like this:

```
<HTML>
<HEAD>
<TITLE>New Page</TITLE>
</HEAD>
<BODY>
User name is Valerie_Gonzales.<P>
Total Hours = 49<P>
Rate per Hour = $17.50<P>
Thanks
</BODY>
</HTML>
```

You'll recall that as we parsed the original name/value pairs, we stored them in our custom **objNameValuePairs** object, using its **Add** method:

```
objNameValuePairs.Add strFieldName, strFieldValue
```

Of course, we don't have to just use values taken from the original name/value pairs. We can add constant values, or ones we've calculated ourselves, inside the DLL. We did this as we processed the contents of the Timesheet, adding the values for the total number of hours worked and the rate per hour to our **objNameValuePairs** object. So we have all the values ready within our object, and all we have to do is parse the template, looking for placeholders which refer to values that we've stored.

Building the HTVB Template Parser

Having seen what it does, we'll see how easy the template parser is to implement. It can save so much time when you are using OLEISAPI, that you might like to consider adding this kind of functionality to your OLE servers. All we have to do is read the contents of the template file from disk into a string, and then run along the string looking for value placeholders.

For each one we find, we retrieve that value from our custom **objNameValuePairs** object and drop it into the string. Afterwards, we can send the string back to the browser as a complete return page. Here's the line from the **Update** method subroutine which sends the **objNameValuePairs** object to our template parsing routine, together with the name of the template. The returned HTML page is assigned to the method's output string, **strResponseOut**:

```
strResponseOut = ParseTemplate(App.Path & "\Template\TimeSheet.htvb", _
                                        objNameValuePairs)
```

Of course, to allow real flexibility, we could design our OLE server to allow the template name to be defined in the name/value pairs that are sent from the browser, rather than being hard-coded like this.

The **ParseTemplate** function looks like this:

```
Public Function ParseTemplate(strTemplatePath As String, objNameValuePairs As
FieldValues) As String

    Dim intFileNo As Integer
    Dim strHTMLOutput As String
    Dim lngFileLength As Long

    strHTMLOutput = ""
    lngFileLength = FileLen(strTemplatePath)
    intFileNo = FreeFile
    Open strTemplatePath For Input Access Read As #intFileNo Len = 32767
    strHTMLOutput = Input(lngFileLength, #intFileNo)
    strHTMLOutput = ReplaceVariables(strHTMLOutput, objNameValuePairs)
    Close #intFileNo
    ParseTemplate = strHTMLOutput

End Function
```

The function **ReplaceVariables** just accepts the 'template-in-a-string' variable, and the name/value pairs object. We find the starting position of the first placeholder in our string by searching for '**<%**', and as long we continue finding placeholders, we replace them with values from **objNameValuePairs**.

Lastly, then, here's the result of our **Update** method, displayed back in the client machine's browser:

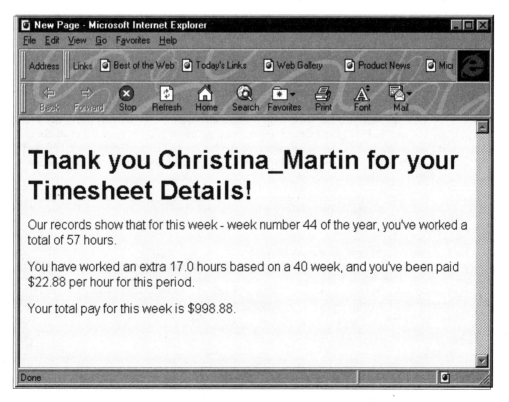

We've seen how the **Timesheet** class in our OLE server is constructed, and how it updates the database and creates the return page. We haven't looked inside the custom object, **FieldValues**, which we've used to store the name/value pairs that arrive from the browser. If you want to see how it's implemented, you can download the complete code from our web site and load it into Visual Basic.

Errors and Debugging in OLE Servers

Everyone knows that bugs in code are a bad thing. In anything more complex than a very trivial program, we can be confident that at least one or two errors will find their way into the code. Some cause mere inconvenience, but others can have a disastrous effect. The problem with software is that it is discrete, and not continuous. That is, if just one bit (binary digit) in a program changes, the results can be catastrophic. There are no engineering tolerances in software—it either works correctly, or it doesn't.

Remember that OLE DLL servers run in the same address space as the IIS, and while this provides many advantages, in terms of performance, it also poses a great threat to the continued integrity of software running on your web server, should something go wrong. We are going to outline some techniques that will help you build robustness into OLE servers, and also deal cleanly with errors should any occur.

Using an HTML Client Control

One of the main functions of an OLE server built for use with OLEISAPI is returning HTML code to the browser. Part of checking that your application is working correctly is viewing the pages this generates. Rather than running a browser on the client, however, you can do this using the HTML Client Control. This is just one of the controls distributed in the Internet Control Pack, which is freely available for download at:

http://microsoft.com/icp/us/icpmain/icpresrc.htm.

Using the HTML Client Control, we can debug our code without ever having to go near Internet Explorer (IE). This is great because IE is heavy on system resources, and by using the HTML client control, we can quickly sort out any errors without having to leave the Visual Basic development environment. We also save ourselves having to switch to IE and click on **Refresh** on every test. As an example, let's turn our attention to the **Timesheet** application once more. We'll use the template that's shown below:

```
<HTML>
<HEAD>
<TITLE>New Page</TITLE>
</HEAD>
<BODY BGCOLOR=#FFFFC0 TOPMARGIN=30>
<H1>Thank you <%PersonName%> for your Timesheet Details!</H1>
Our records show that for this week - week number <%WeekNumber%> of the year,
you've worked a total
of <%HoursWorked%> hours.<P>
<%OvertimeLine%>
Your total pay for this week is $<%Pay%>.
</BODY>
</HTML>
```

Most of this is straightforward, but we've included a variable **<%OvertimeLine%>** that doesn't appear in a normal sentence like the rest. It is, in fact, a single value which was calculated in the **UpdateDatabase** routine, and stored in a name/value pair in our **objNameValuePairs** object. However, it's only added if the employee has worked overtime. By doing this, we can output a line of text only when it's applicable. Here's what our feedback window looks like from this template:

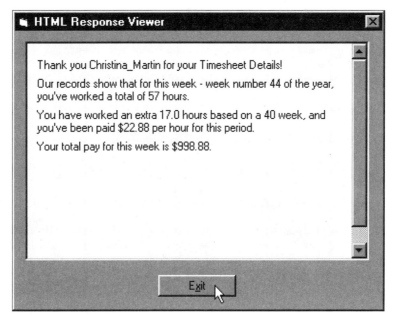

Creating the File for the HTML Viewer

To use the HTML control to view our code, all we have to do is load the file into the HTML Client Control. We pass the output string to the following routine, which writes it to a file on disk:

```
Private Sub WriteToFile(strHTMLResponse As String)
   Dim intFileNo As Integer
   intFileNo = FreeFile
   Open App.Path & "\Response.htm" For Output Access Write As #intFileNo
   Print #intFileNo, strHTMLResponse    '<- the HTML output string
   Close #intFileNo
   End Sub
```

This can then be loaded into the HTML Client Control. And, of course, we also have a tangible HTML file that we *can* load into a browser, rather than a virtual HTML document. This becomes more important if we've decided to incorporate VBScript into the template, which is designed to be executed in the browser. Simply viewing the text for the page will not indicate if it is working properly.

We load the file into the HTML control by invoking its **RequestDoc** method, and pass the location of our file:

```
frmHTMLViewer.HTML.RequestDoc ("File:///" & App.Path & "/Response.htm")
```

One thing that you're bound to have noticed is the *three* present in the code. Microsoft's *HTML Client Control* uses this as the main distinguishing feature of file access, as opposed to normal HTTP.

Using Conditional Compilation

Our HTML Client Control is implemented on a VB form, which is then displayed to show the HTML code. Of course, having forms popping up on the screen is not a great idea for the compiled OLE server. We've got to find a way to restrict this behavior so that it only occurs when it's being run as a client process, i.e. inside the VB run-time environment. In this section, we'll discuss how this is possible, and how we can enforce appropriate client/server behavior simply and easily.

Modifying Client/Server Behavior when Testing

When we're building and testing an OLE Server DLL, we run the project in the Visual Basic environment. By adding code to **Sub Main()**, which is the entry point for the OLE server, we can create an object based on a class, and invoke its methods explicitly. In this way, we can see the type of result that would have occurred—had we used OLEISAPI to create our object directly.

Of course, we only want to do this when we're running the project as a client, and it's really important to make sure our OLE server would never be installed on the web server with testing code still residing in **Sub Main()**. We can use conditional compilation to achieve the results we're after, and this only requires modifications in three places: **Sub Main()** to determine if our code there runs or not; in the HTML return string generation (the method OLEISAPI will invoke in our class); and lastly, some part in our project that will ensure that it will only compile to an OLE server with the client-based bits removed from the final server-based DLL.

We've used a conditional compilation variable called **flgDebug**, whose value is set in the Tools | Options | Advanced tab. When we are setting up the project to run as a client, we set the flag value to 1; and when we're ready to make the OLE server, we set it to 0. In this way, no conditionally compiled code is included.

Modifications to Sub Main()

If the **flgDebug** flag is set when we run the project, the code between the **#** markers is executed. This creates the variables we need, and the **Timesheet** object. Then it calls the **Update** method, writes the results to a file, and displays it in our HTML viewer form.

```
Sub Main()
#If flgDebug Then
  Dim objTimeSheet As New TimeSheet
  Dim strIn As String, strOut As String
  strIn = "Field1=Value1&Field2=Value2&Field3=Value3"
  objTimeSheet.Update strIn, strOut
  WriteToFile (strOut)
  frmHTMLViewer.Show
  frmHTMLViewer.HTML.RequestDoc ("File:///" & App.Path & "/Response.htm")
#End If
End Sub
```

Modifications to the Update Method

When we are generating HTML that is going to be sent to a client browser, we need to tell the browser that it is, in fact, receiving an HTML document. This is done by specifying the content-type of the returned document. However, we only need to do this when our OLE server is running under a web server. In debugging mode, the output goes to our HTML viewer control. This expects HTML by default, and if we do include the content-type in the document, this appears as literal text. Here's how we've modified the **Update** method of our **Timesheet** class:

```
Public Sub Update(strFieldValuePairsIn As String, strResponseOut As String)
    ParseFieldValuePairs strFieldValuePairsIn, objFieldValuePairs
    ProcessUpdate
#If flgDebug Then
    strResponseOut = ""
#Else
   strResponseOut = "Content-Type: text/html" & vbCrLf
#End If
   strResponseOut = strResponseOut & ParseTemplate(App.Path _
                & "\Template\TimeSheet.htvb", objFieldValuePairs)
End Sub
```

Enforcing OLE Compilation Compatibility

There's just one more place where we've introduced conditional compilation into our code, and that's to ensure that we can't accidentally compile our project as an OLE server with **flgDebug** set to **1**. Just imagine that you've completed your project, and you're confident that your OLE server works as intended. It's time to install and register it on NT. However, if you've forgotten to reset the **flgDebug** variable to **0**, your OLE server will freeze as soon as the screen form is displayed. Clearly, we would like to safeguard against this happening.

OLE servers support practically all the functionality available in Visual Basic. It's also possible to write OLE servers that will try to pop windows up on the server, and hence freeze. However, there is one statement that *isn't* supported by OLE servers, and that's the **End** keyword, which stops program execution as soon as it's encountered. We can use this to our advantage. In our HTML viewer form, we've included the following code for the E̱xit button:

```
#If flgDebug Then
   Private Sub cmdExit_Click()
      End
   End Sub
#End If
```

If we try to compile the project into an OLE server with **flgDebug** set to **1**, we get an error message stating that we've tried to include invalid functionality in our OLE server.

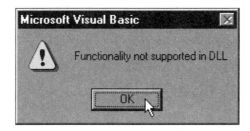

Handling Errors and Exiting Cleanly

What happens if an error occurs inside our OLE server? Imagine, say, that the database which the OLE server is manipulating gets corrupted and causes a run-time error in our OLE server. If we don't handle this error, our OLE server will hang until the problem that causes it is corrected. And because it's running in the same address space as the web server, it could well damage that, leaving you to restart IIS.

At the very least, we want to make sure that our OLE server will always terminate cleanly. This means that we must handle any errors that occur—even if we don't correct the problem that caused it. In such a case, we can detect within the OLE server if an error has occurred, and return an HTML page to that effect.

There are three top level areas where errors can occur: **Class_Initialize()**, **Class_Terminate()**, and the method being invoked—in our case **Update()**. We must handle the error in all these, and return an indication to the user. We must always make sure an error is not propagated back to **OLEISAPI.DLL**. Handling it before it reaches **OLEISAPI.DLL** ensures that our OLE server exits cleanly and thus doesn't cause any problems to executing code in the IIS address space.

In the VB code, you'll find a routine called **CreateHTMLError**. All it does is generate a suitable HTML page that indicates the nature of the error, and where it originated. By assigning this to the return string **strResponseOut**, instead of the normal acknowledgment page, it is passed back as the return HTML document.

Summary

In this chapter, we've been examining one way of using the interface that Internet Information Server provides to create our special purpose web server applications. These free us from the limitations of using the Internet Database Connector (IDC) methods. We can, instead, introduce more complex ways of manipulating the information, and at the same time exert more control over the HTML pages that are returned to the browser following a query operation.

As well as the extra control OLEISAPI offers us, over and above that of most other Internet database technologies, it has another advantage. Once we are using a 'real' programming language (rather than a scripting language like IDC) we have the rest of that language's functionality available as well. We saw how easy it is to include the current time and date in the page we return to the client browser, as well as manipulating a database using SQL statements.

We also took some time to examine the methodology of object design, to give you some pointers towards developing your own object-based applications. By using classes and object-oriented programming methods, when you build OLE servers or other applications, you are able to produce re-usable objects. These can be dropped easily into future projects, saving both time and development effort.

In the next chapter, we take in a totally different type of technology. This requires no actual programming knowledge, so it may make a refreshing change from the way we've taxed your brain in this chapter.

Microsoft dbWeb

In the previous two chapters, we've looked in depth at a couple of the tools which allow you to connect a database to the Internet or your company intranet. The first of these, Internet Database Connector (IDC), provides an easy, non-programming route for creating quite complex, dynamically-generated web pages, using values retrieved from your database. We also showed you how you can use OLE/ActiveX methods to work directly with the Internet Server Application Programming Interface (OLEISAPI). This is a far more powerful method, which allows you to exert extra control over the results and incorporate functionality from outside Internet Information Server. Of course, it does require more in the way of programming effort.

In this chapter, we'll be looking at another technology which is closely linked with the ones you've already seen. However, this is more focused, and requires less in the way of actual programming—it is, rather, an application in its own right. Microsoft dbWeb is used in a very similar way to a normal database application like Microsoft Access.

In this chapter, we'll be looking at:

- The background to Microsoft dbWeb
- How dbWeb's Schema Wizard is used to create a basic report
- Ways we can use dbWeb to create more powerful information systems
- How dbWeb works, and how we can extend it for more specialized uses

First, an introduction to what it looks like, and what it can do.

Introducing Microsoft dbWeb

Microsoft dbWeb is just one of the database publishing tools, and builds directly on several existing technologies. It makes creating dynamically-generated web pages much easier than most other methods, using the familiar Wizard-style approach to guide you through the process. Before we can see it in action, though, we must have a data source available. Like most other new Microsoft technologies, dbWeb uses ODBC to connect to a data source.

Preparing a dbWeb Data Source

To connect to a data source, and create a **System Data Source Name**, you use the ODBC 32 Manager. This is found in Windows NT Control Panel; we have described the stages required to set up a System DSN in Appendix A.

*A **Data Source Name** (DSN) is the name by which a data source, such as an Access or SQL Server database, is identified to the whole operating system. It provides the link between the actual database and the application that wants to use it through ODBC. It means that you only have to supply the DSN, instead of all the connection information (such as the path and format), each time you access the database.*

If you haven't defined the DSN already, dbWeb simplifies things for you. As soon as you start the **dbWeb Administrator** program, it provides a list of the **Data Sources** you've already used in dbWeb. If the one you want isn't there, you can add it, or create a new one with the **New Datasource** button. In our example, you can see the data source **INTRANET** listed. (The 'folder' icon indicates that it is a data source, and not a schema.) This is a System DSN which we've linked to the database that holds the data from the **Timesheet** page in our **Wrox Information Manager** application.

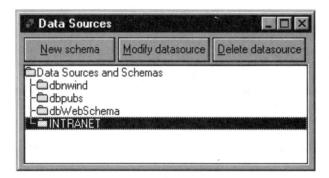

Linking to an Existing Data Source

The **New Datasource** button opens the dbWeb **Data Source** dialog. Now we can enter a **Data Source Name**, or click the ellipsis (browse) button. This opens a list of all the existing ODBC System DSNs, and we can select the one we want. Notice our **INTRANET** DSN in the list. In this case, we're connecting to an Access database file (**.mdb**).

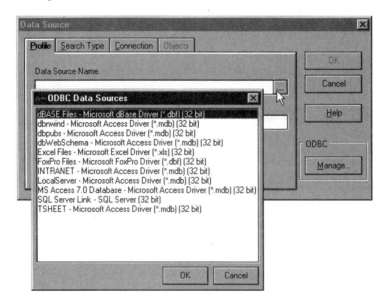

Creating a New Data Source Link

If you haven't already created the DSN, the data source you need won't be in the list. In this case, you need to use the ODBC 32 Manager in Control Panel to define it. dbWeb does, fortunately, provide a link to this. Clicking the Manage button in the Data Source dialog opens ODBC 32 Manager automatically.

Refer to Appendix A for details of how you create a new System DSN in ODBC 32 Manager.

Using Schema Wizard

Once the data source is organized, we can start using it to create our web pages. The quickest way to start, and to get an understanding for what dbWeb can do, is to use Schema Wizard. We'll use it to create a simple query on our **Timesheet** table. To start Schema Wizard, select the Data Source you want to use and click New Schema. In the New Schema dialog, click Schema Wizard.

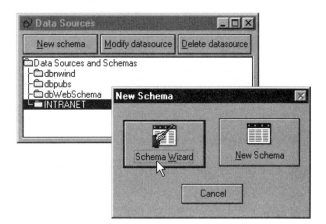

A series of Wizard dialogs now appears. The first shows a list of all the tables in our data source. In this case, we want the one holding our timesheet data. It's called, appropriately enough, **Timesheet**.

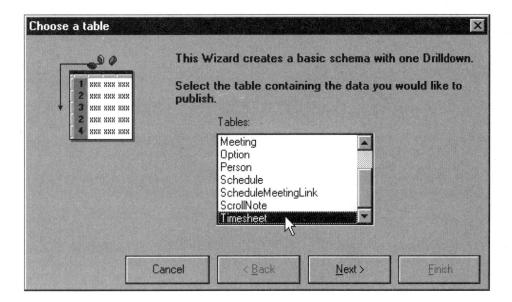

In the next dialog, we select which fields we want to allow the viewer to specify values for in the query page, where they enter the criteria for the query. They'll see a 'Query By Example' page containing a text box for all the fields we specify here, and can then select the records they want to see by entering criteria in these text boxes. Here, we've specified all of them except the key field TSKEY:

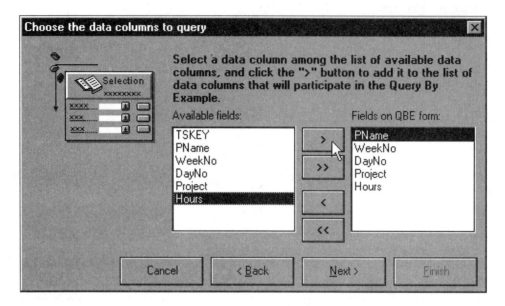

Now we select the fields we want to appear in the 'results' page. These don't have to be the same as the ones in the 'query' page—we've just selected the name, day number, project description and number of hours fields:

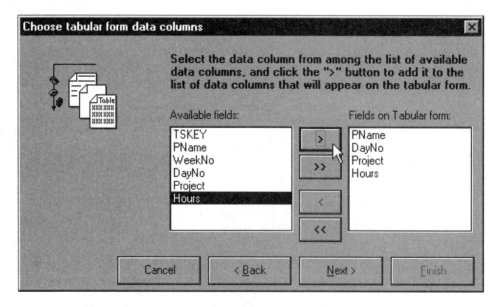

To make the results more useful, we can also specify a Drilldown Automatic Link. This allows the user to select a record in the 'results' page and get a different view of the information. In our case, we'll allow them to 'drill down' on the **Project** field. You'll see what this actually does when we look at the pages that the Wizard creates.

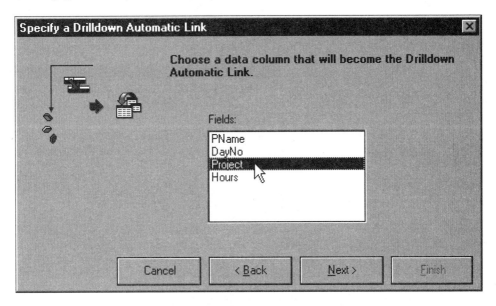

The final step is to save the schema by entering a name, and clicking the Finish button. Because dbWeb stores it in its own data store, we don't have to worry about supplying a path.

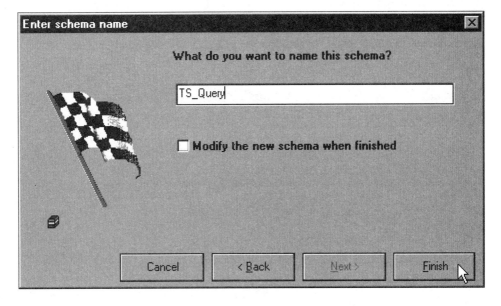

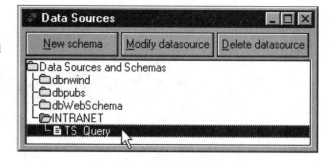

That's our first schema created. Now all we have to do is see what it looks like in a browser. Here's the **Data Sources** window again, now showing our newly-created schema.

*As you'll see later, the **schema** is just the settings and options for a particular query system that we create. It is stored by dbWeb in its own special format, inside a database called **dbweb.mdb**. The schema is linked to a specific data source via the System DSN we provided, and we can create several schemas based on one data source if required.*

Viewing the Results of Schema Wizard

Once we've created a schema, we can use it to view the results from within a standard web browser. The data is, of course, just embedded into an HTML web page. The browser can be on the server itself, or on any machine connected to it. However, there is one more job we have to do before the information can be viewed. Unlike IDC, where we can always access information when Internet Information Server is running, we need an extra process to be available for dbWeb. This is the special **dbWeb Service** application, which provides the interface between IIS and dbWeb itself. It runs as a separate background process on the Windows NT Server operating system.

Starting the dbWeb Service

To start the dbWeb Service, open **Control Panel**, and then open the **Services** window. In the list of available services, select **dbWeb Service** and click the **Start** button. The **Service Control** dialog appears, and after a few moments its **Status** changes to **Started**.

Services

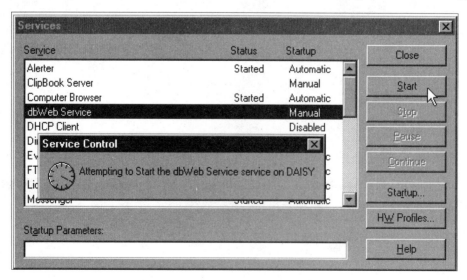

*You can set up Windows NT to start the dbWeb Service automatically each time the server is started. Click the Sta*r*tup... button, and select* Automatic *for the Startup Type.*

Opening the Query Page in a Browser

At last, we're ready to run a query on our data. Normally, you would place a link in one of your pages to reference the query, but in this case we'll just open it directly. The URL we need is:

http://[*host-machine*]**/scripts/dbweb/dbwebc.dll/**[*schema-name*]**?**[*method*]

[*host-machine*] is the IP address or domain name of the server. The **scripts** directory will be (by default) in **InetPub**, and dbWeb creates its own directory within this which holds **dbwebc.dll**. The [*schema-name*] is the name we gave to the schema when we created it—in this case **TS_Query**. Finally, the [*method*] defines what we want dbWeb to do. To generate the query page, we use the **getqbe** method that is built into the DLL. The final URL, then, is:

http://[*host-machine*]**/scripts/dbweb/dbwebc.dll/TS_Query?getqbe**

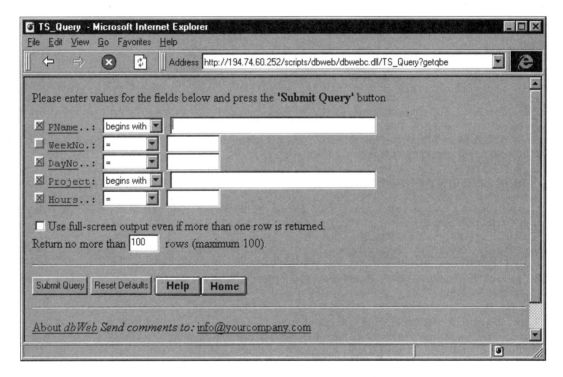

Well, it's not the prettiest page we've ever created, but it is highly functional. For each field that we decided to include in the query page, there is a text box where we can enter a criterion, and a drop-down list containing operators which we want to apply. We can apply criteria to as many of the fields as we want for each query.

99

For **text** fields, these operators allow us to search for records which start with, end with, match completely, or just contain the criteria in that particular field.

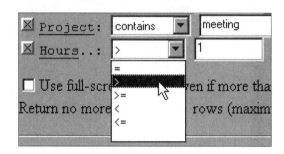

For **numeric** fields, the operators allow us to search for records where the field value is equal to, greater than, greater than or equal to, less than, or less than or equal to the criteria.

It's possible that some fields in the query page may not be correctly identified by type. This is normally due to incorrect property settings in the original table, and you'll see later how to overcome this if it occurs in your schemas.

Normally, if the query returns more than one record, the results are displayed in a tabular form—with the fields across the page like a database table. If only one record matches the criteria, however, it is displayed showing the values of all the fields down the page. This is called freeform format. At the bottom of the query page is a check box which allows the user to select Freeform (full-screen) output if more than one record is returned. There is also a text box where they can limit the total number of records returned.

Apart from these controls, there are buttons to Submit the information and run the query, Reset the controls to their default values, or jump to a Help or Home page. Some of the field names are also hyperlinks. At present all these links display pages that are the defaults supplied with dbWeb, but you'll see later how we can set up our own Help and Home pages.

The Query Results Page

OK, we've talked enough about the query page. Enter some criteria to limit the records returned, and hit the Submit Query button to see the results. This causes dbWeb to automatically call its built-in **getresults** method, which performs the query and displays the results. Here, we've used the criteria **Project contains meeting** and **Hours > 1**. The result is a list of all the people who attended a meeting of any kind which lasted more than one hour.

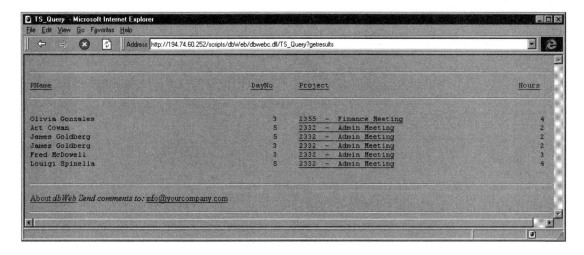

Again, the formatting of the results page is pretty rough. And because it uses the original maximum length properties of the fields, it will probably be too wide to fit on screen all in one go. However, it does provide us with what we want—a list of all the people attending meetings which lasted longer than an hour.

Notice that the display only contains the four fields **PName**, **DayNo**, **Project** and **Hours**. These are the four that we specified in Schema Wizard. If you look back at the query page, you can see that the fields which are included are marked with a cross next to their name.

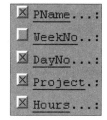

Drilling Down for a Project

You'll also notice that the values in the **Project** column are hyperlinks, rather than ordinary text. We can use these to get more information from our data. For example, there seem to be a lot of admin meetings going on. In the Wizard, we specified that the Project field was our drill-down field. By clicking on one of these hyperlinks we get another results page. This time, it only contains the records for Admin Meetings.

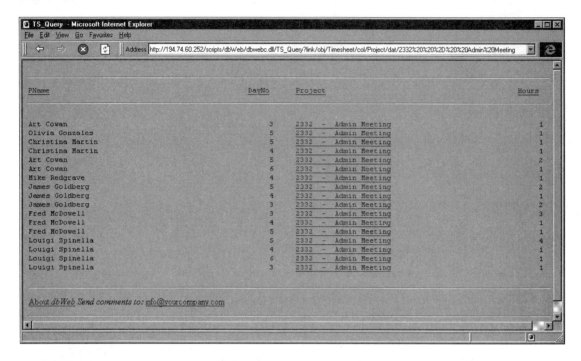

At this point, the **Project** field is again represented as hyperlinks. However, we've already displayed all the Admin Meeting records, so clicking these just produces the same results.

Click the Back button on your browser, and we can follow a different **Project** drill-down. This time click on the Finance Meeting link at the top of the list. Now we get a different display, showing only a single record, and laying the fields out underneath each other. This is the freeform mode, which occurs automatically if there is only one record in the results.

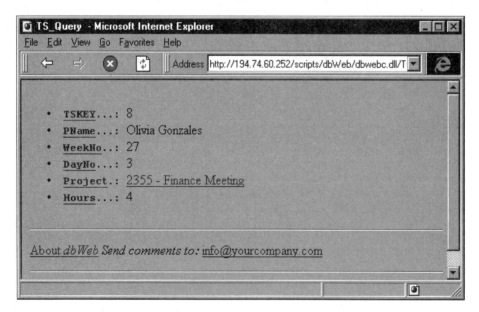

To start a new query, you'll have to click the Back button again to get back to the 'query' page.

Modifying an Existing Schema

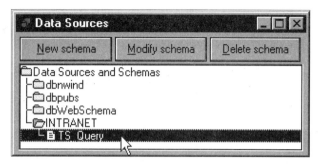

Now that we've created a first, albeit pretty rough-looking query capability, we'll see how we can improve it. To open an existing schema, we just select it in the **Data Sources** list and click the Modify Schema button.

This opens the tabbed schema dialog, where all the various properties of the schema are set. By editing these, we can change the whole behavior of the query that **Schema Wizard** created.

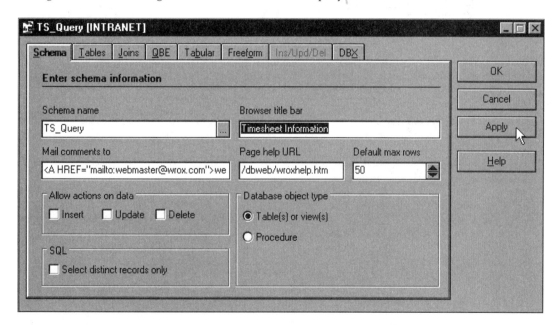

For example, in the first tab of the dialog (Schema), we've changed the Browser Title bar text, the HTML that creates the Mail comments to hyperlink, and the URL that is used when the Help button is clicked. We've also reduced the Default max rows from **100** to **50**.

Linking Fields from Another Table

At present our schema only contains the one table, **Timesheet**, which we selected when we used Schema Wizard to create the schema. We can easily link other tables to our query and use the fields in them to get more information. For example, we have the total number of hours worked on each project, but it would be nice to know how much this cost as well, because each employee is on a different hourly rate.

103

In the **Person** table of our database, we have an **HourRate** field, which contains the rate per hour for each employee. By linking this to our existing **Timesheet** table in the schema, we can use it in our reports as well. To add more tables to a schema, we use the Tables tab of the Schema dialog. Double-clicking on a table in either list opens it so that we can see the fields it contains. Here, we've added the **Person** table to our existing schema:

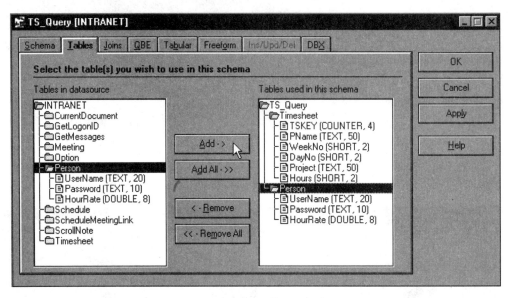

The next step is to link the new table to one of the existing ones. In our case we only had one table so we just need to link the two together. This is done in the Joins tab of the dialog. Clicking the New Join button opens the Joins dialog, and in it we select the two fields that form the join— just like we would in a normal database system. In this case it's **UserName** in the **Person** table and **PName** in our existing **Timesheet** table:

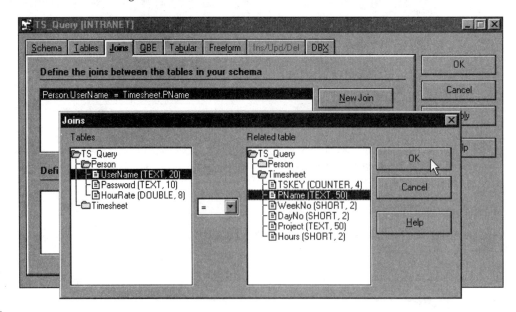

Once the join is complete, we can use any of the fields in either table in our query and results pages.

Changing the Behavior of the Query Page

One thing of interest to us at the moment is how we can change the appearance and behavior of the query and results pages. The QBE (Query By Example) tab of the dialog defines which fields are included in the 'query' page; it looks similar to the page in the Wizard that we used to create the schema. We can add fields to, or remove them from, the query page that's displayed in the browser. Here, we're adding the **HourRate** field from the **Person** table:

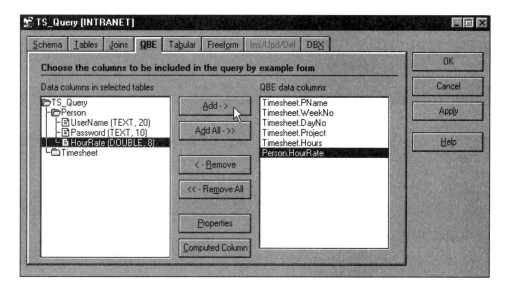

However, we can do a lot more than this. Selecting a field in the QBE data columns list and clicking the Properties button displays a property sheet for that field. Here, we can change the way that the field controls in the query page are displayed.

For example, we can arrange for the **PName** field to be shown in the query page as a drop-down combo list, rather than just a text box. To do this, we've set the Control Type to **Combo**, and used the special value **#autofill+#** for the Data value property. This fills the control with all the values in the table, plus a **Null** value for use when the contents of that column are not being used as a criteria (the value **#autofill#** works the same way, but does not include a **Null** value). Other properties we've changed are the Column width and Column label, and we've set the value of Sort priority to **1** so that the results are sorted by the values in this field:

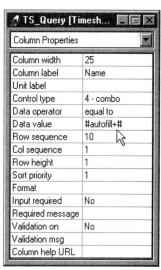

The Data Operator property defines the list of comparison operators that appear in the drop-down list for each field. There are different default sets for **Text** and **Number**-type fields, as we saw in the original query page that Schema Wizard created. However, we can select which ones we actually want for any field—so if Schema Wizard gets it wrong, we can select the ones we want. Clicking the 'ellipsis' button in the Data Operator property opens the Operators dialog:

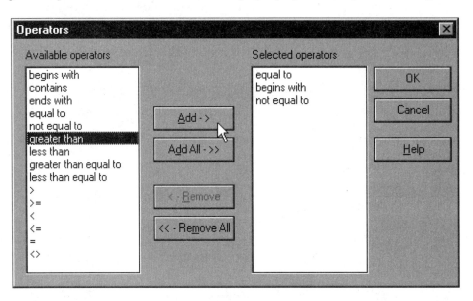

The rest of the properties allow us to control other aspects of the field controls used on the query page. For example, here we've set the Format of the **HourRate** field to display the value as currency.

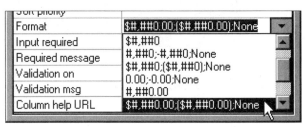

We can also validate the criteria that the user enters. Here, we're requiring an input for the **WeekNo** field, so that they cannot query the database without specifying a week number. At the same time, we're checking to see that the criteria they enter is a valid numeric value. In both cases, we can specify the message that's displayed if they don't follow the rules.

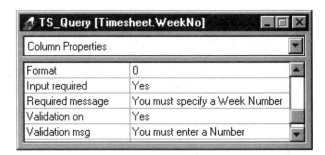

106

Changing the Appearance of the Query Page

Now that we've sorted the mechanics of the query page, we need to be able to change the appearance to suit our own site. The properties dialog we get when the QBE tab is open contains a set of Column Properties which we've been working with, plus a set of QBE Form Properties. We display these by selecting QBE Form Properties in the drop-down list at the top of the properties dialog.

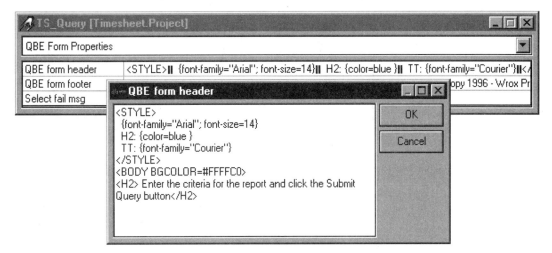

In this dialog, we can enter HTML code which is inserted at the top or at the foot of the **<FORM>** section on the query page. If we don't supply any code, the default is used, including the instruction to '...click the Submit Query...' button. Instead of typing directly in the property dialog, select the property you want, then right-click and select Zoom. Here, we've changed the background color of the page, and the format of the text.

> *The third form property, Select fail msg, is the text displayed if the SQL query, that dbWeb creates to retrieve the data, fails with an error.*

Here's the result of all our modifications to the schema:

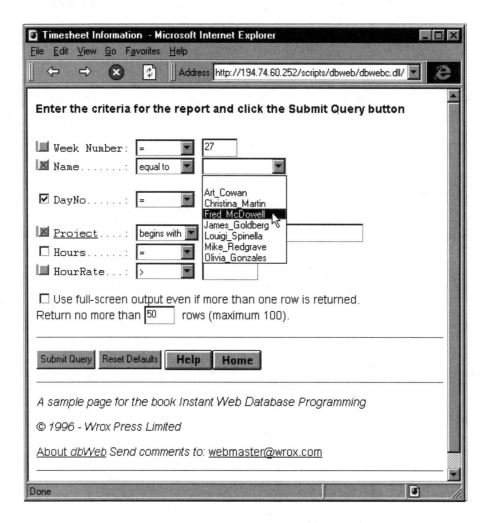

We've included a sample dbWeb schema like this in our Wrox Information Manager application. To run it open the Samples Index Page at:

`http://www.wrox.com/books/0464/samples/webdb.htm`

One of the things you should notice about the new query page, is that some of the fields now have a 'real' check box to their left, rather than the dummy ones we got from Schema Wizard. This allows the user to choose whether they want to include that field in the results page or not. We define where these check boxes appear by setting the field properties, but this time in the Tabular tab of the Schema dialog, rather than in the QBE tab. We'll look at these properties next.

Changing the Behavior of the Results Pages

We've already mentioned that the results of a query are displayed by dbWeb in one of two forms: tabular or freeform. We define the properties and settings for the report forms using the Tabular and Freeform tabs in the Schema dialog. They are very similar, though there are a couple of differences in the field properties.

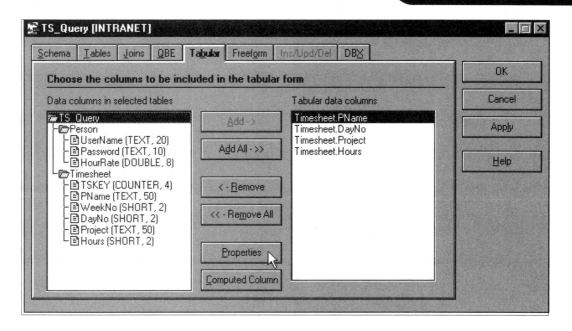

Among the Tabular properties is Display When. Setting this to Always produces the fixed cross next to the name of the field in the query page. However, the other two options, Default on and Default off, produce a real check box which is appropriately set, and which the user can change to control the inclusion of that field in the final results page.

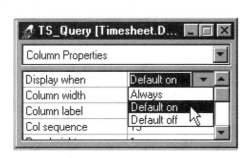
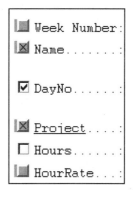

Other than that, we use the rest of the properties in a similar way to the QBE tab. We can change the order in which they are displayed with the Col sequence property, the number of lines used for the information from each record with the Row height property, and the sorting order of the results with the Sort priority property.

The Column help URL property is the address of the page that's opened when that heading is clicked—it's only displayed as a hyperlink if you enter a value here. Also notice, in the properties for the **Project** field, that there's an entry for the Automatic Link URL. This is the 'address' of the page that's opened when you drill down into the results by clicking on a hyperlinked value.

109

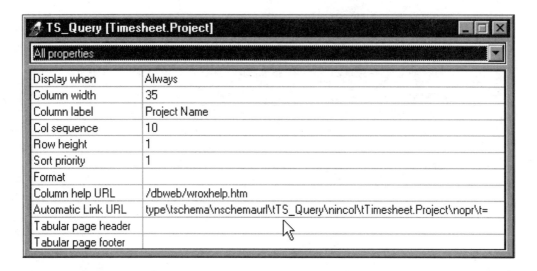

In this introduction to dbWeb, we won't be going into details of how you create linked schemas. However, there is a Link Expression Builder dialog which opens when you select the Automatic Link URL property and click the ellipsis button that appears.

Creating Computed Columns

As well as displaying data that is actually stored in the database, dbWeb lets us create computed (or calculated) columns in the results pages. Clicking the Computed Column button opens an Expression Builder dialog where we can create an expression which will be evaluated to provide the values for the new column.

In our case, we want to display the total cost of each project period, using the number of hours and the hourly rate. This is a relatively simple example, but you can, of course, use more complex expressions. Double-clicking a field in the left-hand list places it into the right-hand expression window. We also need to select the data type for the result at the bottom of the window:

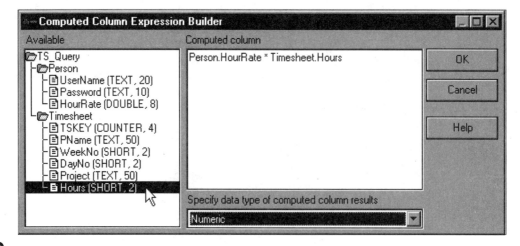

This new column has all the properties of the original ones, except that it can't be an optional column in the query page. Its Display When property is always set to Always (if you see what we mean!). We can use this new column just like any other in our results pages.

Changing the Appearance of the Results Pages

We'll take a look at a couple of ways that we can change the appearance of the results pages that dbWeb generates. The easiest way is to use the same method as we saw with the query page. There, we placed HTML code on the QBE form header and QBE form footer properties. We can do the same in the results pages. The Tabular tab of the Schema dialog allows us to enter HTML code for the Tabular page header and Tabular page footer properties. For the Freeform results page, we can place HTML code in the Freeform page header, Freeform page footer, and Freeform record header properties.

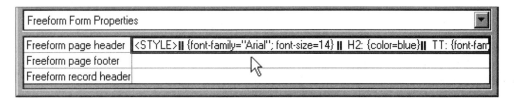

Here's how the Tabular results page looks after these few modifications:

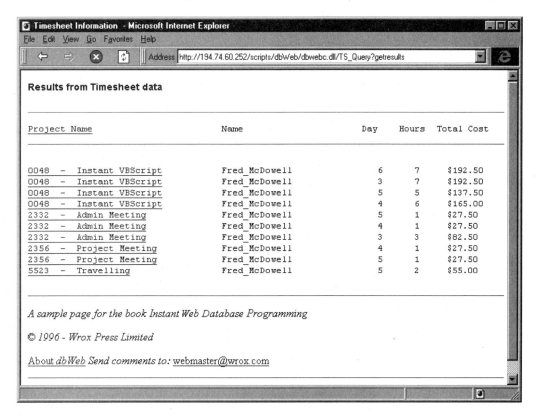

And here's the Freeform results page:

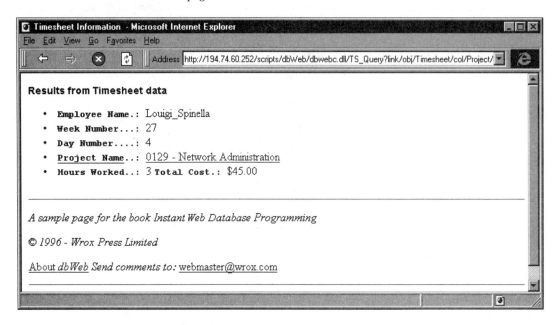

Using DBX Templates

Instead of just adding code in the Tabular or Freeform property boxes of the results page, we can specify two HTML documents and have these used as templates for the Tabular and Freeform results pages. This is done in the DBX (dbWeb Extended Template) tab of the Schema dialog:

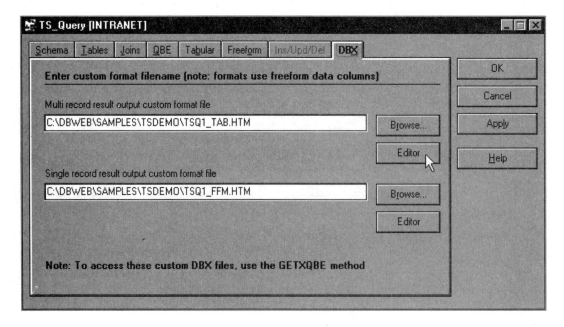

These templates allow us to create our own, complete, HTML representation of the returned page, just like an HTX template does with IDC. We can, therefore, include our own graphics, headers and footers, and our own corporate design. This is somewhat removed from our earlier approach of dbWeb as a programming-free system, but it does allow us a lot more freedom over the final page design.

The easiest way to create these templates is to click Editor, and use the built-in DBX-Editor. This inserts the correct field codes into the HTML page automatically. Of course, there's no reason why you shouldn't use your favorite HTML editor to create the page first, and then edit it with DBX-Editor to insert the actual fields. Looking at DBX-Editor with the file **TSQ1_TAB.HTM** loaded shows, as you can see, that it's not the most elegant or well-equipped HTML editing environment!

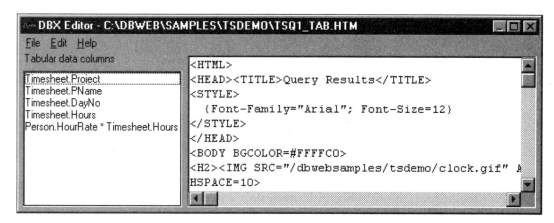

The Tabular DBX Template

Here's the full code of the custom template **TSQ1_TAB.HTM**, which is used to format the values returned by the query. After the usual leading sections is a table which will contain the results. Notice how we first create the heading row including the names of the columns:

```
<HTML>
<HEAD><TITLE>Query Results</TITLE>
<STYLE>
  {Font-Family="Arial"; Font-Size="12"}
</STYLE>
</HEAD>
<BODY BGCOLOR=#FFFFC0>
<IMG SRC="/dbwebsamples/tsdemo/clock.gif" ALIGN=LEFT WIDTH=50 HEIGHT=52 HSPACE=10>
<H2>Query Results from the <I>Timesheet</I> file.</H2><HR>

<TABLE>
<TR>
<TH ALIGN=LEFT><I> Project Name </I></TH>
<TH ALIGN=LEFT><I> Day </I></TH>
<TH ALIGN=LEFT><I> Name </I></TH>
<TH ALIGN=LEFT><I> Hours </I></TH>
<TH ALIGN=LEFT><I> Total Cost </I></TH>
</TR>

<!--The following line turns banding on-->
```

```
\tbon\tmatch\tTimesheet\tProject\t
<TR>
<TD ALIGN=LEFT>\tobj\tTimesheet\tcol\tProject\t</TD>
<TD ALIGN=CENTER>\tobj\tTimesheet\tcol\tDayNo\t</TD>
<TD ALIGN=LEFT>\tobj\tTimesheet\tcol\tPName\t</TD>
<TD ALIGN=CENTER>\tobj\tTimesheet\tcol\tHours\t</TD>
<TD ALIGN=RIGHT>\tobj\tComputed\tcol\tC135425\t</TD>
</TR>
<!--The following line turns banding off-->
\tboff\t

</TABLE>

<HR>
A sample page from the book Instant Web Database Programming<P>
<CITE>&copy; 1997 - Wrox Press</CITE>
</BODY>
</HTML>
```

After the heading row, we need to repeat the detail row for each record returned. This is equivalent to the way IDC uses a **<%BeginDetail%> <%End Detail%>** section. The line

```
\tbon\tmatch\tTimesheet\tProject\t
```

turns on **banding**, like the statement **<%BeginDetail%>** does with IDC, so that the following HTML code is repeated for each record. You can see the name of the table (**Timesheet**) and the name of the field they are to be sorted on (**Project**). For each record, within the banding section, we retrieve the value of the **Project** field using:

```
<TD ALIGN=LEFT>\tobj\tTimesheet\tcol\tProject\t</TD>
```

This statement refers to the **Project** field in the **Timesheet** table, and we can refer to any of the fields in this way. (The computed column uses an internally-generated number for the field name.) Then, to define the end of the repeating section, we use the 'banding end' statement, which works like the **<%EndDetail%>** statement does in IDC:

```
\tboff\t
```

When we execute a query, our new template page is populated with the returned values and sent back to the browser:

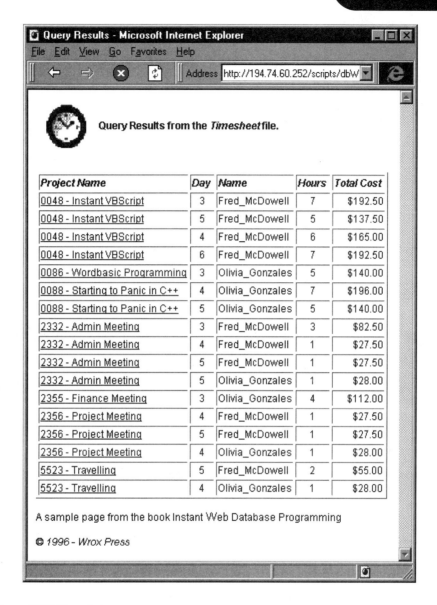

The Freeform DBX Template

The **Freeform** template is a lot simpler. There is no 'banding' in this case, as it's expected that there will only be one record. If there is more than one record, because the user selected the Freeform option in the query page when they ran the query, the template is used repeatedly—once for each record.

```
<HTML>
<HEAD><TITLE>Query Results</TITLE>
<STYLE>
  {Font-Family="Arial"; Font-Size="12"}
</STYLE>
```

```
     </HEAD>
     <BODY BGCOLOR=#FFFFC0>
     <IMG SRC="/dbwebsamples/tsdemo/clock.gif" ALIGN=LEFT WIDTH=50 HEIGHT=52 HSPACE=10>
     <H2>Query Results from the <I>Timesheet</I> file.</H2><HR>
     <CENTER>

     <TABLE WIDTH=70%>
     <TR><TD><I>Project Name:</I></TD><TD><B> \tobj\tTSREC\tcol\tProject\t </B></TD>
     <TR><TD><I>Day:</I></TD><TD><B> \tobj\tTimesheet\tcol\tDayNo\t </B></TD>
     <TR><TD><I>Name:</I></TD><TD><B> \tobj\tTimesheet\tcol\tPName\t </B></TD>
     <TR><TD><I>Hours:</I></TD><TD><B> \tobj\tTimesheet\tcol\tHours\t </B></TD>
     <TR><TD><I>Total Cost:</I></TD><TD><B> \tobj\tComputed\tcol\tC135425\t </B></TD>
     </TABLE>

     </CENTER>
     <HR>
     A sample page from the book Instant Web Database Programming<P>
     <CITE>&copy; 1997 - Wrox Press</CITE>
     <HR>
     </BODY>
     </HTML>
```

Here are the results of this template:

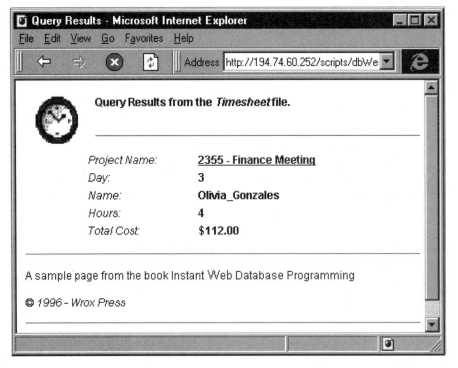

In order for dbWeb to use the new templates we've created, we need to use a slightly different address. The method is **getxqbe**, rather than **getqbe**. This tells dbWeb to use our custom DBX Tabular and Freeform templates for the results pages, instead of its own default ones. In effect, it means that the results page is automatically opened with the **getxresults** method rather than **getresults**.

So to start our new DBX-template query we would use:

http://[*host-machine*]**/scripts/dbweb/dbwebc.dll/TS_Query?getxqbe**

Creating a New Schema by Hand

You can create a new schema by hand, without using the Wizard, but it's generally easier to let the Wizard do the spade-work. You can then modify it afterwards, as we've done. If you do want to create one from scratch, however, the process is very similar.

When using the Wizard, we selected our Data Source in the main dbWeb Administrator dialog and clicked the New Schema button. In the New Schema dialog, we selected Schema Wizard. As you'll no doubt have realized, selecting the New Schema option just creates a 'blank' schema containing various default values.

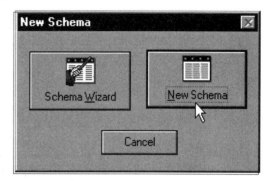

For example, it will include dummy URLs for the Mail comments to and Page Help, and a value of 100 for Default Max Rows, but little else. From there, you have to do all the rest of the work of selecting fields, defining links, and settings the field properties yourself.

How dbWeb Works

After seeing IDC and OLEISAPI in the earlier chapters, you probably find a little light coming on somewhere upstairs which says 'that looks familiar'. The way that dbWeb uses HTML files as templates, and allows you to add HTML code to the various tabs in the schema dialog, should have suggested to you that what we're seeing is really just some specialist implementation of the IIS interface, and the technologies we've looked at earlier.

When we used IDC in Chapter 2, we saw how easy it is to retrieve values from a database and format them in a web page using an Extended HTML Template (HTX) file. This saves having to code all the HTML each time we want to write a query. Instead, we can set up standard templates and modify them as required. It also allows us to use an HTML editing application to create the page. All we need do then is add in the IDC variables and references which are replaced by the actual values from the database when the page is loaded by the browser.

Like IDC, dbWeb allows us to create a template file and, within it, use special codes as placeholders for the actual values from the records. In IDC, we used **<%FieldName%>**, while in dbWeb we used **\tobj\tTableName\tcol\tFieldName\t**. IDC uses **<%BeginDetail%>** and **<%EndDetail%>** to define a section which is repeated for each record, while in dbWeb it's **\tbon\tmatch\tTableName\tSortField\t** and **\tboff\t**. So we can create our own dbWeb templates and make the reports as complex as we like.

But dbWeb uses a **DLL**, **classes**, and **methods** just like we saw with OLEISAPI in Chapter 3. To call an OLEISAPI application, and pass it data, we used:

http://[*host-machine*]**/scripts/oleisapi.dll/**[*custom*.**dll**]**/**[*class*]**?**[*method*]

In dbWeb, we use:

http://[*host-machine*]**/scripts/dbweb/dbwebc.dll/**[*schema-name*]**?**[*method*]

This tells the dbWeb DLL which schema to use, and which method to apply—for example, the **getqbe** method which displays the 'query' page. Then, using the information in the schema, it builds the SQL statement and executes it against our data source. The values in the records which are returned are plugged into the default internal dbWeb templates (or the user-defined DBX templates in the case of the **getxresults** method) and sent as an HTML page to the browser.

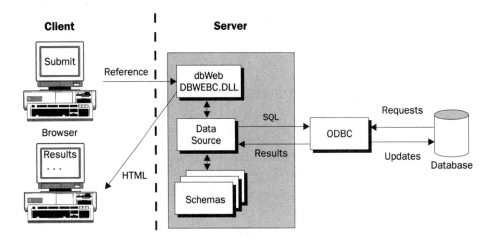

What dbWeb Does and Doesn't Do

The one thing that dbWeb does well is to hide away the actual process of retrieving the data from the tables. In IDC, we have to specify our own SQL statements, while in dbWeb there is no sign of them. However, this is also a major failing. There is no obvious way to perform anything other than a normal **SELECT** query when retrieving information. So summarizing information is not really possible. For example, we can list all the projects for each person, and the cost of each one, but not a total for all the people, or all the projects.

However, dbWeb does allow us to create results pages where the data in the tables can be updated. In the first page of the Schema dialog are the options which set this up and enable the Ins/Upd/Del tab of the dialog. To do this, however, we *must* create individual DBX templates for each operation.

We can also create more complex queries by linking more than one schema together. This means that clicking on a result field in the first schema can jump to another schema which provides different views of the same, or other, data. As you start to work with dbWeb, you'll find it is a very powerful tool underneath an easy-to-grasp (though a little outdated) interface.

Summary

In this chapter, we've looked at another of the technologies designed to enable you to publish data from your database system on the Web or your corporate intranet.

While we haven't covered all the ways you can build reports with dbWeb, you can see just how powerful it can be when building any kind of web site which has to convey real information to the users, rather than just glossy advertising. On the company intranet, it can make information retrieval much more intuitive, and hence make your staff that bit more efficient.

Now it's time we moved on to see how we combine all the technologies we've looked at so far, in a real application.

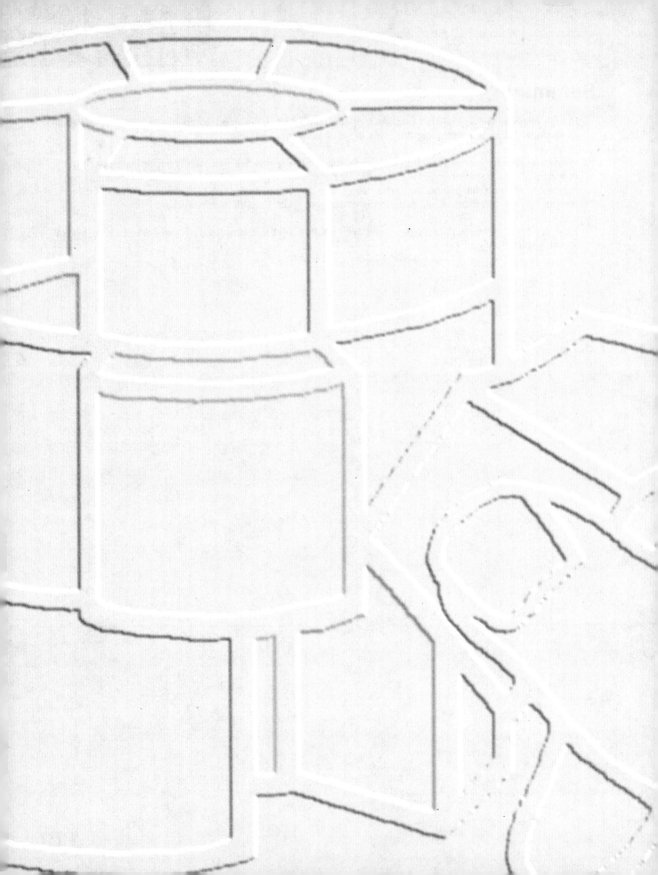

Building Applications

So far in this book, we've been looking at individual technologies which allow us to publish information on a web site or company intranet. In particular, we've been looking at information which is stored in a database; this is likely to be one of the prime areas of interest as you build and maintain your own site. The technologies we've covered—IDC, OLEISAPI and dbWeb—can each, in their own way, provide all the functionality you need for a reasonably simple data retrieval system.

However, if you've tried our sample Wrox Information Manager application, you'll have seen that there is more than just simple data retrieval going on. We call it an *application*, because it attempts to integrate several different informational needs within one page. It uses a fixed menu frame, and other frames which display the various user-interaction documents. On top of that, it allows users of the application to send short text messages to each other, which are almost immediately visible, without the need to fire up their messaging software.

In this chapter, then, we'll step back a little and see how we use the different server-side methods to build client-server applications. To do this, we'll incorporate some of the new technologies which are shaping up on the client side as well—primarily VBScript and ActiveX controls. We'll also be looking at methods of securing your system to protect it from unwanted visitors.

So we'll be looking at:

     How we blend different server-side technologies into a single application.

     Ways of incorporating client-side functionality into our dynamic web pages.

     Types of more complex server-side scripting methods.

     The important issues of good design and system security.

First, we'll look at how the Wrox Information Manager application fits together as a single tool, combining the separate parts we've been working with so far in this book.

Designing the Wrox Information Manager

In this book, we set out to build a single-page web application, which offered a range of functions. So far, it's not complete in all the respects we originally envisaged, but what we have done is provide you with some useful ways of combining the technologies we've been discussing in the book up to now. The final functions in Wrox Information Manager will, ultimately, include:

- Access to regularly used files and resources (our Current Documents page) and the ability to search for them.

- A Timesheet page, where users can provide information on their daily tasks.

- The ability to query this information, so as to simplify project management and costing.

- An on-line Diary and meeting scheduling system, allowing meetings of several people to be set up easily.

- A system for storing and retrieving address information, so that each person has access to all the company's contacts.

- A simple messaging system, allowing short messages to be sent quickly to one or more people.

You've seen screen shots of several of these functions throughout the book, and may also have tried using the application from our web site. In this chapter, you'll see how the different parts fit together, and learn about some of the techniques we've used to make the application more powerful, while still keeping it user-friendly.

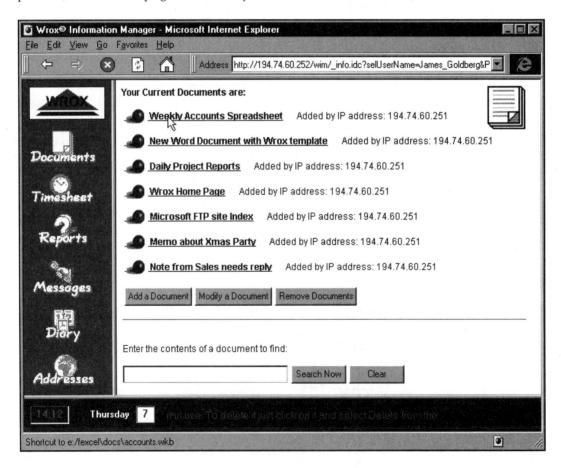

If you haven't tried out the Wrox Information Manager yourself, point your browser at:

http://www.wrox.com/books/0464/samples/webdb.htm

From there, you can start the application. In this specially tailored trial version, you don't need to enter a password to gain access.

An Overview of our Application

The first step in designing our application is to try and get some overall idea of what we're looking for. We know there are several tasks that need to be achieved, but how do we present these to the user and how do we store information that they supply? We've already decided that we want all the tasks to be accessed from within a single browser window, which contains multiple frames—including a 'menu' page of some type which allows the user to select the task they need.

An advantage of doing it like this is that by keeping the menu frame in view all the time, we can provide a quick and easy way for users to switch between the different tasks.

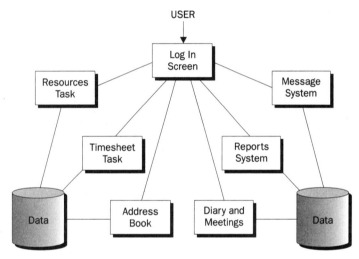

It also makes updating the site easier. It's a simple job to add a new page, or series of pages, and slot a menu item into the existing menu frame to load it. If we didn't have a fixed reference frame like this, we would have to decide which other pages should carry a link to the new ones—and then make sure each user knows where to find those links.

Lastly, there is one other aspect to consider. The protocol of the Web, HTTP (Hypertext Transfer Protocol), is generally anonymous. Once you've loaded a page from the server, it goes off and forgets about you until you make another request. Each time your browser asks for a new page, a graphic, or other object stored on the server, you reconnect to it afresh. Although you can store information between connections, using **cookies**, it's not like a local network where the server knows who you are when you log in, and maintains a persistent connection.

> ***Cookies*** *are items of information generated by the server and stored locally on your hard disk. They can be accessed from the browser using VBScript or JavaScript, and can also be manipulated at the server end. They are often used to hold information about visitors to a site (so that they don't have to log in each time they visit), or to store other information.*

The server can collect some information about the connection using HTTP variables, but in the real world, you'd want to send a password to identify the actual *person*, rather than just the machine they're using.

Deciding on the Components Required

The next step in designing our application, given that we know the tasks it must accomplish, is to figure out what components we might need. Obviously, we need a database of some type—we decided to incorporate all the data for our application into a single one. By using ODBC and SQL, we've kept the implementation of the application scripts and code as separate as possible from the actual database. We used Microsoft Access to build our database, but there's no reason why any other system that provides an ODBC driver shouldn't be used.

The other components of our application are basically all HTML files, scripts, and templates—with some exceptions for OLEISAPI and dbWeb. With these, we need to implement DLLs or schemas to handle the transition between our data and the Internet Server API. Here's a listing of the different components we know we'll need to implement:

- A database containing various tables which hold our data.
- A main frame page, containing the menu for the various function pages.
- A log-in page where the user identifies themselves, so that we update the correct records.
- An IDC script and template to create the Current Documents page, plus scripts to allow the contents to be updated.
- An Index Server script and template to allow users to search for documents and resources.
- An IDC script and template to create the Timesheet page, and an OLEISAPI DLL to handle updates to the information.
- A dbWeb schema which allows managers to query the Timesheet information, and the related templates to display the results.
- A separate area of the page to dynamically display the messages sent between users.
- A Diary system, storing the allocated times of meetings and events for each user.
- A system of collecting information about meetings, and updating the relevant users' diaries.

We won't actually be implementing the diary and meeting system in this book, so we've purposely left the details rather vague here.

Connecting the Components Together

Once we've discovered what we need to incorporate into our application, we can consider how it all fits together. Here's a plan of the various parts of the Wrox Information Manager application, showing the links to the tables. We've omitted any reference to the diary and meeting scheduler for the moment, because we will not be implementing them in this book. However, as you'll see from the modular nature of the design, dropping them in later will be no problem. We'll just need to add the relevant tables to the database, or connect to other databases which contain them, and slot the pages and scripts into the application with a reference to them in the main menu.

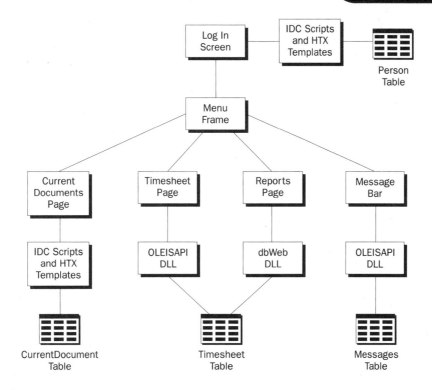

However, this is still a rather simplistic view. Once we've recognized the user, and validated their password if required, we will allow them to select the function they want from the menu in the main window. But we can't always just load a static page here. We may want to pre-populate the page with values from the database, or even the current time and date; and so we need to dynamically generate a page to be sent back.

As an example, look at the **Timesheet** page. In it, we allow users to select from any of the pre-defined list of projects. They can't just enter their own descriptions. This keeps the data in the tables tidy, and prevents incorrect code numbers or descriptions from upsetting the integrity of the data. It also makes life easier for the user, of course, and produces a much more professional-looking page.

So instead of loading Timesheet.htm, a static page, we actually run an IDC script when the user clicks on the **Timesheet** menu option. This script queries the database to get a list of projects, and creates a page containing this list of project descriptions inside rows of combo boxes.

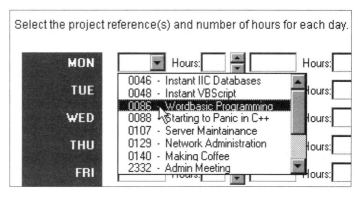

When they have filled in all the details, and click the Update button on the page, we reference an OLEISAPI DLL. This takes the values from the page, and updates or adds records in the Timesheet table reflecting the settings in the controls on the page.

So the process, just for this operation, requires several server interactions. The log-in page runs an IDC script which checks the user name and password against the **Person** table. If successful, the script calls an HTX template which creates and returns a page welcoming them to the application.

In our sample application, you don't need a password to log in. If you did, and gave the wrong one, the application would need to include code to handle this event, and display a warning page.

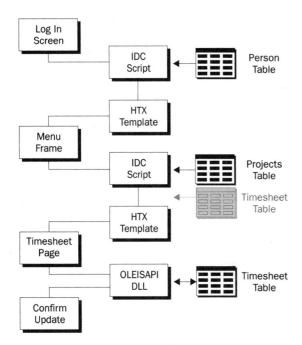

At this point, they select the Timesheet option, and this runs another IDC script which creates the Timesheet page, pulling in the project names from the **Projects** table. Finally, when they update the entries in this page, we can call the OLEISAPI DLL, like you saw in Chapter 3, to update the **Timesheet** table.

Of course, when we load the Timesheet page, we could include any existing details for the current week, so that users could fill it in daily, and correct entries as required up to the end of that week. This would make the task more complex, but it would be quite possible since the existing values could be pulled out of the **Timesheet** table as the page was generated.

Organizing and Storing the Data

Before we can build an application like this, we need the base data to be available. Because we originally built this application from scratch, we could design the database to suit our needs. This isn't always possible, though, and you may find that getting access to the data is the hardest part of the whole job.

We've used ODBC where possible, and this is usually the best way to accomplish the task. In fact, IDC and dbWeb will expect a **Data Source Name** to have already been assigned, as you saw in earlier chapters. When you use the ISAPI directly, though, things are a little different. You may be able to connect to a data source like SQL Server using ODBC, and then execute SQL statements directly against it. Alternatively, you can use the built-in record handling abilities of Visual Basic to talk directly to your database, like we've done with Microsoft Access.

The trick is to separate, as far as possible, the parts of the application that perform the querying of the data from the parts that create the dynamic pages. Using SQL makes this task easier. If you create an OLEISAPI DLL which uses the VB **Edit** and **Update** commands to directly manipulate the tables in a database, then you'll have a lot of work to do maintaining that DLL as the format of the tables change.

If your DLL or IDC script uses an SQL statement, however, you can alter this more easily to accommodate changes in the underlying data source. For example, imagine you currently retrieve the values from a single table with the statement:

```
SELECT DISTINCT CustName, CustRef FROM Customer ORDER BY CustRef
```

When the **Customer** table is divided up to allow more than one delivery address per customer, you can just change the statement:

```
SELECT DISTINCT CustName, CustRef FROM CustRefs JOIN CustAddr ON ...
```

However, if you were retrieving the values directly, by opening the tables and searching for matching records, you would have to change the whole structure of the code to suit the new table designs.

The Wrox Information Manager Tables

We've taken advantage of the flexibility that using SQL offers us, to keep our first attempt as simple as possible. Our database is built in Microsoft Access and contains all the tables we'll need. And, of course, the tables don't have to be all in the same database. You can allocate different Data Source Names for each table, if you wish, providing each one has all the information you need for that query. Here are the tables in our Microsoft Access database:

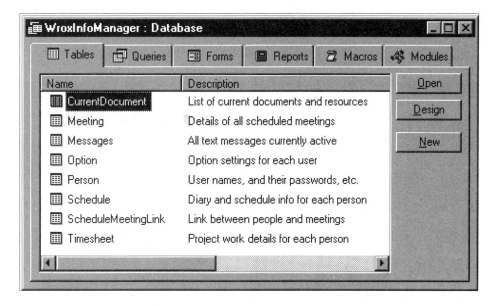

In order to keep our design simple, we've used a text identifier for each person, rather than using a separate key, and this is also used as the look up value for that person in other tables. It's not the most efficient way of doing things, but here we're concentrating on how the server technologies are used, rather than teaching you database theory. We've also omitted the **Projects** table, because we can get the same information for our simple needs from the **Timesheet** table at present.

Loading Pages in our Application

So, by now, we've covered a couple of walls of the office with detailed drawings of each step of the process, and we're ready to start building the components. In our case, we've already seen the working parts of the main ones—the Current Documents, Timesheet, and Reports pages. But how do we actually get these pages loaded when we want them, and how do we go about passing information between them?

The Current Documents page, as you've seen, is really an HTX template. We reference an IDC script in the hyperlink in the menu, and include the user name and password as arguments. These values are then available in the IDC script, and are used to retrieve the correct records from the **CurrentDocuments** table. It's all quite easy really. Look back at Chapter 2 again if you want to see how this is done in detail.

However, when we load the Timesheet page, we have to do a bit more than this. We need to collect a list of projects from the **Timesheet** table and return them to the browser. But because we want to display them inside several drop-down lists, which are in ActiveX controls in a separate file, it's not quite as simple as in the Current Documents page. In this case, we have to employ some client-side script to make it all work together. This is the subject of the next section.

Overall, however, you can see how our application was fitted together using components which can quite easily be developed by different teams (as in fact ours were), and then combined together into a main menu-type interface.

Using VBScript and ActiveX

There are often times when we need to carry out tasks within our pages that just aren't possible using ordinary HTML. New client-side technologies, such as the VBScript and JavaScript scripting languages, combined with Java applets and ActiveX objects, allow far more functionality to be added to an HTML page. There's no reason why we can't include this functionality in pages we create dynamically. The browser doesn't know how the pages that it receives are actually being created anyway—it just interprets the string of characters that arrive. In this book, we're going to look at some possibilities using VBScript, but there is no reason why you can't use JavaScript in the same way.

VBScript and HTX Detail Sections

There are two basic ways we can take advantage of VBScript and ActiveX in our dynamically generated pages. The first is to create 'inline code', for example by including scripting language statements within a **<%BeginDetail%> <%EndDetail%>** section of an HTX template, so that the statement is repeated in the page: once for each record that is returned by a query. The second way, which we'll come to later, is to create 'over-loaded' script routines and variables.

We'll start by looking at inline code—as an example, we'll see how the Timesheet page of our sample application is loaded, and how information from it is sent back to the server.

Returning to the Timesheet Page

The Timesheet page contains a series of list boxes, text boxes, and spin buttons, where users can record how much time they spend on individual projects during the week.

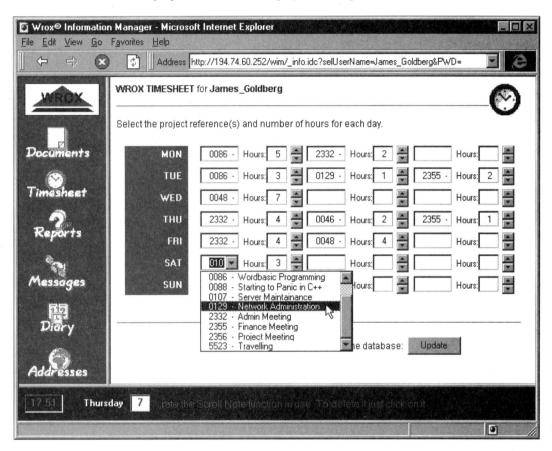

At the top of the Timesheet page is the current user's name, which we collected when they logged on, and which we've been passing between pages as we load them. We showed you how this worked in Chapter 2. It's pretty obvious, though, that the page you're looking at isn't created with just the normal HTML-style controls. The drop-down list is wider when open than closed, for example, and there's no **"SPIN-BUTTON"** option available for an **<INPUT>** tag. In fact, the page uses ActiveX **layout controls**, populated with other types of ActiveX control.

> *ActiveX layout controls are just a special kind of ActiveX control that you can use in a web page. They can act as a container to hold other ActiveX controls, which is what we've done here. Microsoft ActiveX Control Pad provides an easy way of inserting and editing layout controls.*

We've created a layout control object called **ProjLay**, which contains seven list boxes, text boxes, and spin buttons—one for each day of the week. To build the main working parts of the page, we incorporate three of these objects into a table, placing them side by side. Also, there is a layout control which contains the day names (in **label** controls), a hidden ActiveX **list box**, a **<FORM>** section containing a hidden text box, and a **SUBMIT** button with its caption set to Update.

```
<B>WROX TIMESHEET</B> for <B><%idc.UserName%></B>
<HR>Select the project reference(s) and number of hours for each day.<P>
<OBJECT ID="hidProjects" WIDTH=0 HEIGHT=0
   CLASSID="CLSID:8BD21D20-EC42-11CE-9E0D-00AA006002F3">
   <PARAM NAME="ScrollBars" VALUE="3">
   <PARAM NAME="Size" VALUE="2928;2928">
</OBJECT>

<TABLE WIDTH=100%>
  <TR><TD ALIGN="RIGHT">
    <OBJECT CLASSID="CLSID:812AE312-8B8E-11CF-93C8-00AA00C08FDF"
       ID="DayNames_alx" STYLE="LEFT:0;TOP:0">
       <PARAM NAME="ALXPATH" REF VALUE="DayNames.alx">
    </OBJECT>
  </TD><TD ALIGN="CENTER">
    <OBJECT CLASSID="CLSID:812AE312-8B8E-11CF-93C8-00AA00C08FDF"
       ID="ProjLay1_alx" STYLE="LEFT:0;TOP:0">
       <PARAM NAME="ALXPATH" REF VALUE="ProjLay.alx">
    </OBJECT>
  </TD><TD ALIGN="CENTER">
    <OBJECT CLASSID="CLSID:812AE312-8B8E-11CF-93C8-00AA00C08FDF"
       ID="ProjLay2_alx" STYLE="LEFT:0;TOP:0">
       <PARAM NAME="ALXPATH" REF VALUE="ProjLay.alx">
    </OBJECT>
  </TD><TD ALIGN="CENTER">
    <OBJECT CLASSID="CLSID:812AE312-8B8E-11CF-93C8-00AA00C08FDF"
       ID="ProjLay3_alx" STYLE="LEFT:0;TOP:0">
       <PARAM NAME="ALXPATH" REF VALUE="ProjLay.alx">
    </OBJECT>
  </TD></TR>
</TABLE><HR>

<FORM ACTION="/oleisapi.dll/wim/Timesheet.Update" METHOD="POST">
  Click here to submit the values to the database:
  <INPUT TYPE="HIDDEN" NAME="hidResults">
  <INPUT TYPE="SUBMIT" NAME="cmdSubmit" VALUE="Update">
</FORM>
```

Loading the Timesheet Page

In Chapter 2 we saw how we can pass values into a web page when we load it, using IDC. We did this by storing the page as an HTX template, rather than as a normal static HTML file, and adding placeholders for the values. Our Timesheet page is loaded in the same way. The **<A>** tag in the menu frame uses this **HREF**:

```
HREF="Timesheet/Tsheet.idc?UserName=<%idc.UserName%>"
```

So the current user's name, which will have been inserted into this **HREF** when the menu page was created, will be passed on to our Timesheet IDC script, **Tsheet.idc**, as a parameter. Here's the IDC script:

```
Datasource:WroxInfoManager
Username: sa
Template: Tsheet.htx
SQLStatement:
+SELECT DISTINCT Project FROM Timesheet ORDER BY Project;
```

This provides us with a list of the project names from the **Timesheet** table, plus our user name, which is available because it was a parameter to the script. To display the user name in the page, we've used:

```
<B>WROX TIMESHEET</B> for <B><%idc.UserName%></B>
```

However, getting the list of projects into the page isn't quite so easy—as you'll see. And getting them out as parameters, when the page is submitted for processing, is no simple feat either. Recall that our Timesheet page uses OLEISAPI to process the information. We'll look, first, at how we can get the information into the lists on the page; and then we'll see how we subsequently get that information back to the server.

Filling the ActiveX Project List Controls

In Chapter 2, we saw how IDC can be used to fill an HTML **<SELECT>** list, by placing the **<OPTION>** tag within the **<%BeginDetail%>** **<%EndDetail%>** section:

```
<SELECT NAME=selUserName>
  <%BeginDetail%>
    <OPTION VALUE="<%UserName%>"><%UserName%>
  <%EndDetail%>
</SELECT>
```

When we use an ActiveX List Control, this method isn't suitable, because the layout control is a separate file, removed from the Timesheet page. However, the list control does support the **AddItem** method, which we can execute using VBScript. Here's a **<SCRIPT>** section from the Timesheet page, which defines code for the **Window_onLoad()** event. It only runs when the page has finished loading, and it adds the list of project names to the hidden list box named **hidProjects**:

```
<SCRIPT LANGUAGE="VBScript">
<!--
Option Explicit

Sub Window_onLoad()
  <%BeginDetail%>
    hidProjects.AddItem "<%Project%>"
  <%EndDetail%>
End Sub

-->
</SCRIPT>
```

If you are used to Visual Basic, you'll have no problems picking up VBScript. Look out for the Wrox Press book, Instant VBScript, which will bring you up to speed in no time.

The only problem, now, is that we want the values to be in the drop-down list boxes in the layout controls, and not in a hidden list box. The list boxes, however, are in a separate file, which defines

131

the **ProjLay** layout control. It's not an HTX template, so we can't include a **<%BeginDetail%>** **<%EndDetail%>** section. Instead, we'll use VBScript code in the page to copy the list across.

Unpredictable onLoad() Events

However, this is where things can go wrong very easily. Most browsers set up several simultaneous connections to the server when they are loading the components of a page, so you can never be sure which ones will finish loading first. So, we can't copy the values across to the ActiveX list box during the main page's **onLoad()** event, because there's a good chance that the **ProjLay** layout control will not have finished loading. The layout control has its own **onLoad()** event, but because it is loaded separately from the main part of the page, the order of these events is again unpredictable.

> *If you find an error message such as* Undefined Property or Method, *or* Object does not support this method, *being displayed when your page loads, look out for this effect as a possible cause.*

We've found two ways of getting round this problem. The simplest way is to place a global variable called, say, **gblnInitialized**, in the main page. Then add a global subroutine called something like **Sub Initialize()**, which copies the values from the hidden list to the list where you want to display them, and sets **gblnInitialized** to **True**.

In the layout control's **onLoad()** event, we can check the value of the global variable. If it's still **False**, we can execute **Sub Initialize()**. We do the same in the main (or any other) window's **onLoad()** event, or in any other event that occurs as the page is loaded or first used.

In our Timesheet case, however, we have an extra problem. We're using three instances of the **ProjLay** layout control, and we need to fill in the values for the drop-down lists in each one. But the previous method will only run once, because after this the variable **gblnInitialized** will be **True**, preventing it running again. However, drop-down lists have a **DropButtonClick()** event, which is triggered when they are first opened. This provides us with an alternative method of filling them with our **Project** values.

We've inserted a subroutine into the actual layout control file, **ProjLay.alx**, which copies the values from the hidden list **hidProjects**, which is in the main Timesheet page, into all the list boxes in that control. Then, for each list box, we use the **DropButtonClick()** event to check if the list is already full. If not, its **ListCount** property will be zero, and we call our **FillALXLists** routine to fill them all:

```
Sub txtProjMon_DropButtonClick()     'repeated for each list box control
  If txtProjMon.ListCount = 0 Then FillALXLists
End Sub

Sub FillALXLists()
  For intLoop = 0 To hidProjects.ListCount - 1
    txtProject = hidProjects.List(intLoop)
    txtProjMon.AddItem txtProject
    txtProjTue.AddItem txtProject
    txtProjWed.AddItem txtProject
    txtProjThu.AddItem txtProject
    txtProjFri.AddItem txtProject
    txtProjSat.AddItem txtProject
    txtProjSun.AddItem txtProject
  Next
End Sub
```

The only effect is a very slight delay the first time a list inside that layout control is opened, while the list is filled. (The browser does this before actually displaying the open list to the user.) After that, it all works as normal.

Sending the Results to the Server

When we come to submit the results to the server, we also encounter a couple of problems. We can't submit values from ActiveX controls just by putting them in a **<FORM>** section, like we do with the normal HTML-style controls. However, ActiveX controls are so darn useful that we have to find other simple ways round this problem.

Probably the easiest way, and the one we've implemented in our Timesheet page, is to build up the return string in a variable, locally, using VBScript code, and then place it in a hidden HTML text control on a **<FORM>**. When the form is submitted, the server won't be able to tell the difference. And because a normal **SUBMIT** button has an **onClick()** event, we can run our code when the button is clicked. The browser will execute our VBScript code in entirety, before it actually submits the information on the form. We can quite happily set the values of the controls on the form while our script is running, and have these values submitted.

Here's part of the VBScript code in the Timesheet page. It runs when the Update button on the page, which is just a normal **SUBMIT** button, is clicked. It builds up a string of values in the correct format for the server to understand, and places it in the hidden text box named **hidResults**:

```
Sub cmdSubmit_onClick()
  Dim strRet

  'user name is put into the placeholder by IDC, when the page is created
  strRet = "PersonName=" & "<%idc.UserName%>"

  'add the values from the timesheet  -  Monday (Day 1)
  If ProjLay1_alx.txtProjMon.Value <>"" And
                              ProjLay1_alx.spnHoursMon.Value > 0 Then
    strRet = strRet & "&1P1D=" & Left(ProjLay1_alx.txtProjMon.Value, 4)
    strRet = strRet & "&1P1H=" & ProjLay1_alx.spnHoursMon.Value
  End If
  If ProjLay2_alx.txtProjMon.Value <>"" And
                              ProjLay2_alx.spnHoursMon.Value > 0 Then
    strRet = strRet & "&1P2D=" & Left(ProjLay2_alx.txtProjMon.Value, 4)
    strRet = strRet & "&1P2H=" & ProjLay2_alx.spnHoursMon.Value
  End If
  If ProjLay3_alx.txtProjMon.Value <>"" And
                              ProjLay3_alx.spnHoursMon.Value > 0 Then
    strRet = strRet & "&1P3D=" & Left(ProjLay3_alx.txtProjMon.Value, 4)
    strRet = strRet & "&1P3H=" & ProjLay3_alx.spnHoursMon.Value
  End If

  'Tuesday (Day 2)
    . . .
    . . .
  'Sunday (Day 7)
    . . .


  frmSend.hidResults.Value=strRet

End Sub
```

All we do is examine each list box and text box on the page to see if there is a value entered for the project name and number of hours. If so, we add the values to the output string. Now you can see where the string we handled in Chapter 3 actually came from.

Warning! Untruth Detected!

A little thought will also reveal, now, that we were somewhat economical with the truth in Chapter 3. We showed how our **Timesheet** DLL on the server had to cope with a set of name/ value pairs, as though it was created by 21 pairs of list and text boxes. The string, we suggested, would be like this:

```
PersonName=Olivia_Gonzales&1P1D=0488&1P1H=2&...
```

What we've actually done in our VBscript code, is to create this string and store it in the **hidResults** control. So it's actually submitted as a *single* name/value pair:

```
hidResults=PersonName=Olivia_Gonzales&1P1D=0488&1P1H=2&...
```

However, it's also URL encoded by the browser first, automatically; so what actually gets sent to the server is something like this:

```
hidResults=PersonName%3DOlivia_Gonzales%261P1D%3D0488%261P1H=2%26...
```

The equals signs and ampersands have been replaced with their ASCII code equivalents, so that the server can decipher where the name/value pairs start and finish. The **Timesheet** DLL actually contains an extra routine which splits off the extra name and equals sign from the start of the string, after it's been decoded.

> *There's a list of the characters affected by URL encoding in Appendix B.*

Overloaded Variables and Routines

Another useful way of using client-side scripting with IDC is by creating an 'overloaded' script. The code in the HTX template stored on the server is not interpreted or executed there directly— the template itself doesn't get sent to the browser. It's only a guide for your Internet server, as to where it should place the values it extracts from the database. So we can create an overloaded script by including several code routines which have the same name, or duplicate global variables and arrays, in the HTX template. All we have to do is make sure that either a **<%BeginDetail%>** **<%EndDetail%>** or **<%If...%>** **<%Else%>** **<%EndIf%>** section removes all but one of these when it generates the final HTML page to send to the browser.

Storing and Setting User's Options

Here's a simple example of using overloaded VBScript. Our database contains a table called **UserOption**, which holds the various options that our users select as they work with our application. When we load a page, we can run an IDC script which retrieves these options and sets them in the page. Here's the script:

```
Datasource:WroxInfoManager
Username: sa
Template: NewPage.htx
SQLStatement:
```

```
+ SELECT BGCOLOR, FGCOLOR, LKCOLOR, TXTFONT FROM UserOption
+ WHERE UserName=<%idc.UserName%>'
```

This selects the values of the options for that user, and places them into the page that's generated by the template—in this case **NewPage.htx**. We can set some of them by using the value we've retrieved directly, such as in the **<STYLE>** tag, and others by using the value in a VBScript statement. Here's part of the template file:

```
<HTM1>
<HEAD>
  <TITLE>Overloaded code example</TITLE>
  <STYLE>{Font-Family="<%TXTFONT%>"; Font-Size="18"}</STYLE>
</HEAD>
<BODY>

<SCRIPT LANGUAGE="VBScript">
<!--
  <%BeginDetail%>
    document.bgColor = "<%BGCOLOR%>"
    document.fgColor = "<%FGCOLOR%>"
    document.linkColor = "<%LKCOLOR%>"
  <%EndDetail%>

  <%If CurrentRecord GT 0%>
    document.write "I've changed the environment options.<BR>"
    document.write "<A HREF=""...""">Click here</A> to change them.<P>"
    document.write "(signed) The WebMaster."
  <%Else%>
    document.write "<A HREF=""...""">Click here</A> to select ... options."
  <%EndIf%>
-->
</SCRIPT>
```

If the user doesn't have any preferences stored, there will be no records returned for the **<%BeginDetail%>** **<%EndDetail%>** section. This is equivalent to using a loop where the test condition is always false so the code inside the loop is never executed.

Then, after the **<%BeginDetail%>** **<%EndDetail%>** section, we can use the value in **CurrentRecord**, within an **<%If ..%>** **<%Else%>** **<%EndIf%>** construct, to display an appropriate message. Remember that the value of **CurrentRecord** is undefined until after the **<%BeginDetail%>** **<%EndDetail%>** section.

So, here's the result for Olivia Gonzales, who has the following settings in the database: **BGCOLOR=0**, **FGCOLOR=#FFFFFF**, **LKCOLOR=#00FFFF**, and **TXTFONT=Deco: Wild Italic**.

135

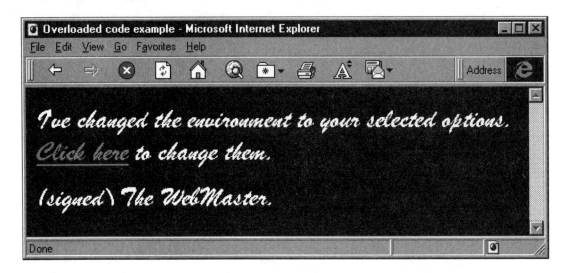

If you include a font name in the **<STYLE>** *tag which doesn't exist on the target machine, or use an empty string (as will be the case if the user has no options set), it defaults to the normal browser fonts. It's generally best to stick to the standard fonts when using* **<STYLE>** *tags, in the traditional way. By using our dynamic method, however, you can allow users to display your pages in any of their local fonts.*

Overloaded Subroutines and Functions

The previous example shows how we can include different VBScript commands in the page, depending on the results of the SQL query carried out in the IDC script. In a similar way, we can include different variable, subroutine, and function declarations as well. Here's a simple case which uses the same IDC script, but this time the template defines a global array variable named **garrUserOptions**, and a subroutine named **GetUserOptions()**.

Using the same principles as the last example, only one of the two available variable declarations will be included in the final page that's sent to the browser, depending on whether a record is returned by the query or not:

```
<SCRIPT LANGUAGE="VBScript">
<!--

<%BeginDetail%>
  Dim garrUserOptions(0, 3)
  Sub GetUserOptions()        'set stored options
    garrUserOptions(0, 0) = "<%BGCOLOR%>"
    garrUserOptions(0, 1) = "<%FGCOLOR%>"
    garrUserOptions(0, 2) = "<%LKCOLOR%>"
    garrUserOptions(0, 3) = "<%TXTFONT%>"
  End Sub
<%EndDetail%>

<%If CurrentRecord EQ 0%>
  Dim garrUserOptions(0, 3)
  Sub GetUserOptions()        'set default options
    garrUserOptions(0, 0) = "#FFFFC0"
    garrUserOptions(0, 1) = "#000000"
```

```
        garrUserOptions(0, 2) = "#0000FF"
        garrUserOptions(0, 3) = "Arial"
    End Sub
<%EndIf%>


-->
</SCRIPT>
```

In reality, this is only the tip of the iceberg. Remember that you can include more than one SQL statement in an IDC script (in version 2.0), and have an equivalent number of **<%BeginDetail%>** **<%EndDetail%>** sections in the template. You can also test the value of **CurrentRecord** as many times as you like, after each **<%BeginDetail%>** **<%EndDetail%>** section. So, you can have numerous different blocks of script in the template, and leave it to the SQL query to ultimately decide which ones will be included in the final page.

Keeping your Users and Data Secure

Once you start to allow access to your stored data through a web server, such as Internet Information Server, you have to start thinking seriously about security. If your only connection is to the office network, as an intranet, then you have less risks to contend with. Compare this to the situation where the entire world can come and play on your server via a TCP/IP link to the Internet as a whole. In the rest of this chapter, we'll be turning our minds to securing your system, so that your application can safely be put to use.

Remember that network security is a complex and very serious business. If it is your responsibility, you should certainly consider taking professional advice which is tailored to your situation. We will only be giving an overview of the issues here.

Assessing the Risks to your System

Before you can look seriously at where your system is at risk, you need to have a plan for the network as a whole. If you have important files scattered all over the various server directories and on the workstation hard drives, you're going to have a difficult job setting up a secure system. You must be able to clearly define which data is sensitive, and where each user should be allowed access, before you can consider surveying the risks or implementing security control methods.

Risks on your Company Intranet

Presumably, your network is as secure as it needs to be to support the running of the company. When you implement an intranet within an existing network, your intention is likely to be to allow your staff better access to corporate information. Passwords, user accounts, and other security methods will already be in force, and you only need to concern yourself (at least in theory) with any new resources you establish.

Protecting Databases

The first point is to be careful that you don't circumvent existing permissions when you go about creating new System Data Source Names. These are required for IIS and other applications to be able to see the database, but you can still implement the normal security techniques which prevent access through other methods (i.e. when they run the database application directly).

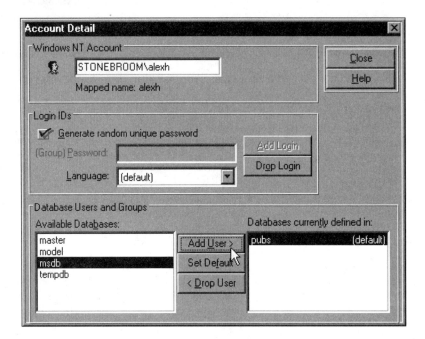

In Microsoft SQL Server, for example, you set up user rights directly, or allow the NT Server permissions to be used, when you create the link to a database. In Access, you can set up the system administration database (**.mda**) and Workgroups which allow password-protected user accounts to be used.

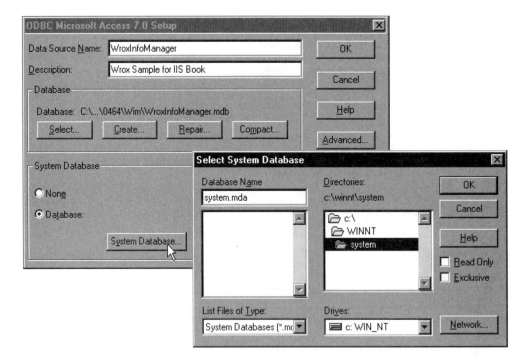

Whichever route you follow, you can generally use the existing account permissions through the ODBC driver you set up. When IIS runs a query, it must supply the correct password for that database, and this password can be placed in appropriate IDC scripts. For sensitive data, however, you can omit it so that the user will be prompted by NT before the query runs. If they don't have permission to access the data, the IDC script or dbWeb query will not proceed. However, this regular prompting is not useful when they are accessing several pages.

Protecting Documents

For more general documents, security on an intranet is generally not so cumbersome. For example, price lists and technical information will need to be available to almost everybody. However, you may have documents for which you need to limit distribution. When users are connecting to the server through a browser, they can freely enter IP addresses or normal physical paths to view all kinds of resources, unless you take steps to prevent them. The easiest way is to use NT Server's existing permissions to limit access to different directories and files for each user or group of users.

If the documents are not HTML files, you can password protect them individually using the security features of their application. In Word, for example, you can protect documents from being opened at all, or make them read-only, using the **Save** tab of the **Options** dialog. You may also wish to take advantage of features like Annotations and Revisions. This is particularly useful, because it allows you to control how users are able to load these files over the network and save changes to them.

Risks from the Internet

If you're worried about the dangers of damage to your files and system from the young prankster in the Accounts department, just wait till you connect your network to the Internet. A few million highly-skilled network specialists could well be out there, trying to break into your system! You still need to take the same steps as you would with your company Intranet, but be prepared to add extra protective layers as well.

Email messages and files are propagated through many different network routers on their way round the Net—and, to make matters worse, TCP/IP is itself inherently insecure as transport protocols go. Almost anyone can examine the headers and routing information in the packets that travel in and out of your network. Unless you take some steps to stop them, people anywhere in the world can, with comparative ease, pretend to be a workstation on your network, and access your server that way.

More skilled visitors may even convince the server that *they* are the administrator, and you could find yourself locked out altogether if they can change the access permissions. So you will need to take a few more steps to protect yourself, and the other users on your internal network.

Whole books are written about network security, and if you are responsible for implementing it on an Internet-connected site, you should be prepared to learn a lot more about it. In the rest of this chapter, we'll try to give you some general advice, and suggest some things you should be thinking about.

Using Existing NT Security Methods

On top of the usual application-specific security techniques we've mentioned, like password protecting documents and setting up user rights in your database programs, you need to be absolutely sure that you've got the best from Windows NT's own security system. NT is (underneath) a C2-rated secure operating system, though you have to do some work to achieve this. For example, you have to prevent the last user name being displayed in the log-in dialogs. Microsoft supplies an application called **C2Config.exe** which will help you set up this extended C2-level security.

NTFS File and Directory Security

For a start, unless there is a particular reason why not, you should be using the NTFS file system on your server's drives, rather than the traditional FAT method. Not only does this provide better performance, but it also adds an extra layer of protection to your files. NTFS can set security permissions on individual files, as well as complete directories, and you can easily update the permissions as needed.

More to the point, you aren't limited to just read-only or full access like a traditional filing system. You can apply a mixture of these attributes to files or directories:

Attribute	Meaning
No Access	No access to the directory or file.
Add	Files can only be added to the directory, and new sub-directories created. The contents cannot be listed. New files cannot replace existing ones with the same name. Files cannot be executed.
Add and Read	Files can be read from, and added to, a directory. New sub-directories can be created. The directory contents can be listed. New files cannot replacing existing ones with the same name. Files can be executed.
Read	Files can be read from, but not added to or deleted from the directory. The contents can be listed. Files can be executed.
Change	Files can be read. Files and sub-directories can be added and deleted. New files will replace existing ones with the same name. The directory contents can be listed. Files can be executed.
Full Control	Files can be read. Files and sub-directories can be added and deleted. New files will replace existing ones with the same name. The directory contents can be listed. Files can be executed. Ownership of the files and sub-directories can be taken, and permissions changed.

*Setting some of these options automatically implies others: for example, granting **Change** permission automatically implies **Read** permission. You can also set up special, user-defined, combinations of attributes if required. For example **Read** can be set to **RX** for Read and Execute, or **RWX** for Read, Write and Execute. As you'll see later, there is a user account set up for the web server itself. Because it needs Read and Execute permission, but not Write, we can set it up to just **RX**.*

Setting Directory and File Permissions

To set the permissions for a file or directory, select it in an Explorer window, and open the Properties dialog. In the Security tab, there are sections for Permissions, Auditing, and Ownership. In the Permissions section, click the Permissions button to open the Directory Permissions or File Permissions dialog.

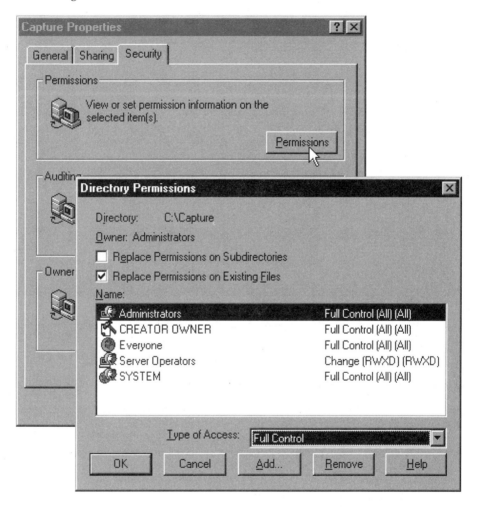

Here, you can set the type of control for each user group. Use the Add button to add other groups, and the Type of Access drop-down list to select the access you want to give that group. Make sure you prevent access to sensitive files for default groups such as Everyone. When setting permissions for a directory, you can specify that those settings replace the current permissions on existing files in that directory by setting the appropriate checkbox at the top of the dialog. You can also update the permissions on all the files in any sub-directories as well.

The Properties dialog also lets you set up Auditing. By adding a group to the Directory Auditing dialog and selecting the Events you want to monitor, NT will create an audit log which can be useful to check for attempted security breaches. Notice, also, that you can add auditing to existing files in the current directory and any sub-directories.

141

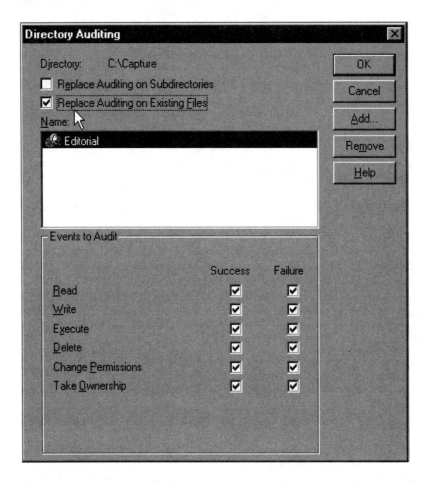

Lastly, the Directory Properties and File Properties dialogs allow you to take ownership of a file, if you already have the correct permission. This means that its permissions will be changed to your own default permissions. If you want to take over a directory, perhaps for site maintenance, you can take ownership as the Administrator, with Full Control permissions, then hand it back to the user account afterwards. Their default permissions, for example Add and Read, will then be restored. This is a useful way to solve the problem of directory security that's gone wrong. Log on as the administrator, take control of the entire directory, then reset the proper permissions.

User Groups, Accounts and Permissions

The main protection for your network and its data is through NT's built-in security. We've mentioned user groups in the previous section, so we'll take a little time to give you a brief outline. Of course, if you are already administering the server, you'll already have set up appropriate user groups and accounts.

You create **accounts** which have specific permissions to access and update data, and add each **user** to an appropriate **group**. Then, by mapping **groups** to **accounts**, you allow each user the required level of file and directory access within your network. However, you need to make sure that they all belong to the correct groups, and that there are no left-over accounts or groups hanging around.

142

All this is done in the User Manager dialog:

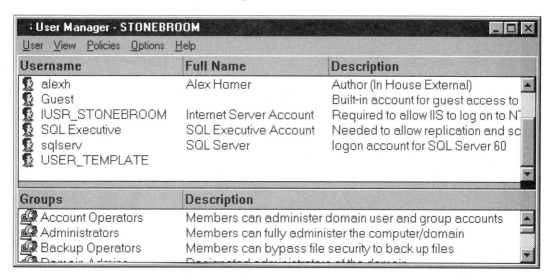

For each user or group, you can specify a huge range of options and controls. For example, you can control what times of day they can log on, which workstations they can log on to, set their password, and specify when they next need to change it. There's also an option to disable accounts altogether—useful if you want to temporarily prevent access by a particular group, or while you get round to removing unused accounts.

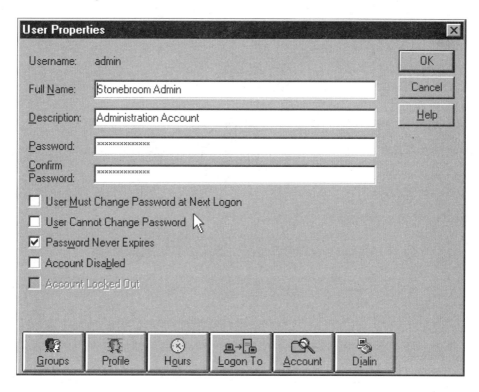

You should also enforce a suitable minimum password length and regular password changes. NT can do this with the **Account Policy** dialog, where you can also prevent the same password being used again, and passwords being changed too often. You can also set up NT so that repeated log in attempts will lock the user out and alert you. And if you have defined the times when users can log on, you can use the settings in this dialog to eject them from the network automatically at the end of these periods.

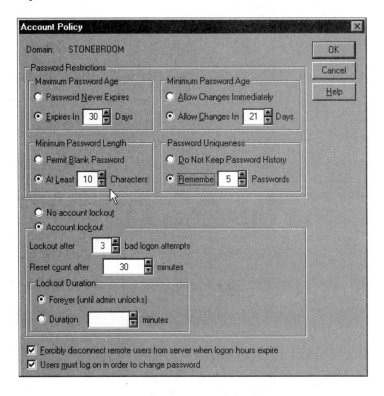

Default User Groups and Group Names

Accounts and groups give you a way of setting the permissions on both files and directories, and on other objects within NT—such as the various **Services** that are available from **Control Panel**. One default group, **Everyone**, is often used to set permissions. A good policy is to remove all default groups and users, or a least give them very low privileges. Then create an entirely new set of groups and users. Default users and groups are ones like Guests, Administrators, Domain Admins, Domain Guests, Backup Operators, etc.

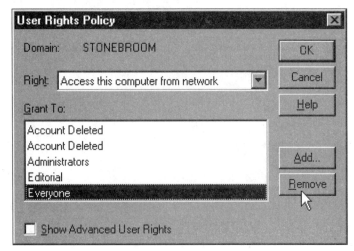

144

You should also encourage users to be as restrictive as possible about which directories and resources they share over the network. The best policy is one of advice—set up standard corporate guidelines. Once into your network from outside, all shared resources become available. And be particularly aware of risks when Windows 95 workstations are in use, rather than Windows NT. Windows 95 does not support the full security model that NT does, especially where client file and print sharing is in use, and this can offer on-site 'visitors' an easy way in.

The IUSER User Account

There is one special user that needs to have appropriate permissions set up on your server. To maintain the security model, Internet Information Server logs on to NT as a user when it needs to retrieve files for transmission across the network or the Internet. By default, this user name will be IUSER_*domain_name* or IUSER_*server_name*. The IIS installation program should have created this account and set the default permissions. However, this may not be the case if it is installed on a domain controller.

This is, in fact, a very brief overview. The way the IUSER account operates depends very much on the security model set up for the user and machine.

The most important requirement is that you allow Internet Information Server to log on to NT as a local user. Select **U**ser Rights from the **P**olicies menu to open the User Rights Policy dialog. Then you need to select the Log on locally right, and make sure that either the Internet Information Server user, or a group of which it is a member, is available.

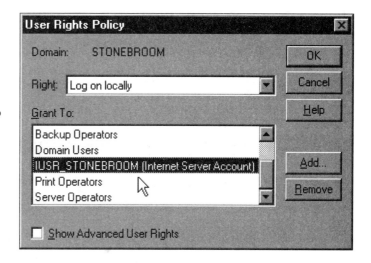

If the Log on locally option is not set, or the IUSER account cannot log on using the password you've supplied (or, of course, if you haven't got an account for IUSER), then you'll find the Log On dialog appearing each time you access a new directory or file with different permissions. Although everything appears to work, you'll still be writing several events to NT's Event Log, because the anonymous log-on failed. After a while, you may find that IIS stops responding, because the log is full.

Once you've created the IUSER account, you can go back to the NT **User Manager** and set the permissions you want for it. Remember you'll have to allow it **Read** permission for any files and directories which contain pages you want to send over the Net, or scripts you want to execute, unless you require a password to be used. If you are using FTP to allow users to send files to the server, you'll also have to set at least **Add** permission as well. If a user requests a document they don't have permission for, IIS will act as though that document doesn't exist.

Having seen how Internet Information Server interfaces with the NT security systems, we'll move on to look at some of the other issues involved in securing your site. This time, though, it's from the web server's point of view.

Securing your Web Server

One of the best ways to protect your data from external risks on an Internet-connected network, is to provide a wall between it and the outside world. You can do this in several ways, the most usual being with a firewall. This allows you to separate the two networks (yours and outside), and selectively pass data through it.

A good firewall will hide your internal network from prying eyes, and can even hide the DNS entries. You'll probably use a proxy server to allow your client machines to see the Internet. The proxy server will, on behalf of the connected client, go and get the requested page through the firewall. This combination effectively removes the identity of the machines on your internal network from the data packets going out on to the net. Hackers can only see the proxy server, and not individual machines. The proxy server has the added advantage of caching requested pages, making access quicker for frequently requested ones.

Hiding Internal Network Data

This also means separating your own internal data from that which you want to publish outside, wherever possible. If they can't be on separate machines, they should at least be on a separate disk or disk partition. If you need to provide access to directories from outside your own network, you can set up virtual paths. Place the files in sub-directories at the end of the tree (not in the root) and set up explicit virtual root paths to them. That way users can't see the directories below. This also allows you to grant everyone access to certain directories, while limiting others to users on your own network and subnet.

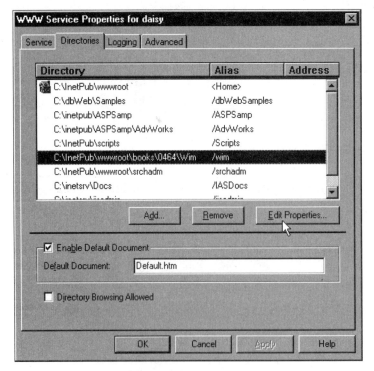

You can also set up discrete permissions to particular mapped directories by specifying the acceptable IP and subnet masks, and creating a virtual server (rather than a virtual path). This means that you have a different IP address for that virtual server, which you'll have to obtain separately from the Internet Naming Authority. Because it's different from your normal domain name, it acts as another way of usefully assigning a different area of your system for public access. Visitors will not be aware that they only have access to a part of your system.

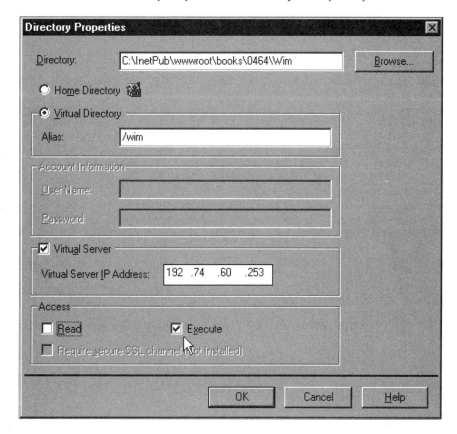

At the bottom of this dialog, you can control the type of access available to that virtual path or server as well. Clearing the Read option, and setting the Execute option, will allow scripts and other programs to run, while preventing users from downloading any of the directory contents. Of course, this only works if you put the files that *must* be read by the browser (i.e. normal HTML pages and templates) in a different directory, which does have Read permission. We'll come back to these options in a while. And if you have obtained a Secure Sockets Layer certificate and key (for which a fee is payable), you can force all connections to that virtual path to use this method.

Using Secure Transmission Protocols

If you intend to transmit and receive sensitive information, such as credit card numbers or other account details, you should consider setting up the Secure Sockets Layer. This can authenticate the individual client and server, encrypt the transmitted text, and add authentication codes to prevent unauthorized changes to the text.

First, you run the Key Manager program that's supplied with IIS, and enter details of your organization. This information is then submitted to VeriSign, or other certification authority, who provide the certificate and software keys required to set it up. For more information, contact VeriSign. Their web site is at **http://www.verisign.com/microsoft/**

Configuring Anonymous Logon

In the Service tab of the IIS Properties dialog you set the user name and password that Internet Information Server will use to log into NT. This should already have been done during installation of IIS, but if you change the account details in NT, you must remember to change them here as well.

The remainder of the dialog deals with how IIS handles client requests from browsers. Visitors to your web site will expect to be able to log in anonymously in most cases. Unless you are charging admission, or performing private transactions, there's no point in asking them their user name and password. In fact, it's generally better not to, because this information is then transmitted across the Net for all to see. So you should always set the Allow Anonymous option for Password Authentication, as well as the default Challenge/Response method, unless it is definitely not appropriate for your site. Although Internet Explorer supports Challenge/Response, it's still the case that some browsers will not.

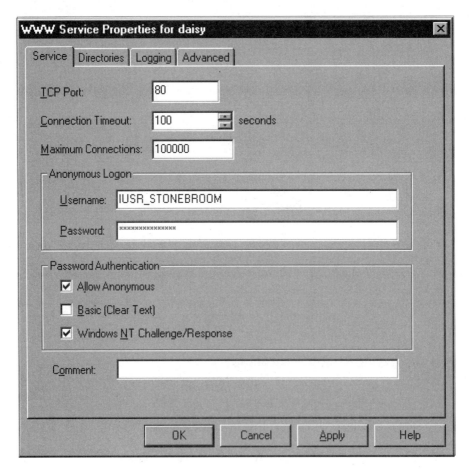

Logging WWW Activity

Actions which violate your system's security are automatically added to the NT Event Log, which also contains information about service failures and general software errors. This logging is performed and controlled by NT, but IIS can also perform logging. However, this is aimed at showing the activity on your web site or intranet, and the results can be sent to either a text file or a database—via a suitable ODBC driver. IIS will create a separate log for each day, week, or month automatically, or when it reaches a certain size.

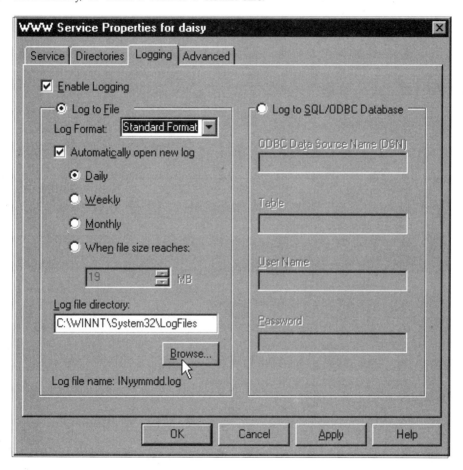

Granting Default Permissions

The final tab in the Properties dialog is most useful if you are working with a limited audience. You can control access to your site by either:

 Setting the default to Granted Access, then adding to the list the IP addresses, or address groups, for which you want to deny access.

 Setting the default to Denied Access, then adding to the list the IP addresses, or address groups, for which you want to permit access.

149

If you are working on an Intranet, with several subnets, then you can easily permit access to the service to just particular groups or users this way. It's not always going to be much help on the Internet as a whole, however, because many providers issue IP addresses from their own range dynamically to their users. Each time they log on, it will be with a different one of these addresses.

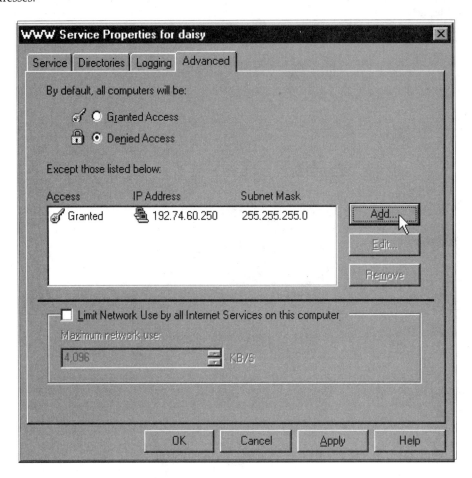

File Transfer Protocol

The properties we've seen above are those for the WWW service on Internet Information Server. There are a broadly equivalent set of properties for the FTP service, and any other services, such as GOPHER, that you may have set up. You can, and should, maintain different settings for each service. In particular, in the Service tab of the dialog, you may want to use a different Username and Password, and set the Allow only anonymous connections option, if it's appropriate. This prevents the user sending passwords over the Net.

```
☑ Allow Anonymous Connections
  Username:  IUSR_STONEBROOMFTP
  Password:  xxxxxxxxxxxxxxxx
  ☑ Allow only anonymous connections
```

Bear in mind, also, that File Transfer Protocol (FTP) gives users far more control over the way they see, and can work with, the files on your system. In a web browser using HTTP, they can only read or execute files. However, FTP will allow them to upload (write) and delete files, and create and delete directories, if you allocate these permissions. You need to ensure that suitable passwords are in place for users who actually do need full access.

> **With FTP it isn't possible to setup virtual servers. Also, there's the little known fact that if you create a virtual directory with the name of a user, then when the user logs on, that directory will be the home directory.**

Creating an FTP Upload Area

One useful way to use the file and directory permissions which we've been considering, is when you need a directory on the server where users can upload files for examination by the administrator. This 'mailbox' facility is popular in situations where various outside contributors have a regular requirement to submit files to your system. The directory they use is set up only with Add permission, so they can upload any file. However, they can't see what files are already there; nor can they download, delete, or execute any of them.

The administrator can then move them to appropriate directories, once they are confirmed to be free from viruses or other risks. The only problem, however, is that users cannot upload files which already exist. They need to rename them to prevent a clash with other files in that directory.

Securing Executable Scripts and Programs

When you create scripts for the ISAPI or IDC interfaces, or schemas for dbWeb, you must include the correct passwords for the data (unless you leave it to the user to enter them when they run the query). In IDC in particular, these scripts are plain text files. However, users will not be able to read or download them as long as you have set just Execute permission (in IIS Server Manager) for the directory where they reside. But bear in mind that if you keep back-up copies elsewhere, as you'll have to do while you develop and maintain the system, users can download them if that directory just has read access.

When using other types of executable programs or DLLs to produce dynamic pages, the information is generally hidden within the executable. But remember that they are fully functional programs which can access your machine at core level. If you don't produce your own, it's worth while considering where they came from, and what else they are doing when you run them. Remove all those you don't need, and while you're about it remove any other applications and scripts that aren't required—including Telnet, FTP, and any other remote access applications.

Finally, bear in mind that the Web allows users to execute applications. If they have FTP and HTTP access to a directory, they can upload a virus-laden file with FTP, and then access it using HTTP as if it was a CGI program or IDC script. If you have **Execute** permission set for that directory, the program will run. Within a few seconds, you'll have more 'nasties' on your server than you can shake a virus scanner at. Keep your FTP and HTTP directories separate at all times!

Summary

In this chapter, we've considered how to build a complete application—including the need to design the system 'up front'. We also looked at the benefits of building the different parts of the application separately and then combining them at the end. If you use a modular based design for your application, you will find it easier to extend it in future—new components can simply be slotted in. We looked at how the Wrox Information Manager is put together, and how it uses some new technologies which are shaping up on the client side: primarily, VBScript and ActiveX controls.

In the second part of the chapter, we suggested some things that you should think about when you come to implement security, to protect your system and data from unwelcome visitors.

In the following and final chapter of this book, we're going to take a look at the newest of all the Microsoft server-side technologies, which is aimed at users of Internet Information Server. If you think IDC and OLEISAPI are clever, then—as the song goes—'You Ain't Seen Nothing Yet ...'

Active Server Pages

In this, the final chapter, we'll be taking a look at one of the most recent developments in web server technologies to come out of Microsoft. **Active Server Pages** the future for server-side programming with Internet Information Server. In many ways, it is a combination of other technologies, yet it adds extra functionality which is either impossible, or just difficult to achieve, with other methods.

This is going to be a brief overview. However, we have implemented parts of our sample **Wrox Information Manager** application using it, so that you can see some of the things that are possible. Why have we left it to the last chapter of the book, rather than describing it earlier as a mainstream technology? The main reason is that, at the time of writing, it is still under development, and only early Beta versions are available. Active Server Pages is included with IIS 3, and can be downloaded from Microsoft's web site.

However, the power and flexibility that it offers does mean that you should be aware of what it can do and how it works. If you are still planning your new web site, or company intranet, you should be looking to evaluate Active Server Pages before you settle fully on other technologies. In this chapter, we'll show you some of the things that you can achieve using it.

We'll be covering:

- What Active Server Pages actually is, and how this web server technology compares to others.
- Why it is so useful, and likely to supersede other methods in the future.
- The background to its design, how it works, and what it can do.
- How we've used it in our **Wrox Information Manager** application.

Bear in mind, as you work through this chapter, that the technology is not yet 'finished'. In other words, much of the structure and syntax, especially in the area of database management, may well change as it approaches a release version.

For a detailed look at how you can use Active Server Pages to produce exciting dynamic and interactive web pages, look out for Instant Active Server Pages, from Wrox Press.

What are Active Server Pages?

To give you an idea of how Active Server Pages fits into the whole scheme of things, we'll first look at a broad overview of the technology. Active Server Pages uses a server-based template file, which is referenced in the client browser—just the same way as you would reference an ordinary HTML page, an IDC script, or a CGI application. And the page that's returned is no different from one created by any of these methods.

The difference, of course, is at the server end. Installing Active Server Pages places a software layer between Internet Information Server and the other components that are used to create dynamic pages. It's not just another separate technology as such, but a way of unifying all the other methods that are available. This is, ultimately, what makes it so powerful. To give you an idea of how it all fits together, here's some of the ways that the Active Server Pages engine can use other methods:

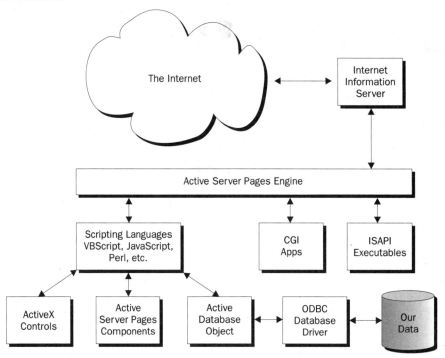

Active Server Pages allows us to continue using existing technologies where they provide the best fit to our needs. Now, however, we can seamlessly combine these methods together, while adding the extra functionality that Active Server Pages itself provides.

What can Active Server Pages Do?

So what, exactly, can Active Server Pages do, and why is it so useful? We'll approach these questions in two ways. First, we'll compare it to the existing methods you have at your disposal and that we've described earlier in this book. Then, we'll take a more detailed look inside the technology.

Active Server Pages vs. IDC and ISAPI

In Chapter 2, we looked at what is, currently, the easiest way to include database information in dynamic web pages. Internet Database Connector uses a script file which specifies where the data comes from, and a template file which formats the returned page. Generally, we provide an SQL statement in the IDC script, which uses ODBC to talk to our database. The returned data is then placed in the HTX file, and the resulting page sent back to the browser as normal HTML.

Internet Database Connector

```
┌──────┐    ┌──────┐    ┌──────────┐    ┌──────┐
│ Web  │───▶│ IDC  │───▶│   HTX    │───▶│ Web  │
│ Page │    │Script│    │ Template │    │ Page │
└──────┘    └──────┘    └──────────┘    └──────┘
                 │ SQL      Results
                 │ (only)   (optional)
                 ▼              ▲
              ┌──────────┐   ┌──────┐
              │   ODBC   │   │ Our  │
              │ Database │◀─▶│ Data │
              │  Driver  │   └──────┘
              └──────────┘
```

*Remember, you don't **have** to return data to your HTX template. If you are just updating or deleting records, you may only want to return an acknowledgment to the browser.*

In Chapter 3, we looked at OLEISAPI. This uses OLE/ActiveX methods to talk to the Internet Server API, through a DLL called **OLEISAPI.DLL**. We created our own OLE Automation Server DLL, which receives the information from the browser and creates the return page itself. This technique offers a lot more functionality than IDC, because it allows us to manipulate the database directly, and use all the other functionality available in the programming language we use to build the DLL. The problem is that we have to cope with writing and compiling the DLL itself, then registering it with Windows so that the OLE link between the components will work correctly. Maintaining and updating it then becomes quite a major task.

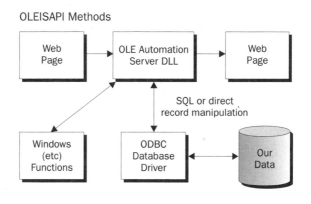

OLEISAPI Methods

157

Now, compare these two methods with Active Server Pages. In broad outline, it looks remarkably like ISAPI or OLEISAPI methods. The main difference is that the executable file, or OLE Server DLL, is replaced by an Active Server Pages script. We also have extra functionality available from pre-built components, which are supplied with Active Server Pages, and we can create our own components as well.

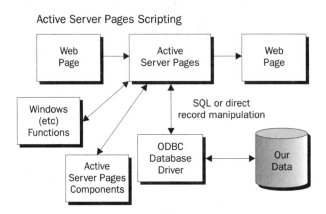

Active Server Pages Scripting

What does an Active Server Pages File Look Like?

It's all very well using vague diagrams to indicate the functionality available from a technology, but at the end of the day you want to know what it actually looks like in real life. We'll attempt to show you in this section. If you are used to using VBScript or JavaScript in the browser, you'll immediately see how Active Server Pages is—as well as being an extension of IDC and ISAPI methods—an extension of these client-side scripting techniques.

The next figure shows some of the ways that you can include dynamic methods in an Active Server Pages file. This file has the extension **.asp** and looks like a cross between an IDC script, and a VBScript or JavaScript page. There are the same placeholders, marked with **<% ... %>**, but here they contain script, rather than just variables. Normal **<SCRIPT> </SCRIPT>** tags also enclose script sections. However, now there is an extra attribute to the **<SCRIPT>** tag, **RUNAT**, which indicates where the script will be executed. And, of course, there's the usual HTML code that builds the non-dynamic parts of the return page:

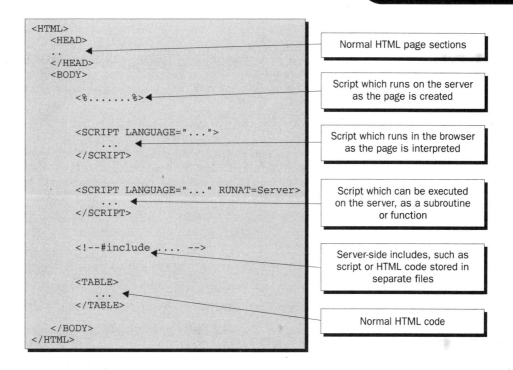

```
<HTML>
   <HEAD>
     ..
   </HEAD>
   <BODY>

        <%.......%>

        <SCRIPT LANGUAGE="...">
           ...
        </SCRIPT>

        <SCRIPT LANGUAGE="..." RUNAT=Server>
           ...
        </SCRIPT>

        <!--#include .... -->

        <TABLE>
           ...
        </TABLE>
   </BODY>
</HTML>
```

Normal HTML page sections

Script which runs on the server as the page is created

Script which runs in the browser as the page is interpreted

Script which can be executed on the server, as a subroutine or function

Server-side includes, such as script or HTML code stored in separate files

Normal HTML code

Notice, also, the Server-side Includes (SSI) which are marked by a comment tag and keyword, such as:

```
<!--#include /asp/myfile.txt-->
```

In the remainder of this section, we'll look briefly at the different elements that can be included in an Active Server Pages file. These can be divided into two broad categories—those that are targeted at the browser and those that are executed on the server. As you'll see, the combination of both in one file starts to provide us with powerful ways of managing true client/server interaction.

Client-side Functionality

We can put anything in the page that Active Server Pages creates, that we would normally include using other methods. This can be normal text and HTML code, client-side scripts, and tags which define objects which are embedded in the page. The page is executed by the server, and the results are then sent back to the browser.

Text and HTML Code

An Active Server Pages file is just an HTML file with extended capabilities. So we can use any HTML tags, plus the text for the body of the page, in our **.asp** file. Active Server Pages also contains methods which can identify the capabilities of the browser that is making the request, so we can create pages where the HTML code is accurately tailored to include only the tags which that particular browser will recognize.

159

Client-side Scripts

All the latest browsers support some method of scripting language. The two most common of these are VBScript and JavaScript, and in both cases, all the script is included in the `.asp` file. The server ignores it, just like it would if we were returning a static web page, or creating it dynamically with IDC or a CGI application. Only when it gets to the browser is the script interpreted and executed as appropriate.

Client-side ActiveX Controls

The increasing use of embedded objects in web pages is fully supported by Active Server Pages. We define the `<APPLET>` or `<OBJECT>` tags in the `.asp` file, just like we would in a static web page, or one that is created dynamically with IDC or a CGI application. Once the page is loaded by the browser, it will reference and download (as required) the objects which are defined there.

Server-side Functionality

Here, we come to the functionality that makes Active Server Pages what it is. It includes both client-side functions (as described above) and server-side functions such as scripts, components and database interaction.

Server-side Scripts

The whole basis of Active Server Pages revolves around the ability to include script sections in the `.asp` file, which are executed *on the server*, rather than in the browser on the client. To make this work, there has to be a way of defining which scripts are destined for the browser, and which should be executed on the server. This is done in two ways.

Code which is written in an extended dialect of VBScript, and which is enclosed in the `<%` and `%>` markers, is interpreted and executed on the server, as the page is processed for return to the browser. This means that we can include the values of existing variables, and perform other script tasks, as the return page is being created:

```
<% = AnnualTotal %>          put the value of AnnualTotal in the page
```

```
<% = AnnualTotal / 12 %>     calculate month average and put it in the page
```

```
<% If MyWalletContents > 4 Then %>
I've got enough for a hamburger.      write normal VBScript code
<% Else %>                            to conditionally create the
Can you lend me $5?                   returned HTML page.
<% End If %>
```

Active Server Pages also supports a new attribute to the `<SCRIPT>` tag, which indicates that the script should be interpreted and executed on the server, and *not* sent to the browser.

```
<SCRIPT LANGUAGE="VBScript" RUNAT=Server>
    ...
    this code will be interpreted by, and executed on, the server
    ...
</SCRIPT>
```

The `LANGUAGE` can be `"VBScript"` or `"JavaScript"`, or any other script language for which an interpreter is installed. The `RUNAT=Server` attribute instructs Active Server Pages to use the appropriate interpreter to execute the script on the server. However, `<SCRIPT>` sections behave

differently on the server to the browser. Script in the browser is always placed within **<SCRIPT>
</SCRIPT>** tags. If it is defined as a subroutine or function, it doesn't get executed until that
routine is explicitly called by other code, or by an event to which it is linked by the name we give
it. However, code which is *not* in a **Sub** or **Function**, is interpreted and executed as the page
loads:

```
<SCRIPT LANGUAGE="VBScript">        NB: this is executed in the browser

    Sub DoSomething()
    ...
    this code will be executed when called by Call DoSomething()
    ...
    End Sub

    Sub btnOK_onClick()
    ...
    this code will be executed when the OK button is clicked
    ...
    End Sub


    ...
    this code will be executed as the page loads
    ...
</SCRIPT>
```

On the server, things are very different. Only code within **<%** and **%>** tags is executed directly
while the page is being parsed on the server; **<SCRIPT> </SCRIPT>** tags can only be used to
define a subroutine or function:

```
<SCRIPT LANGUAGE="VBScript" RUNAT=Server>   this is executed on the server

    Sub DoSomething()
    ...
    this code will be executed when called by Call DoSomething()
    ...
    End Sub

    Sub Session_onStart()
    ...
    this code will be executed when a new session is started
    ...
    End Sub

    code cannot be placed here

</SCRIPT>
```

Notice, also, that we don't need to use comment tags to hide the code from older browsers.
Because it's executed on the server, the browser never sees it. This gives us another advantage. If
we are implementing some calculations that we don't want other people to see, we have a problem
with client-side scripts. Because the script is downloaded to the browser, and executed there, our
visitors can select View Source and examine the code. With server-side scripting, only the results
are sent to the browser, and so our secret is safe.

Server-side Includes

To make the creation of complex web sites simpler, Active Server Pages lets us specify the inclusion of a range of things in the page, before it is processed. These are called Server-side includes (SSI), and have long been available with other server scripting languages, such as Perl, as part of the services provided by the server. SSI allows us to run other applications, such as CGI or ISAPI programs, or execute SHELL scripts. We can also use them to configure the way that variables are formatted, or to include the values of things like the HTTP header information, or the file date and size in the page.

One of the most useful SSI options is to include the contents of another file. This can be a plain text file containing almost any kind of code. We've used this method in our sample programs, as you'll see a little later. It allows us to create re-usable libraries of scripts, or sections of HTML code, and then drop them into any page with just one SSI instruction. It's perfect for creating such things as a standard **<STYLE>** section (without resorting to external style sheets), default page footers, and often-used VBScript or JavaScript subroutines and functions.

Server Components

Lastly, Active Server Pages comes with a set of useful server component objects, which we can use to perform certain pre-defined tasks. In particular, there is an object which allows us to access any database for which an ODBC driver is available. Active Server Pages also supports reading and writing to text files on the server. This means that it's easier to save information on the server, and perform more complex tasks.

As an extension of this, Active Server Pages includes components which use text files to provide an easy way of displaying different advertisements, and nested text menus in our pages. We'll be looking in more detail at the Active Server Pages components that are provided by Microsoft, as part of the technology, later in the chapter.

The fact that Active Server Pages uses components means that it is a completely open and easily expandable system. You can easily create your own components in whatever environment or language you are comfortable with, and use them to extend the power of the server.

Referencing Active Server Pages

As far as the browser is concerned, the only difference between an Active Server Pages script and any other HTML page, script, or CGI application, is the filename. Active Server Pages uses the **.asp** (**Active Server Page**) file extension. So Active Server Pages files can be used as the **ACTION** attribute of a **<FORM>** tag, the **HREF** attribute of an **<A>** tag, or the **SRC** attribute of a **<FRAME>** tag. And you can send arguments to the server in the same way as other technologies, by adding them to the end of the reference:

```
<FORM ACTION="http://myserver.com/scripts/asp/myapp.asp" METHOD="POST">
```

```
<A HREF="/asp/myapp.asp?UserName=Olivia_Gonzales"> Do it now </A>
```

```
<FRAME SRC="../asp/myapp.asp" SCROLLING=NO NORESIZE>
```

The server creates a normal HTML page in return, so the browser displays it just like any other page. There's nothing in the returned page which is different to one created by IDC, OLEISAPI, a Perl script, or a CGI application.

The Active Server Pages Object Model

If you've used VBScript or JavaScript within the browser (and we'll be presuming you have in this chapter), you'll find that creating Active Server Pages scripts is a relatively simple extension to this. To be able to program using a script language, you had to learn about the browser's **object model**. This defines the relationships between all the objects that are displayed in, and form part of, the browser—such as the **window**, **documents**, **forms** and **elements**.

> *To learn more about VBScript and the browser's object model, look out for the Wrox Press book, Instant VBScript.*

It will be no surprise, then, to find that working with Active Server Pages means you need to know about the *server's* object model. In this section, we'll outline how the client and server communicate using the new **Active Server Pages object model**. The model is a great deal simpler than that of the browser, mainly because there are, of course, no visible elements to contend with. The object model contains four main objects: the **application**, the **server**, the **request**, and the **response**.

In any site, the two most common requirements for server programming are usually a **visit counter**, and a generic **form handler**. In the next sections, we'll look at the server's object model, and see how it allows us to implement both of these easily.

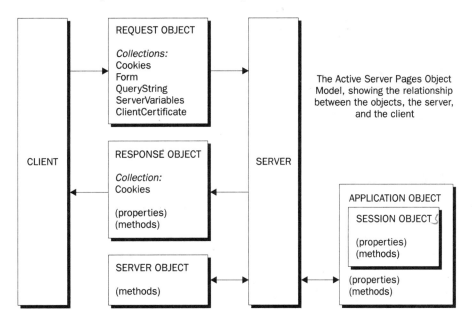

The Active Server Pages Object Model, showing the relationship between the objects, the server, and the client

Applications and Sessions

Active Server Pages defines an **application** object, and within it a collection of **session** objects. We create an application simply by assigning a virtual path, or **alias**, to the root directory where the **.asp** pages that make up the application reside. Active Server Pages automatically creates a new session for each user when they first reference a page in the application, by sending a unique session ID to their browser as a cookie. Each time they reference another page or resource in the application, Active Server Pages reads the header, looking for this cookie.

*For browsers that don't support cookies, Active Server Pages automatically adds a parameter to all the references in pages it creates, which refer to the current application. That way, it can correctly maintain the **session** object.*

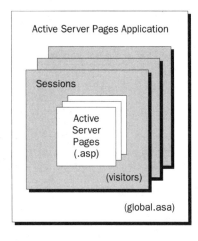

The **application** object provides methods that we can use to store global variables for all users, and each **session** object can be used to store variables global only to that particular user. Both of these give us a useful way of passing information between pages, and between users. The **application** is current permanently, or until Internet Information Server is re-started. A **session** is only current while that particular visitor is using the application, and it ends (by default) 20 minutes after their last reference to a page within the application.

An application can also have a single file called **global.asa**, which must be stored in the virtual root directory for that application. This contains code for the events of the application and session object only, but otherwise looks like a normal **.asp** file. It means, for example, that we can write code that is executed when a session is started or when it ends.

Whenever we need, we can create **custom properties** within the **application** or **session** objects, simply by referencing them. For example, we can create a custom property called **VisitCount** within the **application** object by simply giving it a value in code—from anywhere in our pages. The values of custom properties are available as long as that object is current. So we could use a custom property of the **application** object to keep a count of the number of users who visit our site.

Implementing a Visitor Counter

As an example of using custom properties, we'll look at how we can implement a visitor counter. You can see this code in action in our Wrox Information Manager application. Just start it up, and watch the lower message bar—you'll see your 'visitor number' appear.

Remember, you can run the Wrox Information Manager application from the samples index page on our web site at **http://www/wrox.com/books/0464/samples/webdb.htm**

To create a custom property for the **application** object or the current **session** object, we just have to reference it. In the case of the **application** object, to prevent more than one user updating the property at the same moment, we use the **application** object's **Lock** and **Unlock** methods while setting the new value:

```
<SCRIPT LANGUAGE="VBScript" RUNAT=Server>   NB: this code is in global.asa
   Sub Session_onStart()
      Application.Lock
      Application("VisitCount") = Application("VisitCount") + 1
```

```
        Application.Unlock
      End Sub
    </SCRIPT>
```

Then, to display the value in any **.asp** page, we can use the code:

```
Welcome, you are visitor number <% = Application("VisitCount") %>.
```

Of course, if IIS is stopped and re-started, the application object is destroyed and re-created again. So you'll lose the value of the existing visit count.

The Server Object

The **server** object implements four methods, and one property, **ScriptTimeout**. Three of the methods provide easy ways to translate strings or paths, and one allows us to create instances of objects on the server:

HTMLEncode   applies HTML encoding to a string, replacing **<B>** with **<B&gt**, for example.

URLEncode   applies URL encoding to a string, replacing **<B> <I>** with **%3CB%3E+%3CI%3E**, for example.

MapPath   translates a virtual path (alias) into a physical path, replacing **/asp/ default.htm** with **c:\InetPub\WWWRoot\ASPapps\default.htm**, for example.

CreateObject   is by far the most useful of the methods. We can use it to instantiate any ActiveX control or OLE Server DLL, including the components that are supplied with Active Server Pages.

We use the **CreateObject** method to create an instance of an object from an external source, and **Set** a variable to refer to it. Then we can use that object in our pages:

```
Set objectname = Server.CreateObject(objectID)
```

To create an instance of the supplied **ADOdatabase** component, for example, we could use:

```
Set objText = Server.CreateObject("ADODB.Connection")
```

The Request Object

All the information that we generally require about the browser's request is stored in the **request** object. There are five collections, which hold various types of information:

QueryString   the parameters sent from the browser, from a **<FORM>** section or as explicit parameters added with the **?** character.

Form   the values of all the controls, if a **<FORM>** section of the page was submitted.

Cookies   the contents of all the cookies sent from the browser for that page.

ServerVariables   the values of the environment; for example, the name of the host, or the HTTP content type.

165

ClientCertificate   the values of various parts of the client certificate which is sent in a Secure Sockets Layer HTTP request.

The **Form** and **QueryString** collections implement a **Count** property, and the **For .. Each** construct which allows us to loop through them. We can refer to a particular value in the collection with:

```
Request.Form("fieldname")
Request.QueryString ("parametername")
```

Therefore, **Request.Form("MyChoice")** will retrieve the value from an HTML control named **MyChoice** on a form submitted to the server. If the control is a multi-select list box, with more than one option selected, the number of selections can be returned by

```
Request.Form("MyChoice").Count
```

and the individual values by

```
Request.Form("MyChoice")(1)    to    Request.Form("MyChoice").Count
```

or by using a **For..Each** construct.

The Response Object

All the information we generally require to manipulate the server's response is stored in the **response** object. There is one collection, and a range of methods and properties. The more useful ones are:

Cookies   a collection of all the cookies being sent back to the browser.

Redirect   forces the browser to attempt to load and display a different page.

Write   places text in the output string being sent to the browser.

Other properties and methods allow us to control how the page is buffered before being sent back to the browser, control writing to the event log, and set the HTTP header, content type, and expiration date.

Implementing a Generic Form Handler

To see how we can use the **request** and **response** objects, and combine them with VBScript on the server, we'll show you how we implemented a generic form handler as part of a simple book survey application.

You can run the examples in this chapter from the samples index page at the following address: **http://www.wrox.com/books/0464/samples/webdb.htm**

As we've seen in the previous section, it's easy to retrieve the contents of any field control if we know its name. The problem comes when we don't know how many controls there will be, or what their names are. With a generic form handler, you expect to be able to send it *any* form, and let it figure out the names and number of controls. For example, the HTML code:

```
<FORM ACTION="myscript" METHOD="POST">
  <INPUT TYPE="TEXT" NAME="UserName">
  <INPUT TYPE="CHECKBOX" NAME="Over18" >
  <INPUT TYPE="SUBMIT">
</FORM>
```

should return information such as **UserName=Olivia_Gonzales, Over18=on**. If the **Over18** checkbox is not set, however, the browser will ignore it—so the result should just be **UserName=Olivia_Gonzales**.

Here's a page containing several check boxes. They're all in a single **<FORM>** section, with a **SUBMIT** button. There's also a checkbox named **ShowQuery**, which allows the user to display the complete query string that's sent to the server if they wish:

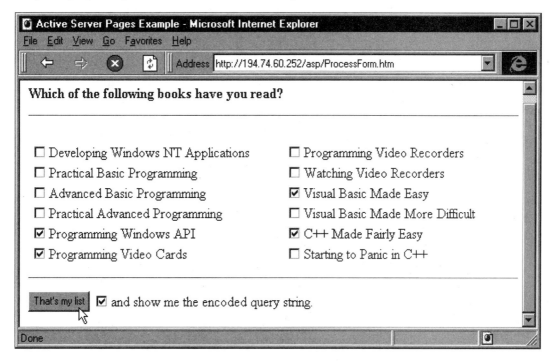

The HTML that makes up the page is not unusual. For each checkbox, we've used the book title as the **NAME** attribute:

```
<INPUT TYPE=CHECKBOX NAME="Visual Basic Made Easy">Visual Basic Made Easy
```

When the form is submitted, Active Server Pages creates a **request** object which holds the values of all the controls on the form and the parameters sent to the server. We can easily get the value of the **ShowQuery** checkbox, because we know its name, by using **Request.Form("ShowQuery")**. However, take a look at the parameters that are passed to the server in the next screen shot:

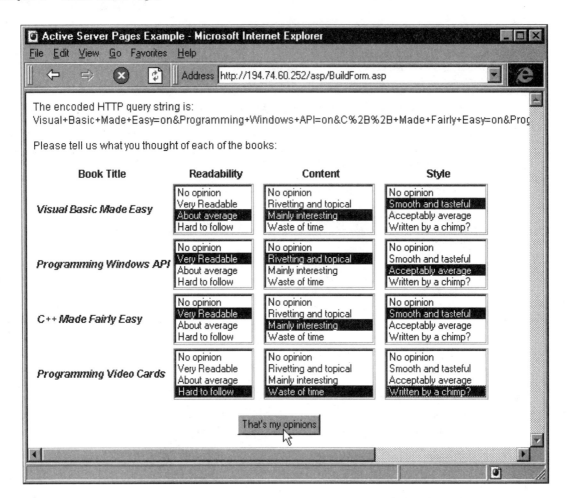

You can see that the only ones that *are* sent, are the values of the check boxes that were set. And, of course, the string of parameters is still URL encoded—the spaces are replaced by plus signs, and the plus signs in "C++" are coded as **%2B**.

We get the complete query string from the **request** object's **Form** collection, using the statement **strQuery = Request.Form**, rather than by specifying a control name. There's no way of getting a list of the control names from the collection, so we have to decode this string to build the list of control names and values. Here's the first part of the Active Server Pages file, **BuildForm.asp**, that receives the query string:

```
<HTML>
<HEAD>
<TITLE>Active Server Pages Example</TITLE>
<!--#include file=Style.txt-->
</HEAD>
<BODY LEFTMARGIN=8 TOPMARGIN=8 BGCOLOR=#FFFFC0>
<!--#include file=URLDecode.txt-->
```

```
<%
strQuery = Request.Form        'get the complete query string
If LCase(Request.Form("ShowQuery")) = "on" Then
  blnShowQuery = -1  'True
  Response.Write "The encoded HTTP query string is: " & strQuery & "<P>"
End If
%>
```

Firstly, notice the two Server-side Includes. One inserts our standard **<STYLE>** tag, and the other inserts a section of code from a separate file. This file, **URLDecode.txt**, contains a function which converts a URL encoded string into its normal form—just like the one we used in Chapter 3. It just contains a pair of **<SCRIPT>** **</SCRIPT>** tags, with the function (written in VBScript) between them:

```
<SCRIPT LANGUAGE=VBScript RUNAT=Server>
Function URLDecode(strToDecode)
  ...  'the VBScript which un-encodes the string, strToDecode, is here.
End Function
</SCRIPT>
```

After this, we declare an array to hold the names and values of all the controls we find. Then we can loop through the query string, storing each name and value:

```
<!-- put names and values into array strResults -->
<%
Dim strResult(50,1) 'array variable to hold control names and values
Dim intNumFields     'number of fields on form

intNumFields = 0
intSep = Instr(strQuery, "&")  'split the string into name/value pairs
Do While intSep
  strNVPair = Left(strQuery, intSep - 1)
  strQuery = Mid(strQuery, intSep + 1)
  intEqu = Instr(strNVPair, "=")           'separate the name and value
  If intEqu > 1 Then                       'and store name in array
    strResult(intNumFields, 0) = URLDecode(Left(strNVPair, intEqu - 1))
  End If
  If intEqu < Len(strNVPair) Then          'store value in array
    strResult(intNumFields, 1) = URLDecode(Mid(strNVPair, intEqu + 1))
  End If
  intNumFields = intNumFields + 1
  intSep = Instr(strQuery, "&")
Loop
intEqu = Instr(strQuery, "=")    'handle the remaining name/value pair
If intEqu > 1 Then
  strResult(intNumFields, 0) = URLDecode(Left(strQuery, intEqu - 1))
End If
If intEqu < Len(strQuery) Then
  strResult(intNumFields, 1) = URLDecode(Mid(strQuery, intEqu + 1))
End If
If (intEqu > 0) And (Not blnShowQuery) Then intNumFields=intNumFields + 1
%>
```

This gives us a generic routine that we can use in any page to build up a list of the names and values of the controls on any form. We just need to change the size of the array to make sure there's enough room for all the controls. You'll see this routine used in our Wrox Information Manager application, later in the chapter.

Once we've got the names and values of the controls, we can create the page you've already seen, where the user enters their opinions of each book they've read. However, if they didn't check any of the boxes, we just return a message instead (we've removed the code that creates the Content and Style lists for clarity):

```
<%If intNumFields = 0 Then %>  <!-- no books selected  -->

<B>You haven't selected any books. Try again, and this time
click on some of the check boxes.</B>

<%Else%>  <!-- create the new form  -->

Please tell us what you thought of each of the books:<P>
<FORM NAME="Form2" ACTION="ProcessForm.asp" METHOD="POST">
<TABLE>
  <TR>
    <TH>Book Title</TH><TH>Readability</TH><TH>Content</TH><TH>Style</TH>
  </TR>
  <% For intLoop = 0 To (intNumFields - 1) %>
    <% strBookName = strResult(intLoop, 0) %>
    <TR>
      <TD><B><I><% = strBookName %></I></B></TD>
      <TD>
        <SELECT NAME="<% = strBookName %>:Readability" SIZE=4>
          <OPTION SELECTED VALUE="-1">No opinion
          <OPTION VALUE="10">Very Readable
          <OPTION VALUE="6">About average
          <OPTION VALUE="2">Hard to follow
        </SELECT>
      </TD>
        . . .    'creates the Content list here
        . . .    'creates the Style list here
    </TR>
  <% Next %>
</TABLE><P>
<CENTER><INPUT TYPE="SUBMIT" VALUE="That's my opinions"></CENTER>
</FORM>

<%End If%>

</BODY>
</HTML>
```

Now, the user can tell us in more detail what they thought of each book. When they click the **SUBMIT** button at the bottom of the page, the values are stored in a database on our server, and an acknowledgment is returned:

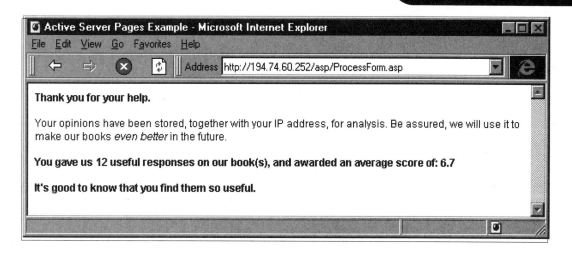

We'll look at how the results are stored in the database a little later in the chapter, when we come to examine the Active Data Object (ADO).

Active Server Pages Components

Active Server Pages components are special-purpose tools that are supplied with Active Server Pages. You can also create your own, which allows you to extend the power of the server by creating highly focused components for your own requirements. In essence, these components are just like the ActiveX controls that are used in the browser. However, they are aimed solely at the kind of tasks that you often need to perform server-side.

At the time of writing, the supplied components are:

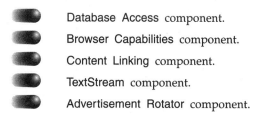

- Database Access component.
- Browser Capabilities component.
- Content Linking component.
- TextStream component.
- Advertisement Rotator component.

By far the most important of these is the first one, the **Database Access** component, which allows us to use Active Server Pages to manipulate a database. It uses ODBC to make the connection, so that we can work with any database for which an ODBC driver is available. We'll be looking in more depth at this component later in the chapter, but we'll first give a brief overview of the others.

> *You'll find documentation about all of the components has been installed by Active Server Pages on your system.*

171

The Browser Capabilities Component

This component uses a text file, and the values returned in the HTTP header by the browser, to allow us to easily determine which features that browser supports:

```
<% Set objBCaps = Server.CreateObject("MSWC.BrowserType") %>
<% If objBCaps.Tables = TRUE Then %>
  'HTML code for tables
<% Else %>
  'text without tables
<%End If %>
```

The information about each browser is contained in a text file called **BROWSCAP.INI**, which can be edited to keep it up to date with new browser capabilities, or to add older ones.

The Content Linking Component

One of the most boring and error-prone tasks in a web site is maintaining the index (or menu) pages which contain links to other resources or submenus and other pages. This is particularly difficult on large, regularly changing sites. The good news is that we can now use the Content Linking component.

A simple text file contains a list of resources or pages that we want to display. For each one, we specify the URL, the text description to be displayed, and an optional comment—separating each with a *Tab* character. Then we can access this text file using a range of methods and properties of the Content Linking component. There are methods and properties that allow us to access any link directly, or retrieve them sequentially.

We've implemented a simple menu for the samples in this chapter. It uses this text file, called **Links.txt**:

```
ProcessForm.htm  Example of handling input from any FORM section.
Style.txt        An inline style section as a text file.
URLDecode.txt    The URLDecode function text file.
Links.asp        This page, demonstrating Content Linking.
```

Then, we display the menu using the following Active Server Pages file, named **Links.asp**:

```
<HTML>
<HEAD>
<TITLE>Content Linking with Active Server Pages</TITLE>
<!--#include file=Style.txt-->
</HEAD>
<BODY BGCOLOR=#FFFFC0>
<B> Listing of available pages </B><P>
<% Set objLinks = Server.CreateObject ("MSWC.NextLink")
intCount = objLinks.GetListCount("/asp/links.txt")
For intLoop = 1 To intCount %>
  <IMG SRC="ball_red.gif">
  <A HREF="<% = objLinks.GetNthURL("/asp/links.txt", intLoop) %>">
    <% = objLinks.GetNthDescription("/asp/links.txt", intLoop) %>
  </A><P>
<% Next %>
</BODY>
</HTML>
```

And here's the result:

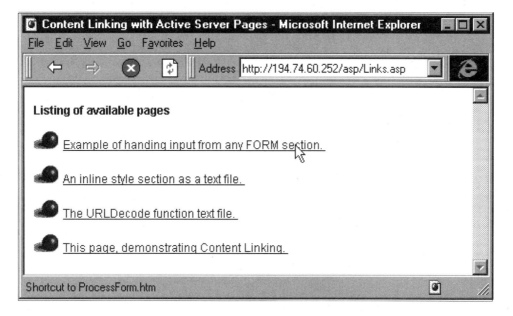

To change the list in future, all we have to do is edit the text file, and not the HTML document. Notice how we've used a Server-side Include to place our standard **<STYLE>** tag, which is stored as the text file **Style.txt**, into the page:

```
<!--#include file=Style.txt-->
```

The Text Stream Component

This component allows us to read and write direct to a text file on the server. There are a whole range of commands that can open an existing file for reading or appending, create a new file, move through the file reading or writing lines, skip individual lines, or read the whole file in one go. We can also use properties which indicate the current position of the file pointer relative to the start or end of the file, and return the column and line number.

Being able to write text files on the server is an important new technique, which opens up some powerful possibilities with Active Server Pages. For example, we can now create a visit counter which doesn't lose count if the server is re-started, like the one based on the **application** object does. It also means that we can create *new* **.asp** files, or any other type of file, directly from an Active Server Pages file. These are, after all, just text files with the extension **.htm**, **.asp**, **.idc**, etc.

In fact, the ability to write files to the server may even be the biggest breakthrough of all the technologies we've described in this book. After all, interactive and dynamic pages that can create their own tailored interactive and dynamic pages must offer all kinds of new opportunities to the imaginative web site builder.

The Advertisement Rotator Component

If we want to include advertisements in our pages, which are different each time the site is visited, we can use the Advertisement Rotator component. It uses a text file which contains details of each image file, including the width and height for its display, plus the site to jump to when it's clicked. It also allows us to specify the relative time to display each image, and the text to display if the browser doesn't support graphics (or if the user has them turned off).

```
Set objAdRot = Server.CreateObject("MSWC.AdRotator")
objAdRot.GetAdvertisement("myadlist.txt")    'the list of advertisements
```

The component can also write an entry to the server's event log each time a visitor clicks on the image to visit the advertiser's site—handy if we're getting paid for each jump we can generate to it.

The Database Connection

To be anything like useful, Active Server Pages has to be able to link to, and manipulate, databases. The Database Access component supplied with Active Server Pages does all the hard work for us. We can use it like IDC, by executing SQL statements against a database, or like ISAPI methods—where we roll up our sleeves and manipulate the records in the database directly. If you are prepared to get your hands dirty like this, there's almost no limit to what you can achieve with it.

The Database Access component implements an object generally referred to as the **Active Data Object** (ADO). We'll take a closer look at this next. ADO is not something that's unique to Active Server Pages, but it's an object database technology which will probably replace the current **Jet** database engine that's used in Microsoft Access, and form the basis for all kinds of database manipulation in the future.

What is ADO?

The Active Data Object provides a fully integrated set of methods and properties for any database which has an ODBC driver available. We first create a **System Data Source Name** (DSN) for the database, like we did in earlier chapters with IDC, OLEISAPI, and dbWeb. Then, in our code, we refer to the database using this DSN.

At the root of the ADO object hierarchy is the **connection** object. This defines the link between the DSN and our code. Inside it are two more objects, the **recordset** object and the **command** object. There are also two collections, which hold the **connection** object's **properties** and details of any **errors** that occur. We can refer to the error collection to find out the number, description, and other information about each error.

The **recordset** object defines the sets of records that we are working with at any one time. Inside the **recordset** object is the collection of **field** objects which represent the fields in each table or recordset, and a collection which holds the **recordset** object's **properties**.

The **command** object represents any stored procedures or query definitions that are in the database. For each one, there is a collection of **parameter** objects, the parameters to that query or procedure, and a collection which holds the **command** object's **properties**.

174

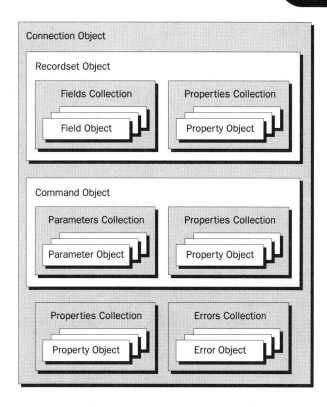

Making the Connection

To use ADO, we have to make a connection with a data source which has a previously defined System Data Source Name defined for it. First, we use the server's **CreateObject** method to create an instance of the **connection** object:

```
Set objConnect = Server.CreateObject("ADODB.Connection")
```

Then, we can link it to our database using the System DSN:

```
objConnect.Open "MySystemDSN"
```

When we've finished with the database, we can explicitly close it and destroy the connection object to save system resources. However, like Visual Basic and VBScript, Active Server Pages is very forgiving. If we don't close and destroy it ourselves, Active Server Pages will do it for us when it's finished creating the page.

```
objConnect.Close
Set objConnect = Nothing
```

Accessing the Data

Once we've made the connection, we can access a database either by executing SQL commands or by manipulating records in the table directly. ADO will retrieve a set of records which we can then access using our code. We can create either forward scrolling, read-only recordsets, or fully scrollable and updatable ones. You'll see what these terms mean in detail a little later.

Note that ADO is an area where the syntax and methods are particularly likely to change between the time of writing, and release of the final version.

Using SQL Queries with ADO

Often the simplest way to access data is with an SQL statement, in the same way as we did with IDC in Chapter 2. If we only want to update the data in the database, we don't even have to return a recordset from it. We just use the **Execute** method of the **connection** object:

```
Set objConnect = Server.CreateObject("ADODB.Connection")
objConnect.Open "MySystemDSN"
strSQL = "DELETE * FROM MyTable WHERE UserName = 'Olivia_Gonzales'"
objConnect.Execute strSQL
objConnect.Close
Set objConnect = Nothing
```

If we want to return a recordset, however, we have to provide a **recordset** object. Then we can retrieve the contents of the fields in this recordset, like this:

```
Set objConnect = Server.CreateObject("ADODB.Connection")
objConnect.Open "MySystemDSN"
strSQL = "SELECT UserName FROM MyTable"
Set rsResult = objConnect.Execute (strSQL)
Do While Not rsResult.EOF
   Response.Write rsResult.UserName
   rsResult.MoveNext
Loop
rsResult.Close
objConnect.Close
Set rsResult = Nothing
Set objConnect = Nothing
```

Using the ADO Methods Directly

Both of the methods we used in the previous section produce a forward scrollable and non-updatable recordset. This means that we can only loop through the records from the first one to the last, and we can't update the database contents by editing the contents of the recordset. To create a fully scrollable and updatable recordset, we have to use a different method:

```
Set objConnect = Server.CreateObject("ADODB.Connection")
Set rsResult = Server.CreateObject("ADODB.Recordset")
objConnect.Open "MySystemDSN"
rsResult.Open "MyTable", objConnect, 1    'adOpenKeySet
...
'process the records
...
```

176

```
rsResult.Close
objConnect.Close
Set rsResult = Nothing
Set objConnect = Nothing
```

The code first creates an instance of a **connection** and a **recordset** object. Next, it opens the database, using its System DSN, and then opens the recordset on the table **MyTable** within that connection object. This time we have a fully scrollable and updatable recordset because we provided the value **adOpenKeySet** (**1**) for the **CursorType** property. The default, which is used when we create the recordset with the **connection** object's **Execute** method, is **adOpenForwardOnly** (**0**).

Once we have an open recordset, we can use a range of methods and properties to get values from it and update the existing values in the database. For example, we can move around using **MoveFirst**, **MoveLast**, **MoveNext**, and **MovePrevious**; add, delete and edit records with the **AddNew**, **Delete**, and **Update** methods; and we can get information such as the field's **Attributes** or the recordset's **RecordCount** and **Bookmark** properties.

If you are used to using Visual Basic with the **Jet** database engine, Access Basic, or Visual Basic for Applications with Access 95, you'll have no problems getting up to speed with ADO. To finish this section, we'll show you how we used it to get the results of our previous book survey into an Access database.

Storing our Book Survey Data in a Database

Earlier, you saw how we can collect information from a user and store it in an array in the server page—before the response is sent to the user. We collected opinions about books that our visitor had read and sent them to another page named **ProcessForm.asp**. This decodes the query string and places the values in an array in this page. Now we just need to store them in our database. We've got an Access database called **ASPTestData.mdb** and we've created a System DSN, **ASPTest**, to refer to it. All we need to do is loop through the values in the array, storing them in the **Opinions** table.

The first section of the page uses the **request** object to get the visitor's name and the host name from the HTTP header that the browser sends. Then it initializes the variables we want to use for the number of responses, and the average score:

```
<!-- now update the database -->
<%
strHostName = Request.ServerVariables("REMOTE_HOST")
strUserName = Request.ServerVariables("REMOTE_USER")
If Len(strUserName) Then strHostName = strUsername & "@" & strHostName
intNumResponses = 0
sngAverageScore = 0
```

The name of each of the list boxes on the form, which contain the opinions, is made up of the book title and the type of opinion (**Readability**, **Content** or **Style**), separated by a colon '**:**' character. The values of the items in the list reflect the opinion:

```
<SELECT NAME="<% = strBookName %>:Readability" SIZE=4>
  <OPTION SELECTED VALUE="-1">No opinion
  <OPTION VALUE="10">Very Readable
  <OPTION VALUE="6">About average
  <OPTION VALUE="2">Hard to follow
</SELECT>
```

177

So for each name/value pair, we have to separate the book title and the type of opinion, then use the value to get the score. Once we've got all the details we need for that opinion, we create an SQL expression which will insert them into the table, and execute it against the **connection** object. Here's the code that does it:

```
Set objConnect = Server.CreateObject("ADODB.Connection")
objConnect.Open "ASPTest"
For intLoop = 0 To (intNumFields - 1)         'for each name/value pair
  strKeyValue = strResult(intLoop, 1)         'score from value part
  If strKeyValue > 0 Then
    intNumResponses = intNumResponses + 1     'update number of respones
    sngAverageScore = sngAverageScore + strKeyValue    'and total score
    strKeyName = strResult(intLoop, 0)            'get the name part
    intPos = Instr(strKeyName, ":")             'and separate at the colon
    strBookName = Left(strKeyName, intPos - 1)      'into the book title
    strOpinionType = Mid(strKeyName, intPos + 1)  'and opinion type
    strSQL = "INSERT INTO Opinions SELECT '" & strHostName _
          & "' AS HostName, '" & strBookName & "' AS BookName, '" _
          & strOpinionType & "' AS Opinion, " & strKeyValue _
          & " AS Score;"
    objConnect.Execute strSQL      'build and execute the SQL statement
  End If
Next
objConnect.Close
Set objConnect = Nothing
```

It's as easy as that. And here's the final table open in Access, showing the opinions and the address of the user. You don't generally get a user-name sent in the HTTP header, unless they have supplied this to log on to the site.

HostName	BookName	Opinion	Score
194.74.60.251	Visual Basic Made Easy	Readability	6
194.74.60.251	Visual Basic Made Easy	Content	6
194.74.60.251	Visual Basic Made Easy	Style	10
194.74.60.251	Programming Windows API	Readability	10
194.74.60.251	Programming Windows API	Content	10
194.74.60.251	Programming Windows API	Style	6
194.74.60.251	C++ Made Fairly Easy	Readability	10
194.74.60.251	C++ Made Fairly Easy	Content	6
194.74.60.251	C++ Made Fairly Easy	Style	10
194.74.60.251	Programming Video Cards	Readability	2
194.74.60.251	Programming Video Cards	Content	2
194.74.60.251	Programming Video Cards	Style	2
*			0

Record: I◀ ◀ 1 ▶ ▶I ▶* of 12

178

Implementing the Messaging System

Before we end, we'll look at one other part of our Wrox Information Manager application. The lower section of the main window contains a page which shows the current time and date, and this is where any messages sent by other users scroll past. When you first open the application, before you actually log on, it shows the visitor counter, as you can see here. We described how this is implemented earlier in this chapter, when we looked at the **application** and **session** objects.

While displaying the time may seem to be rather a waste of resources, and it might seem that it is only there to make the application look pretty, there is actually some reasoning behind it.

Working To Network Time

On a network, you tend to make sure that your file server clock keeps the correct time. This is important if you depend on a file's time and date stamp to check which is the most recent. In theory, you can set up your connected workstations so that their internal clocks are matched to the server each time the users log on. However, this is not always normal practice.

We aren't going to try and update the workstation's internal clocks, but instead we'll display the time from the server's clock on the user's screen. If nothing else, this removes one excuse for being late for meetings.

The message bar page in our application is reloaded on a regular basis, so that it can collect any new messages for that user. We reload it like this simply by setting a suitable value in the **<META HTTP-REFRESH>** tag at the top of the message frame page—in our case every three minutes (or 180 seconds):

```
<META HTTP-EQUIV="REFRESH" CONTENT="180">
```

Each time it's refreshed, it also collects the time and date from the server's clock and displays these on the page. In between page refreshes, we use an ActiveX **Timer** control, with the **Interval** set to **60** seconds, to increment the time. Even if it gets out of step, because the browser or another busy application steals cycles from it, the clock will be corrected at the next page refresh.

The Message Bar

Here is the part of **Mesg.asp** which collects the time and date from the server's clock, and puts it into the returned page. **lblDate**, **lblTime**, and **lblDayName** are the controls you see in the message bar:

```
lblDate.Caption = "<% = Day(Date) %>"      'get the day number and the time
strHour = "0<% = Hour(Time) %>"            'from the server's clock, and put
strMins = "0<% = Minute(Time) %>"          'them in the page.
```

```
lblTime.Caption = Right(strHour, 2) & ":" & Right("0" & strMins, 2)
intWeekday = <% = Weekday(Date) %>
Select Case intWeekday
   Case 1: lblDayName.Caption = "Sunday"
   Case 2: lblDayName.Caption = "Monday"
   Case 3: lblDayName.Caption = "Tuesday"
   Case 4: lblDayName.Caption = "Wednesday"
   Case 5: lblDayName.Caption = "Thursday"
   Case 6: lblDayName.Caption = "Friday"
   Case 7: lblDayName.Caption = "Saturday"
End Select
```

We also need to collect any messages for this user. We know the **UserName**, because it's sent to the page as a parameter from the browser each time the page is loaded. All the messages are stored in the **Messages** table of our application's database. This table holds the **UserName** of the sender and the recipient, plus the time and date it was sent and the text of the message.

So the first step is to collect the messages for the current user from the table, and build up a string holding all of them which we can then scroll across the page in a **<MARQUEE>** control. We separate each message in the string by a series of dots (full stops), like this:

```
<%
ServerUserName = Request.QueryString("UserName")

If Len(ServerUserName) Then      'we've got a user logged in

   Set objConnect = Server.CreateObject("ADODB.Connection")
   objConnect.Open "WroxInfoManager"  'link to the database
   strSQL = "SELECT * FROM Messages WHERE ToUser='" & ServerUserName & "';"
   Set rsResult = objConnect.Execute(strSQL)  'and get the messages
   ServerMesg = ""
   Do While Not rsResult.EOF   'build the message string
      strMesgIn = "From " & rsResult("FromUser") _
                & " - Sent: " & rsResult("Sent") _
                & " - Message: "& rsResult("Message")
      ServerMesg = ServerMesg & strMesgIn & String(15, ".")   'include dots
      rsResult.MoveNext
   Loop
   rsResult.Close
   objConnect.Close
   Set rsResult = Nothing
   Set objResult = Nothing

Else  'the user hasn't yet logged in, just disply the visit count

   ServerMesg = "Welcome to Wrox Information Manager. " _
              & "You are visitor number " _
              & Application("VisitNumber") & "."
End If
%>
```

If the user has not yet logged on to our application, there will be no **UserName** parameter sent to this page, from the main **<FRAMESET>** page that loads it, so **ServerUserName** will be an empty string. In this case, we use the visit counter to put their visitor number in the message string instead. Then, once we've got the complete message string, we display it in a **<MARQUEE>** control on the page:

```
...
<MARQUEE WIDTH=65% HSPACE=10 SCROLLAMOUNT=2 SCROLLDELAY=100>
  <% = ServerMesg %>
</MARQUEE>
...
```

Remember that this will only work with browsers that support the **<MARQUEE>** *tag, of course.*

The Messages Page

The menu bar of our application contains a Messages icon, and clicking this displays a list of the user's messages, sorted in descending order by date and time. Against each message is a 'Delete' check box, which is ticked by default. Clicking the Delete Messages button removes all the messages which still have this option checked.

This is the page where our users can send messages to other users. There is a list of the other users available in the drop-down list, and a text box where they enter the text for the message. Clicking the Send Message button creates a new message record in the database. When the recipient next logs on, or when their message bar is next refreshed (i.e. within three minutes), they will see the message scroll across the bottom of their browser window.

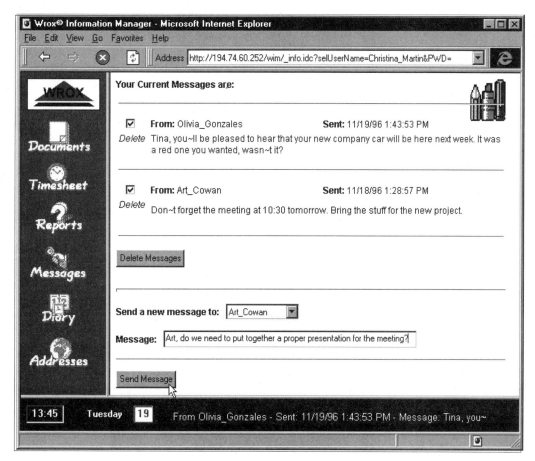

Listing Messages

The Messages page you see here is created with IDC, rather than Active Server Pages, so we won't go into it in great detail. We covered IDC in depth in Chapter 2. The IDC script just retrieves any available messages, and the HTX template displays them in a table with a checkbox control next to each one. If there is one or more messages, it adds the Delete Messages button. If there aren't any, it just displays text to this effect. All this is contained in the first **<FORM>** section of the page, which has its **ACTION** attribute set to **DeleteMesg.asp**:

```
<FORM ACTION="DeleteMesg.asp" METHOD="POST">
<B><IMG SRC="../Images/write.gif" WIDTH=50 HEIGHT=55 ALIGN=RIGHT>
Your Current Messages are:</B>
<TABLE>
  <TR><TD COLSPAN=3><HR></TD></TR>
<%BeginDetail%> <!-- one row for each message from first IDC SQL part -->
  <TR>
    <TD ALIGN=CENTER>
      <INPUT TYPE="CHECKBOX" NAME="<%FromUser%>|<%Sent%>" CHECKED> 
    </TD>
    <TD><B>From: </B> <%FromUser%></TD>
    <TD><B>Sent: </B><%Sent%></TD>
  </TR>
  <TR>
    <TD ALIGN=CENTER><I>Delete  </I></TD>
    <TD COLSPAN=2><%Message%></TD>
  </TR>
  <TR>
    <TD COLSPAN=3><HR></TD>
  </TR>
<%EndDetail%>
</TABLE>

<%If CurrentRecord EQ 0%> <!-- No messages defined -->
  There are no messages for you at the moment.
<%Else%>
  <INPUT TYPE="SUBMIT" VALUE="Delete Messages">
<%EndIf%>
<INPUT TYPE="HIDDEN" NAME="hidUser" VALUE="<%idc.UserName%>">
</FORM>
```

Next, we add the controls which enable the user to send a new message. These controls are in another **<FORM>**, this time with the **ACTION** attribute set to **SendMesg.asp**. To get a list of user names for the drop-down list control, we use the methods you saw in Chapter 2. The IDC script has two SQL statements which return records, and the second set is used in this part of the page:

```
<!-- Now to add the ability to send a message -->
<FORM ACTION="SendMesg.asp" METHOD="POST">
<B>Send a new message to:</B>  
<SELECT NAME="selToUser">
  <%BeginDetail%>    <!-- use list of users from second IDC SQL part -->
    <OPTION VALUE="<%UserName%>"><%UserName%></OPTION>
  <%EndDetail%>
</SELECT>
<P><B>Message:</B>  
<INPUT NAME="txtMesg" SIZE=65 MAXLENGTH=255 VALUE="<%idc.MesgText%>"><HR>
<INPUT TYPE="SUBMIT" VALUE="Send Message">
```

```
<INPUT TYPE="HIDDEN" NAME="hidUser" VALUE="<%idc.UserName%>">
</FORM>
```

Deleting Messages

When the Delete Messages button is clicked in the Messages page, the Active Server Pages file **DeleteMesg.asp** is referenced by the form containing the list of messages. This form also contains a hidden control whose value is set to the **UserName** of the current user. There is also a check box next to each message. When the page was created, the time and date of the message, plus the sender's **UserName**, were combined to give each check box a unique name:

```
<INPUT TYPE="CHECKBOX" NAME="<%FromUser%>|<%Sent%>" CHECKED> 
```

All we have to do is loop through the messages on the page, deleting each one where the check box is still set. This task, as you'll see, serves to indicate just how useful Active Server Pages is, compared to IDC.

Active Server Pages vs. IDC, again

We had a similar task to this that we wanted to achieve in the Current Documents page of our application. There, we had a list of the user's current documents displayed in a page, and we wanted to allow them to delete those that they no longer needed.

We used IDC in that case, and we had to open a separate page which displayed the documents in a multi-select list box. When the Delete button was clicked, we took the comma-separated list of selected values from the list box control, and put it directly in the SQL statement that removed them from the database. Then we re-loaded the original Current Documents page. Look back at Chapter 2 if you want to see this.

With Active Server Pages, we don't need any of these tricks. We can read the query string that's sent from the browser when the form is submitted, and build up a list of messages that we need to delete. Then we just loop through these, deleting each one from the table. To get the list of messages to delete, from the query string, we use the same method as we did in the generic form handler described earlier in this chapter. It creates an array holding the names and values of all the controls on the form.

Then, it's a simple matter of looping through them. We check that we've got the proper '**on**' value for each one as we go, and split up the name part of the name/value pair to get the sender's **UserName**, and the date and time the message was sent. These values, together with the current user's name, are used in the **WHERE** part of the SQL statement to make sure we delete the correct messages from the database:

```
If intNumFields > 1 Then      'got some messages to delete
  Set objConnect = Server.CreateObject("ADODB.Connection")
  objConnect.Open "WroxInfoManager"      'link to the database
  For intLoop = 0 To (intNumFields - 1)      'for each name/value pair
    strKeyValue = strResult(intLoop, 1)      'get the control's value
    If LCase(strKeyValue) = "on" Then      'and check it returned 'on'
      strKeyName = strResult(intLoop, 0)      'then get the control's name
      intPos = Instr(strKeyName, "|")      'and separate out the
      strFrom = Left(strKeyName, intPos - 1)      'sender's UserName
      strSent = Mid(strKeyName, intPos + 1)      'and the date/time sent
      strSQL = "DELETE * FROM Messages WHERE FromUser='" _
             & strFrom & "' AND ToUser='" & strUserName _
```

183

```
                  & "' AND Sent='" & strSent & "';"
     objConnect.Execute strSQL              'execute the SQL query
   End If
 Next
 objConnect.Close
 Set objConnect = Nothing

 'now we can reload the original page, and the messages bar
 strMainRefresh = "CurrentMesg.idc?UserName=" & strUserName
 strMesgRefresh = "Mesg.asp?UserName=" & strUserName
%>

<SCRIPT LANGUAGE=VBScript>
   Location.HRef="<% = strMainRefresh %>"
   Top.Frames("Mesg").Location.HRef="<% = strMesgRefresh %>"
</SCRIPT>

<%Else%>     <!-- just simulate the Back button being clicked -->

<SCRIPT LANGUAGE=VBScript>History.Back 1</SCRIPT>

<%End If%>
```

Notice that the code returns the user to the original Messages page, after we've deleted the messages. Here, we've done it by including VBScript code in the page that's returned to the browser. There's no **RUNAT=Server** in the **<SCRIPT>** tags, so the server doesn't interpret it—it just drops it into the return page as it is.

As this return page is loaded by the browser, it executes the script, and reloads (or refreshes) the Messages page and the lower messages bar. We need to refresh this as well, so that any deleted messages are removed from it. If there were no messages deleted, the script that's written to the page simply simulates the user clicking the browser's Back button, so they get back to the original Messages page that way.

Sending Messages

Lastly, we'll look at how our application sends new messages. In outline, it's a simple process. All we need to do is collect the values for the recipient from the drop-down list, and the text for the message from the text box. We already know the current user's name, and we can find the date and time from the server's clock.

There's one small difficulty. We'll be using the value of the message text, taken from the message box, in our SQL query. If it contains an apostrophe, which is used in the SQL statement as a text field identifier character, we'll get an error from the ODBC driver. As an easy way round this, we've chosen to replace any apostrophes with a tilde '~' character instead.

Here's the 'working parts' of the **SendMesg.asp** page. We know the names of all the controls this time, so we can use the **Request** object's **Form** collection to retrieve their values in the usual way. Then we parse the string for apostrophes, replacing them with tildes, and create and execute the SQL string against our **Messages** table:

```
<%
strUserName = Request.Form("hidUser")    'the current user's username
strToUser = Request.Form("selToUser")    'the recipient's username
strTime = Now                            'the date and time
```

```
strMesg = Request.Form("txtMesg")           'the message text

intPos = Instr(strMesg,"'")                 'replace any apostrophes with
Do While intPos > 0                         'tilde characters
  If intPos = 1 Then
    If Len(strMesg) > 1 Then
      strMesg = "~" & Mid(strMesg, 2)
    Else
      strMesg = "~"
    End If
  ElseIf intPos = Len(strMesg) Then
    strMesg = Left(strMesg, intPos - 1) & "~"
  Else
    strMesg = Left(strMesg, intPos - 1) & "~" _
            & Mid(strMesg, intPos + 1)
  End If
  intPos = Instr(strMesg,"'")
Loop
%>

<!-- now update the database -->
<%
Set objConnect = Server.CreateObject("ADODB.Connection")
objConnect.Open "WroxInfoManager"
strSQL = "INSERT INTO Messages SELECT '" & strUserName _
       & "' AS FromUser, '" & strToUser & "' AS ToUser, '" _
       & strMesg & "' AS Message, '" & strTime & "' AS Sent;"
objConnect.Execute strSQL
objConnect.Close
Set objConnect = Nothing
```

All that's left is to return the user to the original **Messages** page again. In theory, we don't need to refresh it, because they don't see messages that they send to another user. However, we want to provide some confirmation that the message had been sent, so we create a special acknowledgment string, which is already URL encoded, and add it to the address of the current page, as the value of a parameter named **MesgText**:

```
strRefresh = "CurrentMesg.idc?UserName=" & strUserName _
           & "&MesgText=Your+message+has+been+sent+to+" & strToUser
%>
<SCRIPT LANGUAGE=VBScript>
  Location.HRef="<% = strRefresh %>"
</SCRIPT>
```

This complete string is used as the **HREF** of the page that the VBScript running in the browser will load, which is, of course, the original **Messages** page. If you look back at the code for this, you'll see that the text box has its value set to that of the **MesgText** parameter (if there is one) as it loads:

```
<P><B>Message:</B>  
<INPUT NAME="txtMesg" SIZE=65 MAXLENGTH=255 VALUE="<%idc.MesgText%>"><HR>
<INPUT TYPE="SUBMIT" VALUE="Send Message">
```

185

Send a new message to: Art_Cowan

Message: Your message has been sent to Art_Cowan

Send Message

Summary

In this, the final chapter, we've been looking at one of the most recent developments in web server technologies to come out of Microsoft. Active Server Pages is the future for server-side programming with Internet Information Server. In many ways, it's a combination of other technologies, yet it adds extra functionality which is either impossible, or just difficult to achieve, with other methods.

We've seen how it can be used to achieve a variety of tasks, including a visitor counter, and a generic form handler. We've also implemented the messaging parts of our sample **Wrox Information Manager** application using it, so that you can see some of the other things that are possible.

At the time of writing, Active Server Pages is still under development, and only early Beta versions are available. Much of the structure and syntax, especially in the area of database management, may well change as it approaches a release version.

However, the power and flexibility that it offers means that you should be aware of what it can do, and how it works. If you are still planning your new web site, or company intranet, you should be looking to evaluate Active Server Pages before you settle fully on other technologies.

We've also come to the end of the book. In six chapters, we've covered a lot of ground, and several different technologies. However, by now, you should have a real feel for how they all complement each other, how they fit into the whole scheme of things, and how they can be used to create useful, exciting, and dynamic web pages for your site.

Appendix A - Creating a System Data Source Name

To use **Internet Database Connector** (IDC), **dbWeb**, or **Active Server Pages** on Internet Information Server (IIS), you need to set up access to the data source by providing the correct **System Data Source Name** (System DSN).

 Launch the ODBC Administrator program by double-clicking on its icon in Windows Control Panel. The Data Sources dialog shows a list of the currently installed ODBC drivers. Here, we're using an Access database, so we select the Microsoft Access Driver (***.mdb**) entry from the list. If you're using a different database system, you'll need to select the appropriate ODBC driver. If an entry for it isn't present, you will need to install the driver from your original setup disk, or a disk provided by the database vendor.

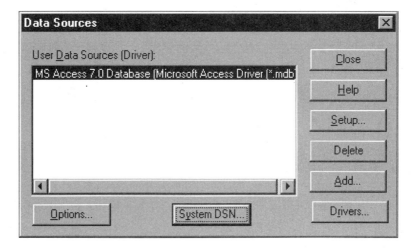

We're going to set up a system **Data Source Name (DSN)** which will allow our database to be accessed by (potentially) all users on the network. Clicking on the System DSN button displays the System Data Sources window which lists all of the system DSNs that are currently installed.

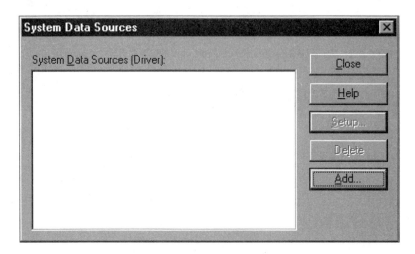

 To set up a new system DSN, click on the Add button to show the Add Data Source window. We want to create an Access system DSN, so we've selected the Microsoft Access driver from the list.

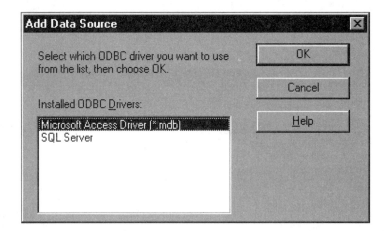

 Click OK to open the ODBC Microsoft Access 7.0 Setup dialog. We now have to enter the name of the data source. This will be the name that our IDC scripts will use as the **Datasource** parameter, and can also be used for ODBC connections in OLE automation servers. We also select the path where our database resides—either by typing it in directly, or clicking the Select button. Because we are using an Access database, we have the opportunity to repair and compact the database as well. We can also specify a workgroup (**system.mdw**) database, to restrict user access if this is required.

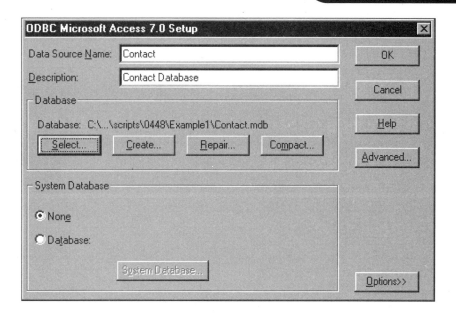

If you are using a different type of data source, such as SQL Server, you will see a different Setup dialog. You'll need to supply the extra details required to access the database, such as the server name and network address.

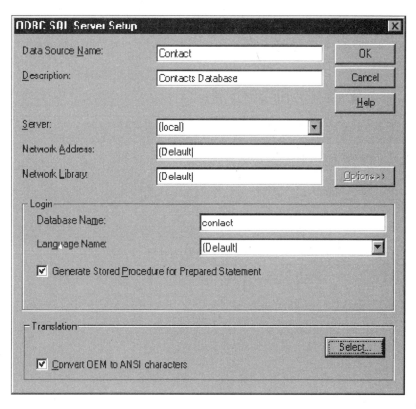

When you've entered all the details, click on OK to return to the System Data Sources screen again. The new System DSN will be shown, and this can be used in an IDC or Active Server Pages or in a dbWeb schema dialog.

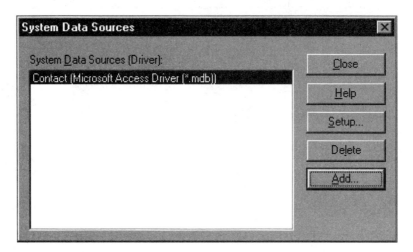

INSTANT

Web Database Programming

Appendix B - URL Encoding Character Translations

Un-encoded	URL-encoded	Un-encoded	URL-encoded
space	+	]	%5D
~	%7E	}	%7D
!	%21	\	%5C
#	%23	|	%7C
$	%24	`	%60
%	%25	'	%27
^	%5E	:	%3A
&	%26	;	%3B
(	%28	/	%2F
)	%29	<	%3C
+	%2B	>	%3E
=	%3D	Chr(13)	%0D
[	%5B	Chr(10)	*ignored*
{	%7B		

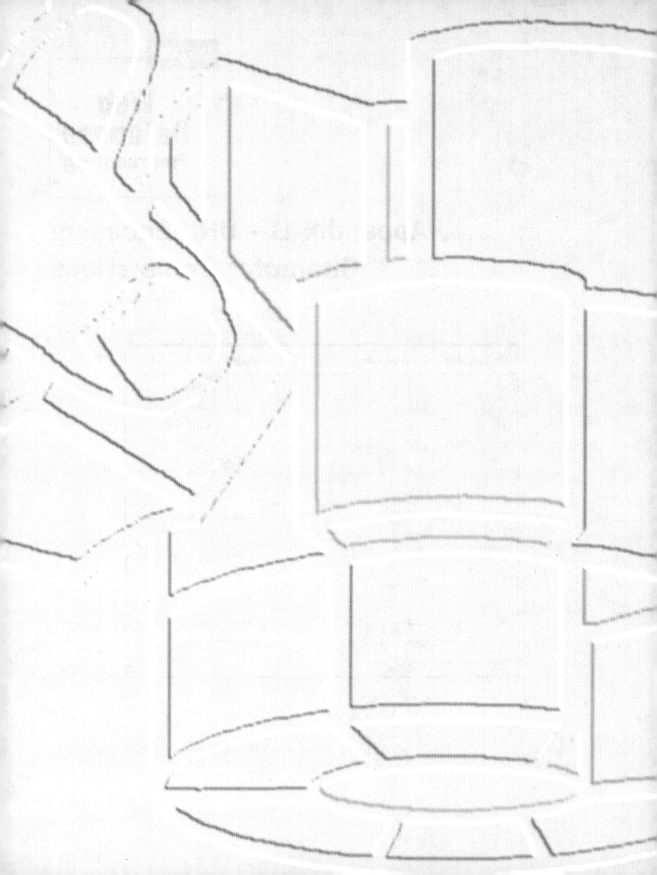

Appendix C - Microsoft Index Server

Although this book is primarily about publishing *database* information, there are often times when you need to publish other types of information. A perfect example is if you have a lot of documentation to manage—such as a technical reference store on the company network, or the code from various projects in a software house. Microsoft Index Server is an application that uses IDC-like methods to provide a powerful searching facility for your web site, intranet, or even just your own hard drives.

Index Server uses a background application that maintains an on-disk catalog, or index, of the content of specified directories on your system. To search the catalog to get information about the indexed documents, you use a query page containing some fairly simple HTML code.

What Index Server Does

Once you've installed Index Server, it is—to a large extent—self-maintaining. During periods of little or no system activity, it trawls round the folders in the selected areas of your system, building and maintaining a catalog of information about each document stored there. When you perform a search in the catalog, it uses the contents of the index to build the HTML result page, and returns it to the client. The whole cataloging and indexing system is practically transparent as far as the user is concerned. It is also very fast, because only the index file needs to be searched each time.

> *Note that the index file can be up to 40% of the total size of the documents on your system, if you have full indexing features in use.*

The Types of Information it Stores

Index Server doesn't just keep a list of file names (if you wanted to do this, you could use the Windows Find dialog), it also stores a multitude of document details. These include all the stored document's properties, the time and date it was created and updated, the size and file attribute status, etc. Plus, and here's the clever bit, it keeps an **abstract** of the contents.

This abstract is a selection of the text in the document, irrespective of what type of document it actually is. And Index Server contains natural language processing systems, dedicated to your own particular spoken language, so it really 'understands', as far as computers can understand, the file contents.

This means that you can search for a word, or group of words, as well as specifying the type of the file and other properties such as the author. The language engine can match words literally, (so that **catch*** will include **catcher** and **catching**), and also grammatically—where **catch**** will include **catching** and **caught**. As well as this, there is a 'noise' list file, which you can edit, that prevents words such as **and**, **or**, **the**, etc. from being included in the index. This makes it a very powerful way of finding information which could be stored anywhere on your system.

Types of Documents that can be Catalogued

Index Server will catalog, by default, all the documents stored in the virtual paths set up in Internet Information Server. These can be HTML files, documents created in Microsoft Word, Excel or PowerPoint, or plain text files. It even maintains non-document files, such as executables, in the catalog, but of course it can't perform searches for meaningful information within these.

You'll find that many document types will not be directly supported by Index Server. At the moment only the Microsoft formats are supported. However, Index Server has a **filter interface** which enables third party software vendors to provide the logic to enable Index Server to support their own application file formats. This means that Index Server can potentially allow any file type to be fully cataloged.

Index Server In Action

To show you what we can achieve with Index Server, with very little effort, here's a sample that we've included in the Wrox Information Manager application. You can run this yourself from our web site—the samples index page is at:

http://www.wrox.com/books/0464/samples/webdb.htm

> *Of course, you won't see the same documents that are shown in the screenshots in this book. Instead, you'll be able to search our site for any documents of interest.*

At the bottom of the Current Documents page in Wrox Information Manager there is a text box and a couple of buttons where you can enter a search criterion and have matching files listed. Here, we've entered the criteria **zip*** to find any documents containing words that start with **zip**.

Enter the contents of a document to find:

| zip* | | Search Now | Clear |

A sample from the book - **IIS Database Programming**

© 1996 - Wrox Press

Clicking Search Now sends Index Server off to look in its catalog, and after a short while a list of matching documents appears. Here, we've found **15** that match, and the list shows details of the first **10** of these.

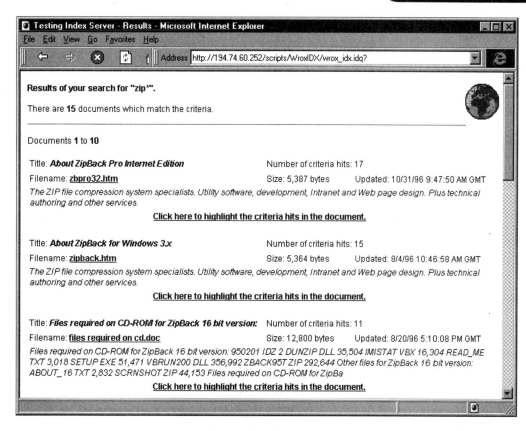

For each one, there's the document title, filename, and some of the abstract information. The page also shows the number of 'criteria hits' which indicates how well it matches our criteria. However, the documents are actually listed in descending order based on their **ranking** by the search engine, not just the number of hits. The ranking is generated automatically and reflects how well the document matches the query, so that the most appropriate ones can be listed first. There's also the size in bytes, and the date and time it was last updated.

Scrolling down to the bottom of the page, we find a button where we can show the next page of results. Notice that it knows there are only five more to look at. Clicking it displays the next page, with the title Documents 11 to 15.

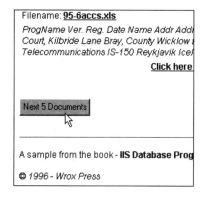

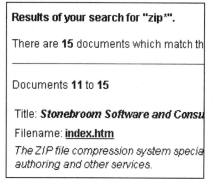

At the bottom of this page, we find a message confirming that there are no more matches, and the controls which allow us to perform a new search. One of the strengths of Index Server is that there are several ways we can specify the documents we want to find. The default, as we've been using here, is to search for the text in the content of the document.

Index Server's Query Language

When composing a query, you need to bear in mind a few simple rules:

Words separated by spaces or ordinary punctuation (which is not listed as a special character in the tables later in this section) are treated as a **phrase**. The search will only return documents which contain this phrase. However, words within the phrase which are listed in the **noise list** (such as **and**, **a**, **but**, **for**, **as**, etc.) are ignored completely, and matching is also **case-insensitive**. So searching for **the State; and the County** will also match **the state of a county**.

To search for a phrase which contains quotation marks (**"**), or one of the special characters such as an exclamation mark (**!**), you have to enclose the whole phrase in quotation marks and then place double quotation marks where you want a quotation mark to appear. For example **"he yelled ""Hello!"" from across the street"**. To search for several individual words in a document, we separate the words with a comma. The result will be documents that contain all, or only *some*, of the words listed. The more that match, however, the better the ranking of the result.

Other than that, you use the normal wildcards and Boolean operators. An asterisk (*) matches any number of characters, and a question mark (?) any single character. There is also the option of a **fuzzy search**. Adding two asterisks to the end of a word will match 'stem words' with the same meaning. A search for **catch****, for instance, will include **catching** and **caught**.

To combine words in the search string, you use Boolean operators like this:

Boolean Keywords	Shorthand	Meaning
Apples **AND** Pears	Apples **&** Pears	**Both** must exist in the document.
Apples **OR** Pears	Apples **|** Pears	**Either** must exist in the document.
Apples **AND NOT** Pears	Apples **&!** Pears	The first word **must** exist in the document, but **not** the second.
Apples **NEAR** Pears	Apples **~** Pears	**Both** must exist in the document, and be **within 50 words** of each other. The closer they are, the higher the ranking in the results.
NOT @size < 2049	**!** @size < 2049	Document must be larger than 2KB

As you can see from the last entry, you can also search by any other of the attributes or properties of the documents that Index Server stores in its catalog, for example:

Attribute or Property	Meaning
Contents	Words and phrases in the document. This is the default if no other attribute or property is specified.
Filename	The name of the file.
Size	The size of the file in bytes.
Path	The actual path and file name of the document.
VPath	The server's virtual path and file name for the document.
HitCount	The number of hits for the content search in the document.
Rank	The relative matching score for the query, from 0 to 1000.
Create	The date and time that the file was originally created.
Write	The date and time that the file was last updated.
DocTitle	The **Title** property for that document.
DocSubject	The **Subject** property for that document.
DocPageCount	The number of pages in the document.
DocAuthor	The **Author** property for that document.
DocKeywords	The keywords specified for that document.
DocComments	The value of the **Comments** property for that document.

The properties starting with Doc are only available for documents created by applications which can store these document properties in their files. In the case of an executable file, for example, there will be no DocPageCount or DocKeywords properties available.

We can search for the value of a property or attribute of a file using the **@** or **#** prefixes. In a relational expression, like the expression **!@size < 2049** we used in the table above, the prefix is **@**. For a normal expression-based search, we use **#**, for example, **#filename *.xlw** will only match Microsoft Excel workbook files. There is one other prefix that you'll find useful, **$contents**. This tells Index Server to treat the query as a 'free text meaning' search. In other words, it will try to interpret the *meaning* of the query string and find documents that best provide a match—even if they don't contain the actual phrase. **$contents tell me how to create a query** will provide a match to any document which covers creating queries.

Index Server on your Intranet

Generally, Index Server will only catalog documents that you specifically place in virtual paths—such as your Internet **WWWroot** and **FTProot** folders and all their sub-folders. However, you can create virtual paths to other directories—dbWeb creates one to its own samples directory, for example.

You can also select which virtual paths to use, and add new ones to point to your existing file resources such as a **My Documents** folder. These can even be on another machine on the network, so long as you can supply the domain or computer name for it.

There are a series of administrative pages supplied with Index Server that can be used to set all the options like this. You can also create your own admin pages, using an `.ida` script file. Check out the Index Server Help pages for more details.

So on a company intranet, you can set up information repositories and point Index Server at them as required. And remember that the files can be of almost any type that filters are available for. Word processor documents and spreadsheets are likely to be a popular choice in this situation, so let's have a look at some of the other features of Index Server that are appropriate. For example, this time we're just looking for documents which have the single word **sales** in them:

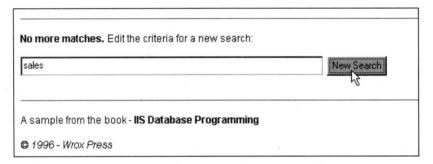

Among the list of hits, we've found a Word document file (called **lynne_cv.doc**) which we'd forgotten was still lurking in a dark and dusty corner of the disk. Underneath the abstract listing is a hyperlink: **Click here to highlight the criteria hits in the document**. This doesn't open the document directly, but sends it to a separate routine which is part of Index Server. It shows an HTML page made up of extracts of the document, with the hits highlighted:

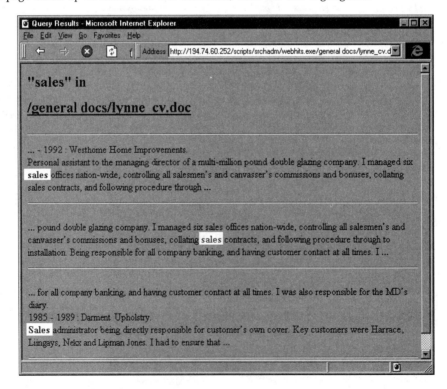

Back in the list of matching files, we've come across the spreadsheet file **excelsample.xls**. Clicking on the filename in the list opens it within a copy of Excel, and inside the Internet Explorer window. We can edit it here and save the changes when we move to another page. How's that for information at your fingertips?

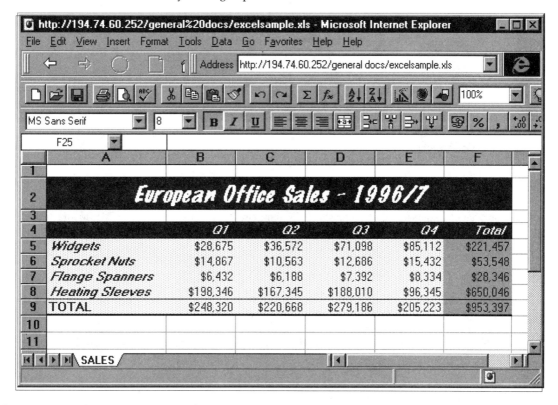

Browsers other than Internet Explorer *will not open the file inside the browser window like this. You'll find that a copy of the original application is opened separately, containing the document.*

How Index Server Works

Having seen just a few examples of what Index Server can do, we'll take an equally brief look at how it works. It is a highly complex query development environment, so we can only hope to cover the basics in this appendix. However, we'll walk through the methods we used to create the query system you've just seen at work.

Index Server Overview

Well, it's a small world. Index Server is, like dbWeb, really just a development of IDC techniques. The diagram shows the principle components, which are an Internet Data Query (IDQ) script and an Extended HTML Template (HTX) file. However, it's a lot more powerful than it may at first appear. The wide range of query syntax that it supports indicates that there's a lot going on.

203

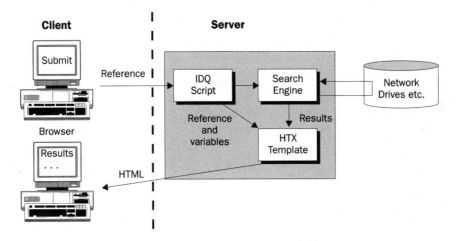

Basically, we reference an IDQ script from the browser, and this controls the whole operation. It instructs the search engine to retrieve the matching document details from the catalog stored on disk, sort them and insert them into the HTX template, then return this as HTML to the browser. Because it only has to search this catalog, and not the whole disk each time, the process is very quick.

Referencing the IDQ Script

Like IDC, we can use a **<FORM>** section in the browser's HTML page to send the contents of the controls in the form to the IDQ script, or we can supply them as parameters in the **HREF** argument of an **<A>** tag. In the sample Current Documents page you've seen, we used this code to create the text box and buttons (we've omitted the server address from the **ACTION** argument for clarity):

```
<FORM ACTION="http://..../scripts/WroxIDX/wrox_idx.idq?" METHOD="POST">
  Enter the contents of a document to find:<P>
  <INPUT TYPE="TEXT" SIZE="70" MAXLENGTH="70" NAME="CiRestriction">
  <INPUT TYPE="SUBMIT" VALUE="Search Now">
  <INPUT TYPE="RESET" VALUE="Clear">
</FORM>
```

Inside the IDQ Script

When the form is submitted, the script **wrox_idx.idq** is referenced. This contains the following code:

```
[Query]
CiColumns=filename,size,characterization,rank,path,hitcount,vpath,DocTitle,write
CiCatalog=c:\IndexServer
CiScope=/
CiFlags=DEEP
CiRestriction=%CiRestriction%
CiMaxRecordsInResultSet=1000
CiMaxRecordsPerPage=10
CiTemplate=/WroxTest/wrox_idx.htx
CiSort=rank[d]
```

It doesn't look much like an IDC script, but that's because it has a very different task to accomplish. **CiColumns** is rather like the **SQL Statement** entry in IDC, however, because it defines which columns (or properties and attributes) are returned from the catalog. These are all ones we've looked at earlier, when we talked about the query language of Index Server, except for **characterization**. This is an **abstract** which Index Server automatically builds from the document, and is intended to indicate its broad contents. You can't use this property in a query, though.

Having specified which properties we want, we have to tell Index Server where to search for the documents. **CiCatalog** is the location of the catalog storing the document details (it's possible to create different ones), and **CiScope** is the virtual root where we want to include documents from. We can select any physical or mapped virtual folder here. In our case, we're starting at the main Internet Server root. To include all the subfolders below it, we've included **CiFlags=DEEP**.

The **CiRestriction** line in the script defines the query we want to use, and because it's sent from the browser as the value of the text box named **CiRestriction**, we use this value in our script by enclosing it in percent signs, as **%CiRestriction%**. Again, it's just like IDC. We can either send the values of these variables from the controls on the form, or preset them in the **.idq** file.

The next two lines then set the maximum number of documents to return, and the number we want to display in each page of our resulting HTML code which is sent back to the browser. Lastly, we specify the location of the HTX template file, and how the matching document details are to be sorted. In this case, we've chosen the usual descending by rank.

As a summary, the next table shows a list of the common variables that can be set in an **.idq** script—either directly, or as a variable of a control on the form section of a page.

Variable	Meaning
CiCatalog	Location of the catalog, if not using the default.
CiForceUseCi	**TRUE** to use the current index, even if out of date.
CiScope	Start directory for the search.
CiFlags	**DEEP** to include all subdirectories below **CiScope**, or **SHALLOW** for only the directory in **CiScope**.
CiColumns	List of all the indexed values to be returned, i.e. the columns for the results set, separated by commas.
CiRestriction	The query to be executed, i.e. what to search for.
CiMaxRecordsInResultsSet	Maximum number of documents to be retrieved.
CiMaxRecordsPerPage	Maximum number of documents to be returned on each page.
CiSort	Order of the returned records, using the column names separated by commas. **[d]** indicates descending order. For example: **State, Size [d], Name**
CiTemplate	Full virtual path to the **.htx** template file.

Inside the HTX Template

All the work of formatting the information to be returned to the browser is done in the HTX template. This is very close to the HTX template used in IDC, in both method and internal format. We use a **<%BeginDetail%> <%EndDetail%>** section which is repeated for each 'record' returned by the Index Server engine, though we do have more options for displaying the information as separate pages, rather than as a single long page. The IDQ variable **CiMaxRecordsPerPage** tells Index Server how many records to retrieve each time.

Index Server HTX templates also support **<%If...%> <%Else%> <%EndIf%>**, and in a template we can retrieve the value of any of the controls on the form which originally referenced the IDQ script, or which are listed in the **CiColumns** line of the script. We can also use the regular HTTP variables, such as **SCRIPT_NAME** or **SERVER_NAME**, as we did with IDC in the Chapter 2.

After running the IDQ script, Index Server returns a set of built-in variables, which indicate the results of the query:

Variable	Meaning
CiMatchedRecordCount	Total number of documents which match the query.
CiTotalNumberPages	Total number of pages used to contain query results.
CiCurrentRecordNumber	Number of current document in the total matched.
CiCurrentPageNumber	Current page number of query results.
CiFirstRecordNumber	Number of the first document on the current page.
CiLastRecordNumber	Number of the last document on the current page. May not be correct until after the **<%EndDetail%>** section.
CiContainsFirstRecord	Set to **1** if the current page contains the first document in the query results, or **0** otherwise.
CiContainsLastRecord	Set to **1** if the current page contains the last document in the query results, or **0** otherwise. May not be correct until after the **<%EndDetail%>** section.
CiBookmark	Reference to the first document on the current page.
CiOutOfDate	Set to **1** if the content index out of date, or **0** if OK.
CiQueryIncomplete	Set to **1** if the query could not be completed using the current content index, or **0** if completed.
CiQueryTimedOut	Set to **1** if the query exceeded the time limit for execution, or **0** if completed.

Here's the 'working parts' of the template file we used to create the query results pages you saw earlier. We've omitted the code which just creates the header and footer:

```
. . .
<B>Results of your search for "<%CiRestriction%>".</B><P>
There are <%CiMatchedRecordCount%> documents which match the criteria.
<HR>
<%If CiMatchedRecordCount NE 0%>
```

```
        Documents <%CiFirstRecordNumber%> to <%CiLastRecordNumber%><P>
<%EndIf%>
<TABLE WIDTH=100%>
   <%BeginDetail%>
     <TR>
        <%If DocTitle ISEMPTY%>
          <TD>Untitled document</TD>
        <%Else%>
          <TD>Title: <I><B><%DocTitle%></B></I></TD>
        <%EndIf%>
        <TD COLSPAN="2">Number of criteria hits: <%HitCount%></TD>
     <TR>
     </TR>
        <TD>Filename: <A HREF="<%EscapeURL vpath%>"><%filename%></A></TD>
        <TD>Size: <%size%> bytes</TD>
        <TD>Updated: <%write%> GMT</TD>
     </TR>
     <TR>
        <TD COLSPAN="3"><I><%characterization%></I></TD>
     </TR>
     <TR>
        <TD COLSPAN="3" ALIGN="CENTER">
        <!-- following must be all on one line -->
        <A HREF="http://<%SERVER_NAME%>/scripts/srchadm/webhits.exe
              <%EscapeURL vpath%>?CiRestriction=<%EscapeURL
              CiRestriction%>&CiBold=YES">
          Click to highlight the criteria hits in the document.</A>
        </TD>
     </TR>
     <TR>
        <TD COLSPAN="3" ALIGN="RIGHT">.</TD>
     </TR>
   <%EndDetail%>
</TABLE>
<FORM ACTION="<%EscapeURL SCRIPT_NAME%>?" METHOD="POST">
   <%If CiMatchedRecordCount EQ 0%>
     Enter the criteria for a new search:<P>
     <INPUT TYPE="TEXT" SIZE="70" MAXLENGTH="70" NAME="CiRestriction">
     <INPUT TYPE="SUBMIT" VALUE="New Search">
     <INPUT TYPE="RESET" VALUE="Clear">
   <%Else%>
     <%If CiRecordsNextPage EQ 0%>
       <HR><B>No more matches.</B> Edit the criteria for a new search:<P>
       <INPUT TYPE="TEXT" SIZE="70" MAXLENGTH="70" NAME="CiRestriction"
                                        VALUE="<%CiRestriction%>">
       <INPUT TYPE="SUBMIT" VALUE="New Search">
     <%Else%>
       <INPUT TYPE="HIDDEN" NAME="CiBookmark" VALUE="<%CiBookmark%>">
       <INPUT TYPE="HIDDEN" NAME="CiBookmarkSkipCount"
                                    VALUE="<%CiMaxRecordsPerPage%>">
       <INPUT TYPE="HIDDEN" NAME="CiMaxRecordsPerPage"
                                    VALUE="<%CiMaxRecordsPerPage%>">
       <INPUT TYPE="HIDDEN" NAME="CiRestriction" VALUE="<%CiRestriction%>">
       <INPUT TYPE="HIDDEN" NAME="CiScope" VALUE="<%CiScope%>">
       <INPUT TYPE="SUBMIT" VALUE="Next <%CiRecordsNextPage%> Documents">
     <%EndIf%>
   <%EndIf%>
</FORM>
. . .
```

207

From your knowledge of HTX files gathered in Chapter 2, it will be obvious how the IDQ variables, such as **<%CiRestriction%>**, and the values obtained from the search, such as **<%DocTitle%>** are used. We create a table to hold the results and, within the **<%BeginDetail%>** **<%EndDetail%>** section, create a table row containing the document title, size, last update time, filename, hit count, and abstract. Because some documents do not have a title, we use an **<%If..%>** **<%Else%>** **<%EndIf%>** construct to display Untitled document in this case:

```
<%If DocTitle ISEMPTY%>
  <TD>Untitled document</TD>
<%Else%>
  <TD>Title: <I><B><%DocTitle%></B></I></TD>
<%EndIf%>
```

*Note that you can't put a **<%BeginDetail%>** **<%EndDetail%>** section inside an **<%If..%>** **<%Else%>** **<%EndIf%>** construct. If you do, you'll get an error message saying that an **<%Else%>** or **<%EndIf%>** can't be found.*

Opening a Matching Document

To allow the user to open a matching document, we make the filename a hyperlink, using the normal **<A>** tag. However, we have to refer to the virtual path, and not the actual physical path if we want it to be loaded using HTTP rather than as a file. And to make sure that any spaces or other non HTTP-legal characters are properly encoded, we **escape** the string by prefixing the variable name with **EscapeURL**:

```
<TD>Filename: <A HREF="<%EscapeURL vpath%>"><%filename%></A></TD>
```

*The **EscapeURL** keyword converts the string following it into a fully URL-encoded version, so that it can be used in the **HREF** or **SRC** argument of an **<A>**, **<FORM>**, **<IMG>**, or **<FRAME>** tag, for example. There are two similar keywords, **EscapeHTML** and **EscapeRAW**. **EscapeHTML** converts the string into HTML format, for example replacing '>' with '>'. In some cases, Index Server executes a conversion automatically, for example in the arguments sent from a form. The **EscapeRAW** keyword can be used to prevent any automatic conversion.*

Displaying Another Page of Documents

Once we've displayed all the documents, we can provide controls so that the user can navigate to the next (or previous) page. In our case, we're just allowing them to display the next page, but you can use the various HTX variables we looked at earlier to control whether a Previous Page button is included.

There are two possibilities where there are no documents on the next page—if there were no matches at all (**CiMatchedRecordCount EQ 0**), or if we have already displayed all the matching documents (**CiRecordsNextPage EQ 0**). In both these cases we just display a message and add the original query text box and Submit buttons again, so that the user can start a new search.

```
<FORM ACTION="<%EscapeURL SCRIPT_NAME%>?" METHOD="POST">
  <%If CiMatchedRecordCount EQ 0%>
    ...
    <!-- no documents found - controls to start a new search -->
    ...
  <%Else%>
```

```
    <%If CiRecordsNextPage EQ 0%>
       ...
       <!-- no documents on next page - controls to start a new search -->
       ...
    <%Else%>
       <!-- more documents on next page -->
       <INPUT TYPE="HIDDEN" NAME="CiBookmark" VALUE="<%CiBookmark%>">
       <INPUT TYPE="HIDDEN" NAME="CiBookmarkSkipCount"
                                 VALUE="<%CiMaxRecordsPerPage%>">
       <INPUT TYPE="HIDDEN" NAME="CiMaxRecordsPerPage"
                                 VALUE="<%CiMaxRecordsPerPage%>">
       <INPUT TYPE="HIDDEN" NAME="CiRestriction" VALUE="<%CiRestriction%>">
       <INPUT TYPE="HIDDEN" NAME="CiScope" VALUE="<%CiScope%>">
       <INPUT TYPE="SUBMIT" VALUE="Next <%CiRecordsNextPage%> Documents">
    <%EndIf%>
  <%EndIf%>
</FORM>
```

If there are more documents, however, we use the value of **CiRecordsNextPage** to set the proper caption of the Submit button. When the form is submitted, we run the same IDQ script, **<%EscapeURL SCRIPT_NAME%>**, again. However, this time we have to include the settings for the internal IDQ variables. We do this in hidden text boxes on the form, and to display the correct page we set the value of **CiBookmark** and **CiBookmarkSkipCount**.

We would usually set **CiBookmark** to the same value as last time, and specify the first document for the new page by setting **CiBookmarkSkipCount** to an appropriate value. To display the next page, we set the contents of the **CiBookmarkSkipCount** control to the value of **CiMaxRecordsPerPage**, and to display the previous page we use **-CiMaxRecordsPerPage**. To jump to a particular page we would use a positive or negative value which is a multiple of **CiMaxRecordsPerPage**.

Notice that we could also change the query, in **CiRestriction**, or the **Scope**, if we wanted to. By providing a complex query results page, which changes these values, the user could be allowed to tailor their search to find a specific document more quickly.

Coping with Errors

Although we haven't done so, you should (to keep our example code as simple as possible) consider including some error checking in your HTX results templates. Before or after displaying the matching documents, you can check the value of the error indicator variables and include appropriate messages:

```
<%If CiOutOfDate EQ 1%>
   <B>Warning: the document indexes are not fully up to date.</B>
<%Else%>
   <%If CiQueryTimeOut EQ 1%>
      <B>Warning: the query could not be completed.</B>
   <%EndIf%>
<%EndIf%>
```

Hit-highlighting the Matching Documents

The final feature we offer users in our sample page is the ability to highlight the matching words within the documents that were found by the query (providing, of course, it was a **content** based search). Below each document displayed on the returned page is a hyperlink which they can click

209

to open a new page in the browser window. This page contains extracts from the document, showing the matching words or highlighted phrases.

To do this, we use a separate program supplied with Index Server, called **Webhits.exe**. It's installed in the **/scripts/srchadmin** folder, which also contains a range of pages you can use to fine-tune the performance of Index Server. To use **Webhits**, we have to supply the virtual path to the file we want highlighted, and the query string that originally found it:

http://[*path to webhits.exe*]**/webhits.exe/**[*document*]**?**[*parameters*]

In our case, the path is **<%SERVER_NAME%>/scripts/srchadm** (we use the HTTP variable **SERVER_NAME** here), and the full path and filename of the document is the same URL-encoded string that we used earlier—**<%EscapeURL vpath%>**. We set the query string using the value of **CiRestriction**, and add a parameter **CiBold** to make the highlighted text, which is colored red by default, display in bold type as well:

```
<A HREF="http://<%SERVER_NAME%>/scripts/srchadm/webhits.exe
           <%EscapeURL vpath%>?CiRestriction=<%EscapeURL
           CiRestriction%>&CiBold=YES">
        Click to highlight the criteria hits in the document.</A>
```

H

223

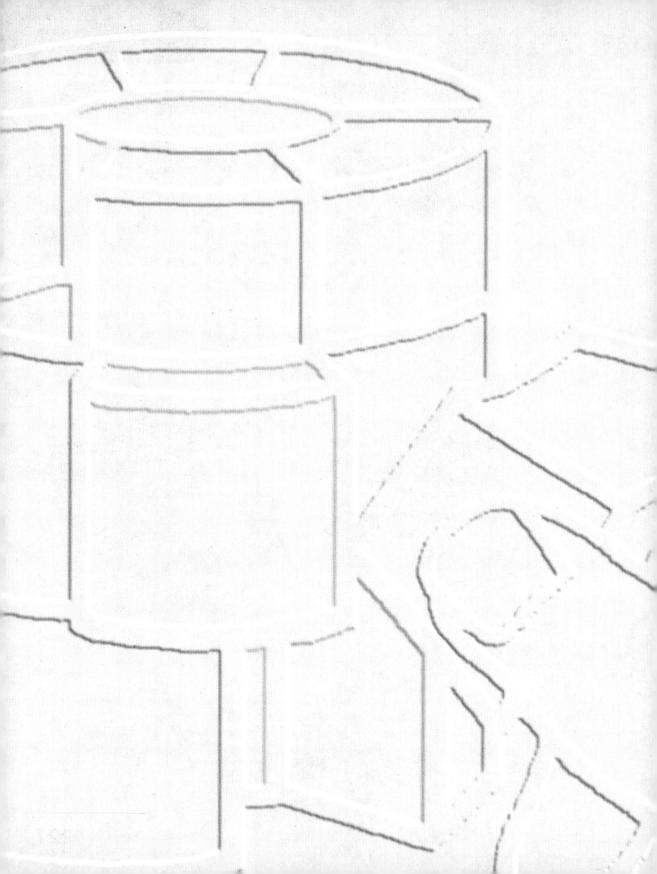

Instant HTML Programmers Reference

Author: Steve Wright
ISBN: 1861000766
Price: $15.00 C$21.00 £13.99

This book is a fast paced guide to the latest version of the HTML language, including the extensions to the standards added by Netscape and Microsoft. Aimed at programmers, it assumes a basic knowledge of the Internet. It starts by looking at the basics of HTML including document structure, formatting tags, inserting hyperlinks and images and image mapping, and then moves on to cover more advanced issues such as tables, frames, creating forms to interact with users, animation, incorporating scripts (such as JavaScript) into HTML documents, and style sheets.

The book includes a full list of all the HTML tags, organised by category for easy reference.

Instant VBScript

Authors: Alex Homer, Darren Gill
ISBN: 1861000448
Price: $25.00 C$35.00 £22.99

This is the guide for programmers who already know HTML and another programming language and want to waste no time getting up to speed. This book takes developers right into the code, straight from the beginning of Chapter 1. The first object is to get the programmer to create their own 'reactive' web pages as quickly as possible while introducing the most important HTML and ActiveX controls. This new knowledge is quickly incorporated into more complex examples with a complete sample site built early in the book.

As Internet Explorer is the browser that introduced VBScript, we also take a detailed look at how to use VBScript to access different objects within the browser. We create our own tools to help us with the development of applications, in particular a debugging tool to aid error-trapping. Information is provided on how to build your own controls and sign them to secure Internet download. Finally we take a look at server side scripting and how with VBScript you can get the clients and server communicating freely. The book is supported by our web site which contains all of the examples in the book in an easily executable form.

Wrox Press
http://www.wrox.com/

WROX

Professional Java Fundamentals

Authors: Cohen, Mitchell, Gonzalez,
Rodrigues and Hammil
ISBN: 1861000383
Price: $35.00 C$49.00 £32.49

Professional Java Fundamentals is a high-level, developer's book that gives you the detailed information and extended coverage you need to program Java for real, making the most of Java's potential.

It starts by thoroughly recapping the basics of Java, providing a language reference, looking at object-oriented programming issues and then at Java's fundamental classes. The book then details advanced language features, such as multithreading, networking, file I/O and native methods. There are five Abstract Windowing Toolkit chapters which provide in-depth coverage of event handling, graphics and animation, GUI building blocks and layout managers. Lastly, the book shows you how to design and implement class libraries in Java.

The book is supported by the Wrox web site, from which the complete source code is available.

Professional Web Site Optimization

Authors: Ware, Barker, Slothouber
and Gross
ISBN: 186100074x
Price: $40.00 C$56.00 £36.99

OK, you've installed your web server, and it's working fine and you've even got people interested in visiting your site - too many people, in fact. The real challenge is just starting you need to make it run faster, better and more flexibly.

This is the book for every webmaster who needs to improve site performance. You could just buy that new T-1 you've had your eye on, but what if the problem is really in your disk controller? Or maybe it's the way you've designed your pages or the ISP you're using.

The book covers web server optimization for all major platforms and includes coverage of LAN performance, ISP performance, basic limits imposed by the nature of HTTP, IP and TCP. We also cover field-proven methods to improve static & dynamic page content from database access and the mysteries of graphic file manipulation and tuning.

If you've got the choice between spending fifteen thousand on a new line, or two hundred dollars in new hardware plus the cost of this book, which decision would your boss prefer?

Beginning Access 95 VBA Programming

Authors: Robert Smith, David Sussman
ISBN: 1874416508
Price: $29.95 C$41.95 £27.99

This book is for the Access user who has a knowledge of databases and the basic objects of an Access database such as tables, queries, forms and reports, but wants to learn how to program. You will need no prior programming experience, in any language.

This book looks in depth at the language that acts as the cornerstone of Microsoft Office 95. Focusing on the sample application provided, it explains the concepts and techniques you need to get to grips with VBA.

The book starts by explaining why you actually need to learn VBA to harness the full power of Access and why macros just aren't enough for some tasks. It then introduces you to the Visual Basic programming environment in Access and explains the common programming techniques and terminology, such as loops, conditions and arrays. Each feature of the language is fully illustrated with practical examples.

The later chapters concentrate on several diverse topics, such as debugging and error handling, multi-user situations, libraries, add-ons and optimization issues. At the end of the book you will have a solid grounding in all the important aspects of VBA. The disk contains the sample application used in the book, plus all the sample VBA code used.

Professional Visual C++ ISAPI Programming

Author: Michael Tracy
ISBN: 1861000664
Price: $40.00 C$56.00 £36.99

This is a working developer's guide to customizing Microsoft's Internet Information Server, which is now an integrated and free addition to the NT4.0 platform. This is essential reading for real-world web site development and expects readers to already be competent C++ and C programmers. Although all techniques in the book are workable under various C++ compilers, users of Visual C++ 4.1 will benefit from the ISAPI extensions supplied in its AppWizard.

This book covers extension and filter programming in depth. There is a walk through the API structure but not a reference to endless calls. Instead, we illustrate the key specifications with example programs.

HTTP and HTML instructions are issued as an appendix. We introduce extensions by mimicking popular CGI scripts and there's a specific chapter on controlling cookies. With filters we are not just re-running generic web code - these are leading-edge filter methods specifically designed for the IIS API.

Beginning Linux Programming

Authors: Neil Matthew, Richard Stones
ISBN: 187441680
Price: $36.95 C$51.95 £33.99

The book is unique in that it teaches UNIX programming in a simple and structured way, using Linux and its associated and freely available development tools as the main platform. Assuming familiarity with the UNIX environment and a basic knowledge of C, the book teaches you how to put together UNIX applications that make the most of your time, your OS and your machine's capabilities.

Having introduced the programming environment and basic tools, the authors turn their attention initially on shell programming. The chapters then concentrate on programming UNIX with C, showing you how to work with files, access the UNIX environment, input and output data using terminals and curses, and manage data. After another round with development and debugging tools, the book discusses processes and signals, pipes and other IPC mechanisms, culminating with a chapter on sockets. Programming the X-Window system is introduced with Tcl/Tk and Java. Finally, the book covers programming for the Internet using HTML and CGI.

The book aims to discuss UNIX programming as described in the relevant POSIX and X/Open specifications, so the code is tested with that in mind. All the source code from the book is available under the terms of the Gnu Public License from the Wrox web site.

Revolutionary Guide to Visual Basic 4 Professional

Author: Larry Roof   ISBN: 1874416370
Price: $44.95 C$62.95 £49.99

This book focuses on the four key areas for developers using VB4: the Win32 API, Objects and OLE, Databases and the VB development cycle. Each of the areas receives in-depth coverage, and techniques are illustrated using rich and complex example projects that bring out the real issues involved in commercial VB development. It examines the Win32 API from a VB perspective and gives a complete run-down of developing multimedia apps. The OLE section includes a help file creator that uses the Word OLE object, and we OLE automate Netscape Navigator 2. The database section offers complete coverage of DAO, SQL and ODBC, finishing with a detailed analysis of client/server database systems. The final section shows how to design, code, optimize and distribute a complete application. The book has a CD including all source code and a hypertext version of the book.

Beginning WordBasic Programming

Author: Alex Homer ISBN: 1874416869
Price: $39.95 C$55.95 £37.49

Starting with an introduction to WordBasic, macros and templates, the first section of the book goes on to look at the language elements of WordBasic. We cover everything from statements, functions and control structures to communicating with your users using dialog boxes. There are clear discussions on the complex issues of the dynamic dialog!

In the second section of the book we look at Word in the workplace covering topics such as creating wizards and add-ins for using Word in a business environment. We show you how to manage large documents and how to automate some of the tasks faced by publishing companies such as controlling changes to documents, creating indexes and tables of contents and improving Word's printing options. We then go into detail on creating Help systems and HTML pages for the Internet. The book takes time out to look at Word Macro viruses and the complexities of DDE with Excel and Access.

All the source code from the book is included on the disk.

Visual C++ 4 MasterClass

Authors: Various   ISBN: 1874416443
Price: $49.95 C$69.95 £46.99

The book starts by covering software design issues related to programming with MFC, providing tips and techniques for creating great MFC extensions. This is followed by an analysis of porting issues when moving your applications from 16 to 32 bits.

The next section shows how you can use COM/OLE in the real world. This begins with an examination of COM technologies and the foundations of OLE (aggregation, uniform data transfer, drag and drop and so on) and is followed by a look at extending standard MFC OLE Document clients and servers to make use of database storage.

The third section of the book concentrates on making use of, and extending, the features that Windows 95 first brought to the public, including the 32-bit common controls, and the new style shell. You'll see how to make use of all the new features including appbars, file viewers, shortcuts, and property sheets.

The fourth section of the book provides a detailed look at multimedia and games programming, making use of Windows multimedia services and the facilities provided by the Game SDK (DirectX).

The final section covers 'net programming, whether it's for the Internet or the intranet. You'll see how to make the most of named pipes, mailslots, NetBIOS and WinSock before seeing how to create the corporate intranet system of your dreams using WinINet and ActiveX technology.

Professional IIS 2 Admin

Author: Christian Gross
ISBN: 1861000480
Price: $40.00 C$56.00 £36.99

This book is a guide for real world, working Administrators who are about to, or have already installed the Microsoft Internet Information Server 2.0 on their NT 3.51/4.0 system.

Rather than regurgitate the install procedure, we take you through the essentials of setting up and configuring your Server for actual robust usage.

Once you're up and running you'll need access to proven techniques for performance analysis, troubleshooting and security - which we cover in dedicated chapters. For super-fine tuning and trimming we walk you through IIS within the NT registry and cover, in extensive detail, how to interpret and respond to the broad logging capabilities within NT & IIS.

Finally, we tackle the black art of multi-homing and load balancing. The Author has applied his experience from the first IIS 1.0 betas thru 2.0 to help you master this function of Inter/Intranet Servers. This book will enable you to run, and expand, a professional Web Site with absolute minimum downtime...and minimum user complaints.

Professional SQL Server 6.5 Admin

Authors: Various   ISBN: 1874416494
Price: $44.95 C$62.95 £41.49

This book is not a tutorial in the complete product, but is for those who need to become either professionally competent in preparation for Microsoft exams or those DBAs needing real world advice to do their job better. It assumes knowledge of databases and wastes no time on getting novices up to speed on the basics of data structure and using a database server in a Client-Server arena.

The book covers everything from installation and configuration right through to the actual managing of the server. There are whole chapters devoted to essential administrative issues such as transaction management and locking, replication, security, monitoring of the system and database backup and recovery. We've used proven techniques to bring robust code and script that will increase your ability to troubleshoot your database structure and improve its performance. Finally, we have looked very carefully at the new features in 6.5, such as the Web Assistant and Distributed Transaction Controller (DTC) and provided you with key practical examples. Where possible, throughout the book we have described a DBA solution in Transact SQL, Visual Basic and the Enterprise Manager.

Wrox Press
http://www.wrox.com/

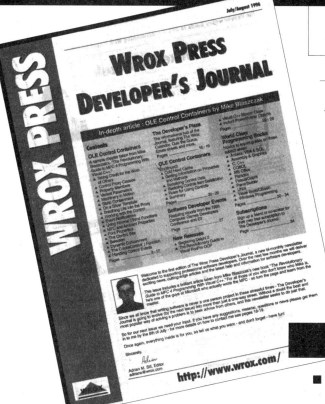

WROX

Register Instant ActiveX Web Database Programming and sign up for a free subscription to The Developer's Journal.

A bi-monthly magazine for software developers, The Wrox Press Developer's Journal features in-depth articles, news and help for everyone in the software development industry. Each issue includes extracts from our latest titles and is crammed full of practical insights into coding techniques, tricks, and research.

Fill in and return the card below to receive a free subscription to the Wrox Press Developer's Journal.

Instant ActiveX Web Database Programming Registration Card

Name _____

Address _____

_____

_____

City _____ State/Region _____

Country _____ Postcode/Zip _____

E-mail _____

Occupation _____

How did you hear about this book? _____

☐ Book review (name) _____

☐ Advertisement (name) _____

☐ Recommendation _____

☐ Catalog _____

☐ Other _____

Where did you buy this book? _____

☐ Bookstore (name) _____ City _____

☐ Computer Store (name) _____

☐ Mail Order _____

☐ Other _____

What influenced you in the purchase of this book?

☐ Cover Design

☐ Contents

☐ Other (please specify) _____

How did you rate the overall contents of this book?

☐ Excellent ☐ Good

☐ Average ☐ Poor

What did you find most useful about this book? _____

What did you find least useful about this book? _____

Please add any additional comments. _____

What other subjects will you buy a computer book on soon? _____

What is the best computer book you have used this year? _____

Note: This information will only be used to keep you updated about new Wrox Press titles and will not be used for any other purpose or passed to any other third party.

WROX

WROX PRESS INC.

Wrox writes books for you. Any suggestions, or
ideas about how you want information given in
your ideal book will be studied by our team.
Your comments are always valued at Wrox.

Free phone in USA 800-USE-WROX
Fax (312) 465 4063

Compuserve 100063,2152.
UK Tel. (0121) 706 6826   Fax   (0121) 706 2967

———— *Computer Book Publishers* ————

NB. If you post the bounce back card below in the UK, please send it to:
Wrox Press Ltd. 30 Lincoln Road, Birmingham, B27 6PA

NO POSTAGE
NECESSARY
IF MAILED
IN THE
UNITED STATES

BUSINESS REPLY MAIL
FIRST CLASS MAIL   PERMIT#64   LA VERGNE, TN

POSTAGE WILL BE PAID BY ADDRESSEE

WROX PRESS
2710 WEST TOUHY AVE
CHICAGO IL 60645-9911